Excel Accounting

Carol Yacht, MA
Software Consultant

Michael Fujita, MAcc, CPA
Assistant Professor of Accounting
Leeward Community College

 **McGraw-Hill**
Irwin

Boston   Burr Ridge, IL   Dubuque, IA   Madison, WI   New York   San Francisco   St. Louis
Bangkok   Bogotá   Caracas   Kuala Lumpur   Lisbon   London   Madrid   Mexico City
Milan   Montreal   New Delhi   Santiago   Seoul   Singapore   Sydney   Taipei   Toronto

About the Authors:

Carol Yacht is a textbook author and educator. Carol contributes regularly to professional journals and is the author of Peachtree, QuickBooks, and Excel textbooks. Carol's teaching career includes Yavapai College; West Los Angeles Community College; California State University, Los Angeles; and Beverly Hills High School and Adult School. Carol is the editor of the *Communicator*, the American Accounting Association's two-year college section publication and is an officer of that section. She worked for IBM Corporation as an education instruction specialist, and served on the Computer Education Task Force for the National Business Education Association. Carol is a frequent speaker at state, regional, and national conventions; technical school consortium meetings; and Department of Education conferences. She earned her AS degree from Temple University, BS degree from the University of New Mexico, and MA degree from California State University, Los Angeles.

Michael Fujita is an Assistant Professor in accounting at Leeward Community College. Michael is a certified public accountant and owns an accounting practice. Michael is also President of the Hawaii Business Education Association. He has worked in the audit and tax departments of Deloitte & Touche LLP and the tax department of Ernst and Young LLP. He earned his BBA in accounting and MAcc from the University of Hawai`i at Manoa.

Excel Accounting
Carol Yacht, M. A. and Michael Fujita, MAcc, CPA

Published by McGraw-Hill/Irwin, an imprint of The McGraw-Hill Companies, Inc., 1221 Avenue of the Americas, New York, NY 10020. Copyright © 2005 by The McGraw-Hill Companies, Inc. All rights reserved.

Vice president and editor-in-chief: *Robin Zwettler*
Editorial director: *Brent Gordon*
Publisher: *Stewart Mattson*
Sponsoring editor: *Steve Schuetz*
Developmental editor: *Andy Set*
Project Manager: *Susan Lombardi*
Senior supplement producer: *Susan Lombardi*
Production supervisor: *Debra Sylvester*
Cover designer: *Kami Carter*
Marketing manager: *Katherine Mattison*
Media producer: *Gregory Bates*

6 7 8 9 0 WDQ/WDQ 0

ISBN 13: 978-0-07-296442-4
ISBN 10: 0-07-296442-1

www.mhhe.com

Preface

Excel Accounting teaches you how to use the spreadsheet program, Microsoft Excel. In this book, you develop spreadsheets to practice accounting procedures.

The instructions in this book were written with Windows XP and Excel 2002. This book can be used with Windows 98 and higher and Excel 97 and higher. This includes Windows XP and Excel 2003. The CD that accompanies this textbook includes Excel files with starting data for selected exercises.

Excel Accounting teaches you how to apply some of the accounting procedures that you learned in your study of accounting. For example, in writing this book, the authors consulted the following textbooks— *Fundamental Accounting Principles 17e* by Larson, Wild and Chiappetta; *Financial Accounting: Information for Decisions 3e* by John Wild; *Managerial Accounting* by Edmonds, Edmonds and Tsay. These textbooks are published by McGraw-Hill/Irwin. When completing projects in *Excel Accounting*, you may want to refer to an accounting textbook that was used in one of your courses.

As you go through *Excel Accounting*, you will see that principles of accounting, financial accounting, and managerial accounting concepts are emphasized.

PART 1: EXCEL TUTORIAL

There are three chapters in Part 1: Chapters 1, 2, and 3.

In Chapter 1, Excel Basics, you start by identifying parts of an Excel screen, then learn how to move around a workbook, enter data, save files, format data, use page setup and print.

In Chapter 2, Using Formulas, you learn about Excel's mathematical features and functions, copy and link worksheets, and the various types of cell references.

In Chapter 3, Formatting, you learn how to change fonts, apply number formats, change cell alignments, use the format painter, apply cell borders, and rename worksheets.

PART 2: ACCOUNTING PROJECTS

There are three chapters in Part 2: Chapters 4, 5 and 6.

Chapter 4, Template Tutorial, you apply the skills that you learned in Chapters 1, 2, and 3 to complete accounting projects. First, you open the appropriate template file included on the CD that accompanies this textbook. Then, you record transactions to change the spreadsheets. After recording the transactions, you analyze the data.

In Chapter 5, Financial Accounting, you use preformatted templates for inventory valuation; recording transactions in the cash receipts journal; completing bank reconciliation; computing an accounts receivable aging schedule; determining depreciation; completing a payroll register; doing a percentage of completion spreadsheet; doing bond amortization; and financial statement analysis.

In Chapter 6, Managerial Accounting, you use preformatted templates to complete a schedule of the cost of goods manufactured; determine the total cost and unit cost of a job; prepare production cost reports; complete break-even analysis; prepare flexible budgets; calculate the price, quantity and total variance for direct materials; and determine make and buy decisions.

PART 3: MODEL BUILDING

There are ten chapters in Part 3: Chapters 7, 8, 9, 10, 11, 12, 13, 14, 15, and 16.

In Chapter 7, Financial Statements, you will build models to solve various problems using Excel. Once you have completed your model, you will be asked to input a new set of data to test your model.

In Chapter 8, Inventory, model-building activities continue. You build a cost of goods sold schedule from scratch.

In Chapter 9, Payroll, you prepare spreadsheets to calculate an employee's earnings record and a payroll register. Similar to the other model building activities that you completed in Chapters 7 and 8, data will be provided so that you can complete the spreadsheets.

In Chapter 10, Depreciation, you prepare a depreciation schedule. You will also prepare a schedule that will calculate depreciation using the units-of-activity (or production) method.

In Chapter 11, Amortization, you will prepare an amortization schedule for a note. You will use a formula to calculate the minimum payment required for a note. You will also calculate the amount of interest being paid with each payment and calculate the remaining principle balance after each payment is made.

In Chapter 12, Cost of Goods Manufactured, you prepare a cost of goods manufactured schedule. Your workbook will contain two linked sheets. One sheet is for input data and the other sheet is the actual cost of goods manufactured schedule which is linked to the input data.

In Chapter 13, Job Order Cost Accounting, you complete job order cost projections.

In Chapter 14, Process Costing, you complete worksheets that show equivalent units as well as production costs.

In Chapter 15, Cost-Volume-Profit, you will determine break-even points using the contribution margin.

In Chapter 16, Budgeting and Analysis, you will use Excel to prepare a master budget.

PART 4: CASE PROBLEMS

The case problems are advanced model-building problems. You build financial and managerial accounting spreadsheets from scratch.

APPENDIX A: ADVANCED EXCEL APPLICATIONS

Appendix A covers two Excel features that were not covered in the textbook: Pivot Tables and Vlookup.

APPENDIX B: GLOSSARY

Appendix B includes a glossary of accounting and Excel terms used in the textbook.

Acknowledgments

The authors would like to thank the following colleagues for their help in the preparation of this book: Steve Schuetz; Melody Marcus; Andy Set; Jacqueline Powers; Greg Bates; Dimpna Figuracion; Matt Lowenkron; and Brice Wood.

We would like to extend a special thank you to the following accounting professors who made many valuable suggestions.

Deborah Bloom, Newbury College
Susan V. Crosson, Santa Fe Community College
Mindy Davis, Oklahoma Panhandle State University
Jeff Decker, University of Hawaii
Shirl Mallory, Coosa Valley Technical College
Sherry Mills, New Mexico State University, Las Cruces
Jack Neymark, Oakton Community College
Cherie O'Neil, Colorado State University
Eddie Metrejean, Texas State University-San Marcos
Judy Pendleton, Flathead Valley Community College
Joel Peralto, Hawaii Community College

We would also like to extend a very special thank you to our students.

Table of Contents

Part 1

Excel Tutorial

In Part 1, you learn about the basic features of Excel. There are three chapters in Part 1.

Chapter 1: Excel Basics

Chapter 2: Using Formulas

Chapter 3: Formatting

In Chapter 1, Excel Basics, you start by identifying parts of an Excel screen, then learn how to move around a workbook, enter data, save files, format data, use page setup, and print.

In Chapter 2, Using Formulas, you learn about Excel's mathematical features and functions, copy and link worksheets, and the various types of cell references.

In Chapter 3, Formatting, you learn how to change fonts, apply number formats, change cell alignments, use the format painter, apply cell borders, and rename worksheets.

The instructions in this book were written using Windows XP and Microsoft Excel 2002. The CD that accompanies this textbook includes Excel files with starting data for selected exercises. Files that are pre-saved and can be used with Excel are called **template** files. These template files can be used with Microsoft Excel 97 and higher.

Windows[1] software uses pictures or **icons** to identify tasks. This is known as a **graphical user interface** (**GUI**). For example, Excel uses common icons or symbols to represent tasks: a file folder for opening a file, an envelope for emailing, an hourglass to show that the program is waiting for a task to be performed, a printer, etc. You use a **mouse**,

---

[1] Words that are boldfaced and italicized are defined in the Glossary. The glossary is on the textbook's website at www.mhhe.com/yachtexcel and on pages 439 - 448.

trackball or other pointing device, in addition to the keyboard, to perform various tasks.

The way personal computer software looks and works can be described by the acronym **WIMP** -- Windows, Icons, Menus, and Pull-downs.

The chart below shows the files saved in Chapters 1, 2, and 3. You can use one blank, formatted disk to save all the files completed in this textbook, Chapters 1-16 and the Case Problems. In the textbook, a floppy disk in drive A is used to save files. You may also save files to a hard-drive location or network drive. If available, you may also save to one Zip™ or Jazz™ drive, or CD-RW drive.

Chapter	File Name	Page Nos.
1	Budgeted Income Statement	16-17
	Exercise 1-1	36
	Exercise 1-2	37
	Exercise 1-3	37
	Exercise 1-4	37
2	Budgeted Income Statement 2	52-53
	Budgeted Income Statement Consol	59
	Exercise 2-1	75
	Exercise 2-2	76
	Exercise 2-3	77
	Exercise 2-4	77
3	Income Stmnt	85; 88; 90; 91
	Exercise 3-1	98
	Exercise 3-2	99
	Exercise 3-3	99-100
	Exercise 3-4	100

Chapter 1

Excel Basics

SOFTWARE OBJECTIVES: In Chapter 1, you will use the software to:

1. Start Microsoft Excel.

2. Identify parts of the Excel screen.

3. Move around the workbook.

4. Create a new spreadsheet.

5. Enter data on your spreadsheet.

6. Clear cell contents, edit data, enter numeric data, and save spreadsheets.

7. Format data, resize columns and rows, and insert rows.

8. Use page setup.

9. Print spreadsheets.

10. Complete the exercises and activities in Chapter 1.

WEB OBJECTIVES: In Chapter 1, you will do these Internet activities:

1. Go to Microsoft Excel's website at http://office.microsoft.com/excel.

2. Use your Internet browser to go to the book's website at www.mhhe.com/yachtexcel.

> **Comment: Setting a Bookmark**
>
> In Chapters 1-16, the web objectives will refer to accessing the book's website (www.mhhe.com/yachtexcel). Since you are going to use this website in every chapter, you should set a **bookmark**. Bookmarks help you keep track of websites that are frequently visited. A bookmarked link is saved on your browser for easy access.
>
> Follow these steps to set a bookmark using Internet Explorer 6.0
>
> 1. Start IE.
> 2. In the "Address" field type www.mhhe.com/yachtexcel.
> 3. From IE's menu bar, click on Favorites, then Add.
> 4. The "Add Favorite" screen pops up. Click [OK]. (If you select [Create in <<], you can create a new folder to save your bookmark.

3. Complete the Internet Activities.

Excel 2002 is part of the Microsoft Office XP suite of applications. Excel is an electronic **spreadsheet**[1] that is used to organize and manipulate numeric data. A spreadsheet is a table of values arranged in rows and columns. Spreadsheets allow users to calculate and correct complicated problems in a fraction of a second. Before the invention of electronic spreadsheets, entire spreadsheets (also known as worksheets) were calculated manually. Electronic spreadsheets allow accountants to save time and be more accurate in their computations.

The ability of spreadsheets to manipulate large amounts of numeric data quickly made them a popular tool; for example, spreadsheets are used by teachers, scientists, engineers, doctors, lawyers, and many other professions.

Excel is one of the most widely used spreadsheet applications. Excel's basic features are shown in this chapter. As you complete the chapters of this book, you will learn much more about Excel's capabilities.

---

[1]Words that are boldfaced and italicized are defined in the Glossary. The Glossary is on the textbook's website at www.mhhe.com/yachtexcel.

GETTING STARTED

Follow these steps to start Excel 2002.

1. Start Windows. If Excel is *not* installed on your computer, refer to Appendix A for installing the software and student data disk that accompanies this textbook.

2. There are two ways to start Excel from your Windows *desktop*.

   a. The Windows desktop shows various *icons* for software applications.

   Double-click on the Excel icon to start the application.

   b. Another way to start Excel, is to click on "Start," then "All Programs" from your Windows *taskbar*. Double-click on "Microsoft Excel" to start the program. If an application is open, the taskbar identifies the open application with a button. For example, when Excel is open, the taskbar includes a 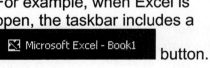 button.

   The All Programs list may differ depending on your computer's configuration. This illustration shows one possible All Programs list; yours will probably differ.

Comment

If you are using an earlier version of Windows (for example, Windows 98 or Windows 95), from your Windows desktop, click on "Start," "Programs," then "Excel." (In this book, the screen illustrations are done with Excel 2002 and Windows XP.) Some differences may occur between the screen illustrations in the text and the ones shown on your screen.

3. A "Microsoft Excel – Book1" screen appears. Compare your screen to the one shown below. (Your screen's toolbars may differ. This is OK; continue with the next section. On page 13, toolbar options are explained in more detail.)

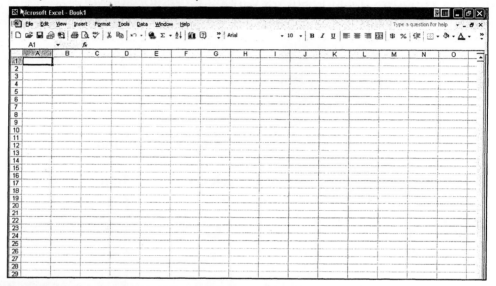

IDENTIFY PARTS OF THE SCREEN

You will begin using Excel with a new ***workbook***. Excel calls the blank screen a workbook. In Excel 2002, the default workbook consists of three sheets. Each sheet is referred to as a spreadsheet or a worksheet. The term spreadsheet and worksheet are used interchangeably.

Comment

There are a couple of ways to begin a new workbook. Using Office XP, you can select "New Office Document" from the "Start" menu, then select "Blank Workbook." A more common way is to click on the Excel icon from your Windows desktop or select "Start," then "Microsoft Excel" from the programs list.

In Excel 2002, the default screen appears similar to this one.

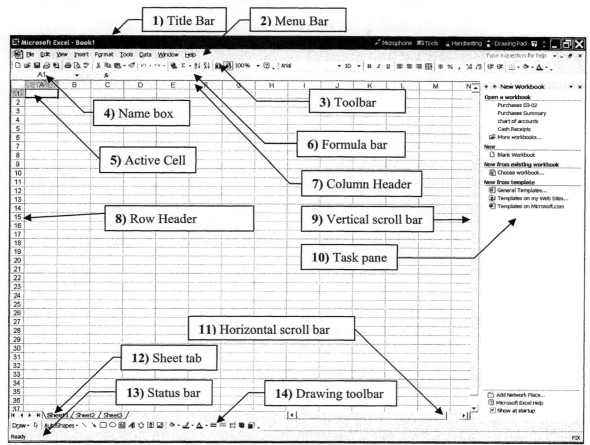

1) Title Bar   2) Menu Bar

3) Toolbar

4) Name box

6) Formula bar

5) Active Cell

7) Column Header

8) Row Header   9) Vertical scroll bar

10) Task pane

11) Horizontal scroll bar

12) Sheet tab

13) Status bar   14) Drawing toolbar

1)   The *title bar* displays the name of the application and the name of the file being viewed. When you open a new workbook in Excel, the title bar will display "Microsoft Excel – Book1." Below the title bar is the menu bar.

2)   The *menu bar* has nine selections: File, Edit, View, Insert, Format, Tools, Data, Window, and Help. As you complete this book, each one of these selections will be studied in more detail.

3)   Below the menu bar is the *toolbar*. The toolbar has icons and buttons that allow the user to perform common tasks by clicking on one of the buttons; for example, clicking on the open folder allows you to open a file or workbook. Excel normally displays a standard toolbar and a formatting toolbar. The standard toolbar displays common tasks such as opening or saving a file, printing, copying and pasting. The formatting toolbar displays formatting tasks that affect the appearance of the document. Remember, toolbars can be customized so your screen's toolbar may look different.

4)   The next row down contains the *name box*. The name box contains information about the selected cell.

5)   The *active cell* is identified by the column and row coordinate; for example, the callout is pointing to vertical column A, and horizontal row 1.

6)   The *formula bar* displays the content of the selected cell.

7)   The *column header* is identified by alphabetic characters: A, B, C, D, etc.

8)   The *row header* is identified by numbers.

9)   The *vertical scroll bar* allows you to move up and down the spreadsheet.

10)   In Windows XP, the *task pane* appears automatically when you start Excel. The task pane lists the last spreadsheet(s) saved and other frequently used features. The task pane can be closed by clicking on the "X" on the "New Workbook" title bar.

11)   The *horizontal scroll bar* allows you to move across the spreadsheet.

12)   The *sheet tab* identifies which worksheet you are using. Excel includes three sheet tabs for each workbook. Think of the sheet tabs as subsidiary (or secondary) workbooks related to the first worksheet or spreadsheet created. The sheet tabs at the bottom of the screen allow the user to select different sheets to view. Just as a book has pages, an Excel workbook has different spreadsheets.

13) The *status bar* includes information about applications that are open, the time and date, and other Windows-related information. The status bar on the illustrated spreadsheet displays "Ready."

14) The *drawing toolbar* allows you to select various shapes that can be added to your spreadsheet.

MOVING AROUND IN A WORKBOOK

You can move around a spreadsheet using either the mouse or the keyboard. Using the mouse, you can click in a cell or click on the scroll bar to scroll up and down or right and left. If using the mouse is not convenient, you may also move around using the arrow keys on the keyboard, or combinations of certain keys. The following table shows the keys you can use to move around in a spreadsheet.

Keys	Action
<Home>[2]	Moves to column A of the current row.
<Ctrl>+<Home>	Moves to cell A1. (Upper left cell of spreadsheet)
<Ctrl>+<End>	Moves to the lower right cell in a spreadsheet.
<Page Up>	Moves the active cell up one full window.
<Page Down>	Moves the active cell down one full window.
<Tab>	Moves the active cell one cell to the right.
<Shift>+<Tab>	Moves the active cell one cell to the left.
<Alt>+<Page Down>	Moves the active cell one window to the right.
<Alt>+<Page Up>	Moves the active cell one window to the left.
<End>+<Arrow key>	If you are in a blank cell, this will move to the next filled cell in the direction of the arrow key. If you are in a filled cell, this will move to the next blank cell in the direction of the arrow key.

---

[2]The less-than (<) and greater-than (>) signs around a word indicate individual keys on the keyboard; for example, <Home> for the "Home" key; <Ctrl> for the "Ctrl" key; <Page Up> for the "Page Up" key, etc.

ENTERING DATA

If you do not have a new workbook open, open one now by clicking on "Excel" from the "Start" menu. You are going to create a quarterly budget for Mike's Surf and Sea.

Before you begin developing a new spreadsheet, you should have a plan. You should know what data you need to input, the calculations you will have to make, and a general idea of what you want your output to be.

Entering Text

Follow these steps to type data into your Excel spreadsheet. Boldface characters indicate the word or words that you should type.

1. Type **Mike's Surf and Sea** in cell A1. Press the <Enter> key or the down arrow to go to cell A2.

2. Type **Budgeted Income Statement** in cell A2. Press the <Enter> key or the down arrow to go to cell A3.

3. Type **for the year ended 2002** in cell A3. Press the <Enter> key three times to go to cell A6.

4. Use your right-arrow or cursor to go to cell B6. Type **January** in cell B6. Press the <Enter> key two times to go to cell B8. Use the left-arrow key to go to cell A8.

5. Type **Revenues** in cell A8, then press <Enter>.

6. Type **Salaries** in cell A9, then press <Enter>.

7. Type **Rent** in cell A10, then press <Enter>.

8. Type **Utilities** in cell A11, then press <Enter>.

9. Type **Total Expenses** in cell A12, then press <Enter>.

10. Type **Net Income** in cell A13, then press <Enter>. Your cursor is in cell A14. Compare your screen with the one shown below.

Clearing Cell Contents

After reviewing your spreadsheet, you realize that you want the columns to be quarters rather than months. In cell B6, you have typed the month of January. Instead of January you want to identify the columns by quarters.

In Excel, there are usually two or three different ways to do things. One way to clear cell contents is to right click on the cell and select "Clear Contents." Another way is to click on the cell and press the <Delete> key.

Follow these steps to clear the cell's contents using the <Delete> key.

1. Move your cursor to cell B6 and press the <Delete> key.

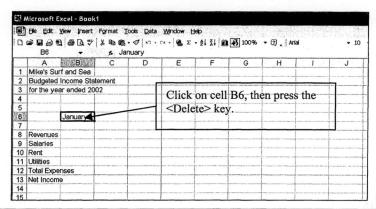

2. The contents of cell B6 are deleted.

Using Undo or Redo

After deleting January from cell B6, you realize that you did not want to clear the cell's contents. Here are three ways to undo a previous action in Excel.

- Click on the Undo button ⬚ on the toolbar (or select Edit, Undo Clear). (Hint: The toolbar has Excel's icons.)
- Or, Use the shortcut keystroke <Ctrl+Z>.
- From the menu bar, click on Edit, then select Undo Clear.

1. After selecting Undo button ⬚, the label "January" returns to cell B6. Since you want to delete it, click on the Redo button ⬚ (or select Edit, then Redo Clear). The label "January" is now removed from cell B6.

Comment: What if my toolbar does not show the Redo button?

If your toolbar does *not* show the Redo button ⟨↻ ▾⟩, from the menu bar, select <u>V</u>iew, then <u>T</u>oolbars. Make sure that "Standard" has a checkmark next to it.

Here are the steps for checking that your toolbar includes the buttons used in this chapter.

1. Click on the "Toolbar Options" button

2. A list drops down. Select <u>A</u>dd or Remove Buttons, then "Standard." Make sure that your screen shows the same checkmarks as the ones shown below.

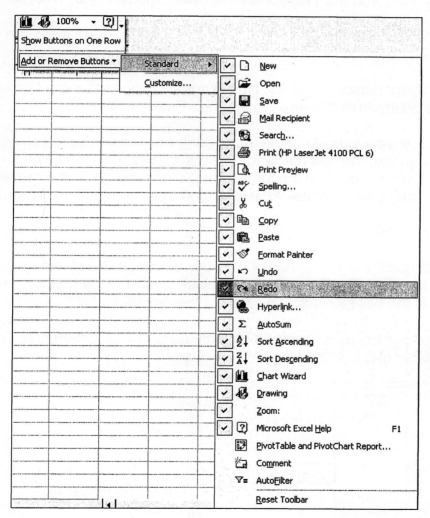

3. When you are finished, press the \<Esc\> key three times.

2. Since you want to display quarters instead of months, type **Quarter 1** in cell B6.

Editing Data

There is more than one way to edit data, too. You can replace the entire contents of a cell by simply selecting the cell and typing the new data. Or, you can edit data by selecting the cell and editing the data in the formula bar. Let's say you want to replace the label "Salaries" with "Wages."

1. Go to cell A9. Notice that "Salaries" is shown in two places: the formula bar and cell A9.

2. With your cursor in cell A9, type **Wages**. Observe that the formula bar also changed to "Wages." Press the <Enter> key.

   Another way to perform the same thing would be to go to cell A9, then click on the "formula bar" and delete the word "Salaries." Then, type the word "Wages" on the formula bar. Once you press the <Enter> key, the contents of cell A9 is changed from "Salaries" to "Wages."

Using AutoFill

You can quickly fill in a series of data by selecting the cell and dragging the *fill handle*. The fill handle is the black square in the bottom right corner of the cell selector. To see how this works, follow these steps.

1. Go to cell B6. Click on the fill handle (little box at bottom right corner of rectangle) and drag it with your cursor to cell F6.

2	Budgeted Income Statement				
3	for the year ended 2002				
4					
5					
6		Quarter 1			
7					
8	Revenues				
9	Wages				
10	Rent				
11	Utilities				

Click on the fill handle and drag to cell F6.

Notice that Excel has determined that you are using a series of quarters. Once you reach the end of the series (Quarter 4), Excel begins the series again (with Quarter 1).

2. Replace the data in cell F6 with **Total**. Compare your spreadsheet to the one shown below.

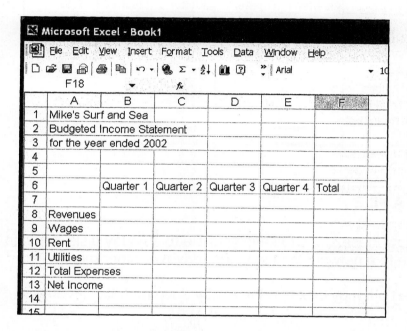

Adding Numeric Data

Follow these steps to add numeric data to your spreadsheet.

1. Type **150** in cell B8, then press <Enter>.

2. Type **25** in cell B9, then press <Enter>.

3. Type **10** in cell B10, then press <Enter>.

4. Type **5** in cell B11, then press <Enter> three times. Compare your spreadsheet with the one shown on the next page.

	A	B	C	D	E	F
1	Mike's Surf and Sea					
2	Budgeted Income Statement					
3	for the year ended 2002					
4						
5						
6		Quarter 1	Quarter 2	Quarter 3	Quarter 4	Total
7						
8	Revenues	150				
9	Wages	25				
10	Rent	10				
11	Utilities	5				
12	Total Expenses					
13	Net Income					
14						
15						

SAVING A FILE

1. Follow these steps to save your file to a floppy disk. You can also save to a network location, hard drive, or other media.

2. Insert a floppy disk into the floppy drive (usually drive A).

3. Click on the save ⊞ icon. The "Save As" dialog box appears.

4. Select 💾 3½ Floppy (A:) from the "Save in" field. Note, if you are saving to a location other than the My Documents folder, you must select the location here before saving.

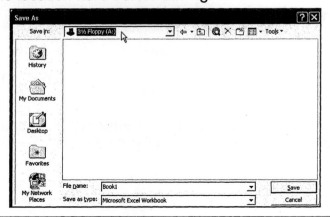

4. Type **Budgeted Income Stmt** in the "File name" field.

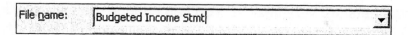

Compare your screen with the one shown below.

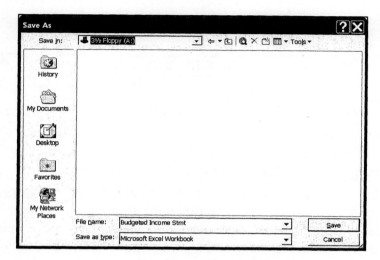

Observe that your are saving to a floppy disk in drive A and that the file name is "Budgeted Income Stmt."

5. Click [Save] or press <Enter>. Your file is now saved as "Budgeted Income Stmt."

FORMATTING DATA

Excel spreadsheets are very flexible. You can change the way they look by changing the font type, font size, font color, alignment of columns, etc. Excel includes a formatting toolbar for that purpose. The illustration below shows Excel's formatting toolbar.

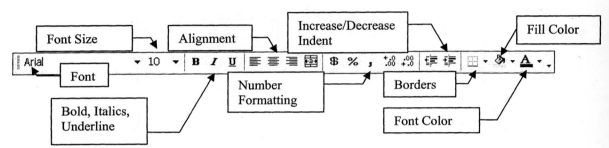

Let's examine this illustration. Starting from the left side, notice that the "Font Size" is "10." There are numerous font size selections. "Alignment" has three selections: left justified, centered, right justified. "Increase/Decrease Indent" is just that – you can increase or decrease indentations. The "Fill Color" is indicated by a bucket. "The Font" is "Arial." There are numerous font selections. The "B," "*I*," and "U" indicate bold, italics or underline choices. "Number Formatting" choices include $, %, etc. "Borders" can be changed, as well as the "Font Color."

Let's begin by centering, bolding and underlining the column headings.

1. Highlight cells B6 through F6. (Hint: Put your mouse in B6, then holding the left-mouse button highlight cells B6:F6. *Or,* you can click cell B6, then use <Shift>+<→ > to highlight cells B6:F6.)

2. Click on the Center ▤ button.

3. Click on the Bold ⬚ᴮ button.

4. Open the Borders drop down list by clicking on the arrow next to the "Borders" button.

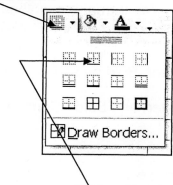

5. Select the Bottom Border button (first row, second column).

	A	B	C	D	E	F
1	Mike's Surf and Sea					
2	Budgeted Income Statement					
3	for the year ended 2002					
4						
5						
6		Quarter 1	Quarter 2	Quarter 3	Quarter 4	Total
7						
8	Revenues	150				
9	Wages	25				
10	Rent	10				
11	Utilities	5				
12	Total Expenses					
13	Net Income					

Next, you will format the Title information so that it is centered across the spreadsheet.

1. Highlight cell A1 through F1.

2. Click on the Merge and Center ▦ button. "Mike's Surf and Sea" is now centered across cells A1 through F1, and the cells have been merged into one cell.

3. Click on the Bold button.

4. Change the font size to 18 points. The formatting toolbar should look now like this. [Arial ▾ 18 ▾ | **B** *I* U | ≣ ≣ ≣ | 🖾]

5. Format row 2 with Merge and Center, Bold and 14-point font size.

6. Format row 3 with Merge and Center, and Bold. Compare your screen to the one shown below.

	A	B	C	D	E	F
1			**Mike's Surf and Sea**			
2			**Budgeted Income Statement**			
3			for the year ended 2002			
4						
5						
6		Quarter 1	Quarter 2	Quarter 3	Quarter 4	Total
7						
8	Revenues	150				
9	Wages	25				
10	Rent	10				
11	Utilities	5				
12	Total Expenses					
13	Net Income					

Resizing Columns and Rows

You may want to resize the columns and rows on your spreadsheet. Follow the steps in the next section which describes how to insert columns and rows.

Inserting Columns and Rows

Whenever you insert columns and rows, keep in mind that Excel will insert columns to the left of the highlighted column and above the highlighted row. To insert a column or row, right-click on the column or row header and select Insert.

The following steps will help you insert a row between "Revenues" (row 8) and "Wages" (row 9).

1. Right-click on the row 9 header, "Wages." A pop-up menu appears. Compare your screen with the one shown on the next page.

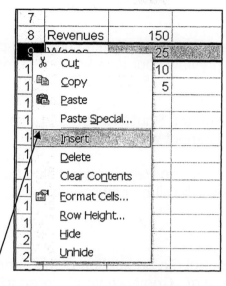

2. Select <u>I</u>nsert. The "Insert" screen pops up. Select Entire <u>r</u>ow, then click on <OK>. (*Hint:* Observe that there is also a selection for inserting a column. In this example, you are inserting a row.)

3. A blank row is inserted after row 8. The former row 9 is now row 10.

4. Move your cursor over the boundary between the column headers A and B (the gray letters at the top of row 1). Observe that the cursor changes to a cross bar. Double click the boundary. Column A automatically widens to the longest cell in column A.

	A	B	C	D	E	F
1	**Mike's Surf and Sea**					
2	**Budgeted Income Statement**					
3	for the year ended 2002					
4						
5						
6		Quarter 1	Quarter 2	Quarter 3	Quarter 4	Total
7						
8	Revenues	150				
9						
10	Wages	25				
11	Rent	10				
12	Utilities	5				
13	Total Expenses					
14	Net Income					
15						
16						

USING PAGE SETUP

Before printing your spreadsheet, you should make sure it will print properly. Follow these steps to preview your spreadsheet before you print it.

1. To view your document, click on the Print Preview 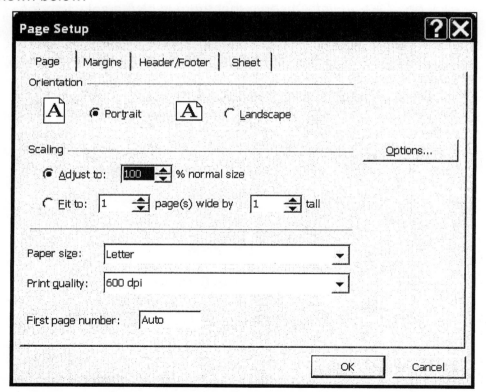 button. This will allow you to see how your document will print.

2. Click on the Setup button to go to the Page Setup dialog box. The first time you do this, the Page tab will be highlighted.

Page Tab

The page tab will allow you to control the orientation of the printed page as well as how many pages you print. Compare your screen to the one shown below.

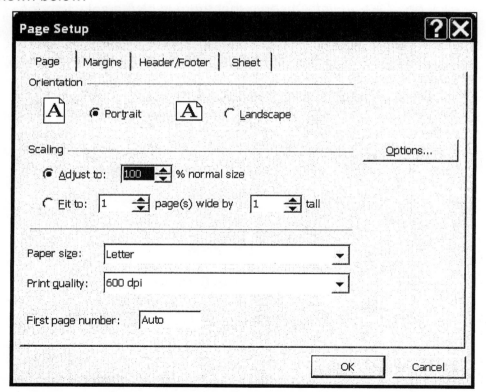

The "Scaling" section allows you to change the size of the spreadsheet. For example, if your spreadsheet is a little too large to print on one page, you can reduce the spreadsheet to a smaller percentage of its original size. Generally, it is not a good idea to reduce the size of the spreadsheet to less than 80% of its original size or the data may be too small for many readers. The "Adjust to" field on your page should show "100% normal size."

You can also choose how many pages to print; for example, if you want to print your spreadsheet on only one page, select the "Fit to" radio button and change the pages to one page wide by one page tall.

The last section controls the Paper size and Print quality. If you are printing on a letter size paper, you should leave this section alone.

Margins Tab

1. Click on the "Margins" tab and this screen appears.

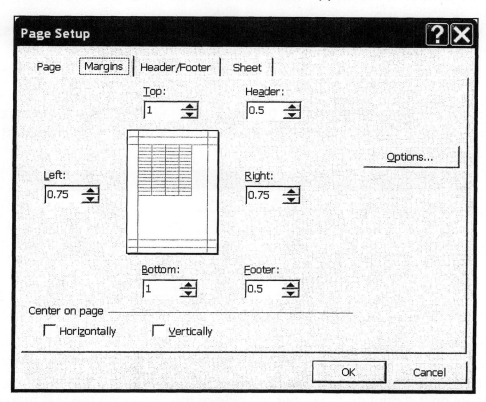

The Margins tab allows you to control the margins on the page. You can also choose to center your spreadsheet horizontally and/or vertically.

2. On most documents, you will want to center horizontally on the page. To do this, click on the box to the left of "Horizontally" to place a checkmark in it.

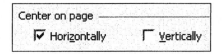

Header/Footer Tab

1. Click on the "Header/Footer" tab. This tab controls what prints in the header and footer sections of each page. You can select from preformatted headers and footers by clicking on the dropdown list for the header or footer.

    If you do not want to use any of the preformatted headers or footers, you may enter information by selecting either the

     buttons.

2. Click on the Custom Header button. The Header dialog box appears. The Footer dialog box is similar to the Header dialog box. Compare your screen to the following image.

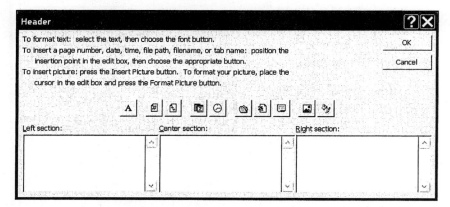

Notice that the box has three sections in it. Everything in the Left section will print on the upper left side of the page with the text being left aligned. Text in the <u>C</u>enter section will print in the upper center of the page and will be center aligned. Text in the <u>R</u>ight section will be appearing on the upper right and be right aligned.

The buttons in this dialog box will allow you to format the data in each section or insert commands.

A	Displays the Fonts dialog box.
#	Inserts page numbers.
	Inserts the total number of pages.
	Inserts the date.
	Inserts the time.
	Inserts the path and file name.
	Inserts the file name.
	Inserts the sheet name.
	Displays the Insert Picture dialog box.
	Displays the Format Picture dialog box.

3. Click on "Cancel" to return to the Page Setup dialog box.

Sheet Tab

1.   Click on the "Sheet" tab. The sheet tab allows you to control what prints on each page.

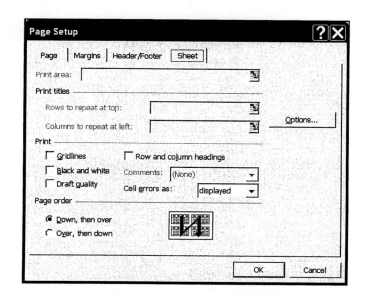

The "Print area" allows you to print certain cells or a range of cells. In the screen illustration above, the "Print area" is grayed out. This indicates it is inactive.

The "Print titles" area will print the same rows or columns on every page.

In the "Print" area, notice that there are a number of check boxes.

Gridlines – allows you to print the horizontal and vertical gridlines.

Black and white – if you are using a black and white printer and have color objects in your spreadsheet, you should check this box.

Draft quality – allows faster printing. This will not print gridlines and graphics.

Row and column headings – selecting this box will print row numbers (1, 2, 3…) and the column letters (A, B, C…).

Comments – this controls how the spreadsheet comments will be displayed.

Cell errors as – sometimes, your screen may display errors. "Cell errors as" controls how these errors are displayed.

2. Click on "Cancel."

PRINTING

Before printing, it is a good idea to save your document. Follow these steps to save your spreadsheet.

1. If your print preview screen is displayed, click on "Close."

2. From the menu bar, select File, Save As.

3. Make sure that the Save in field shows "3½ Floppy (A:)."

4. Highlight "Budgeted Income Stmt."

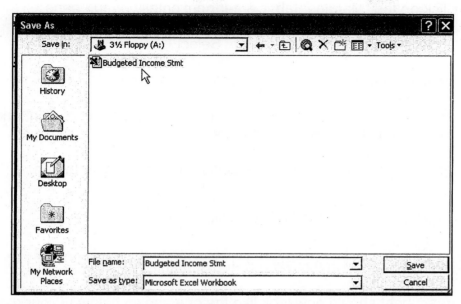

5. Click on <u>S</u>ave. A "Microsoft Excel" warning screen pops up.

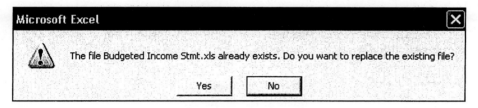

6. Read the information on this screen, then click on "Yes." Your spreadsheet is saved to the disk in drive A.

Checklist Before Printing

You should always use "Print Preview" before printing any document. Follow these steps to do that.

1. Click on the "Print Preview" 🔲 button.

2. Click on the <u>S</u>etup button and perform the following tasks:

    a. If necessary, click on the "Page" tab. Make sure scaling to print is set at 100% of normal size.

b. Click on the "Margins" tab. Center horizontally on the page.

c. Click on the "Header/Footer" tab. Select Custom Header.

d. Type your name in the Left section.

e. Insert the spreadsheet's file name in the Center section. (Hint: the name of this file is "Budgeted Income Stmt.")

f. Insert today's date in the Right section using the date button.

g. Click [OK] in the Header dialog box.

h. Click [OK] in the Page Setup screen.

Your spreadsheet should now look like the one shown below. (Your date will differ from the one shown.)

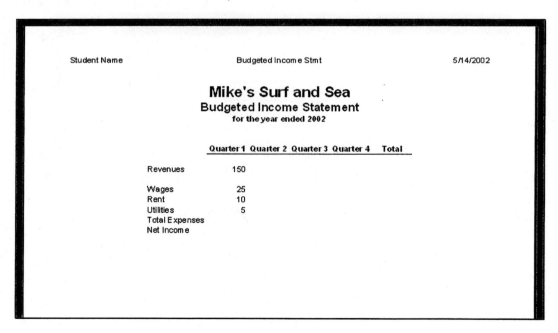

i. Click on the Close [Close] button.

j. Click on the Save ⊞ button now. Notice that the file is automatically saved to your floppy disk in drive A. The file name and drive was selected on pages 26 and 27, steps 4 and 5.

k. Click on the Print 🖨 button. Your spreadsheet starts to print. Compare it to the one shown above.

l. Click on File, Exit to exit Excel.

INTERNET ACTIVITIES
The *Internet* is a worldwide electronic communication network that allows for the sharing of information. The *World Wide Web* (WWW) or Web is a way of accessing information over the Internet. To read about the differences between the Internet and the Web, go to www.webopedia.com/DidYouKnow/Internet/2002/Web_vs_Internet.asp. To make an Internet connection, your computer must be equipped with a *modem*. The word modem is an abbreviation of **Mo**dulator/**Dem**odulator. A modem is a device that translates the digital signals from your computer into analog signals that can travel over telephone lines. There are also wireless radio modems, cable modems, DSL (digital subscriber lines), and T-1 lines for faster connections. *Websites are time and date sensitive. When using the Internet, be aware that changes are the rule.*

1.	From your Internet browser, go to the textbook's website at www.mhhe.com/yachtexcel. Go to the student link.
2.	Link to Internet Activities, then WEB EXERCISES, PART 1 – Chapter 1.
3.	Complete the ACCOUNTINGWEB activity at www.accountingweb.com.
4.	Access this website http://office.microsoft.com/excel.
5.	For purposes of this assignment, go to two links from the Excel website; Using a word processing program, write a summary about the links you selected. Include the website address of each link. Your summary should be no more than 75 words or less than 50 words.

SUMMARY AND REVIEW: In Chapter 1, you used the software to:

1. Start Microsoft Excel.

2. Identify parts of the Excel screen.

3. Move around the workbook.

4. Create a new spreadsheet.

5. Enter data on your spreadsheet.

6. Clear cell contents, edit data, enter numeric data, and save spreadsheets.

7. Format data, resize columns and rows, and insert rows.

8. Use page setup.

9. Print spreadsheets.

10. Complete the exercises and activities in Chapter 1.

WEB OBJECTIVES: In Chapter 1, you did these Internet activities:

1. Went to Microsoft Excel's website at http://office.microsoft.com/excel.

2. Used your Internet browser to go to the book's website at www.mhhe.com/yachtexcel.

Multiple-Choice Questions: In the space provided, write the letter that best answers each question. You may refer to the textbook to complete these questions.

_____1. The website for *Excel Accounting* is:

    a. http://office.microsoft.com/excel.
    b. www.mhhe.com/business/accounting.
    c. www.accountingweb.com.
    d. www.mhhe.com/yachtexcel.
    e. None of the above.

_____2. Electronic spreadsheets are used to:

   a. Organize word processing documents.
   b. Complete application utilities.
   c. Organize and manipulate numeric data.
   d. Access work-related websites for research.
   e. None of the above.

_____3. An advantage of using an Excel spreadsheet is that complicated data is:

   a. Calculated quickly.
   b. Organized in an attractive way.
   c. Able to be reformatted.
   d. All of the above.
   e. None of the above.

_____4. The name of the application and the name of the file being viewed is shown on the:

   a. Toolbar.
   b. Menu bar.
   c. Active cell.
   d. Title bar.
   e. None of the above.

_____5. Information about a selected cell is found in the:

   a. Toolbar.
   b. Menu bar.
   c. Name box.
   d. Active cell.
   e. None of the above.

_____6.   The coordinate of a column and row, for example, A1, is known as the:

    a. Active cell.
    b. Name box.
    c. Formula bar.
    d. Task pane.
    e. None of the above.

_____7.   The column header is identified by a/an:

    a. Numeric character.
    b. Alphabetic character.
    c. Alphanumeric character.
    d. Coordinate of a column and row.
    e. None of the above.

_____8.   The row header is identified by a/an:

    a. Numeric character.
    b. Alphabetic character.
    c. Alphanumeric character.
    d. Coordinate of a column and row.
    e. None of the above.

_____9.   You can add shapes to your spreadsheet by selecting the:

    a. Toolbar.
    b. Vertical scroll bar.
    c. Drawing toolbar.
    d. Horizontal scroll bar.
    e. None of the above.

____10. Information about which applications are open; for example,
the time and date, and other Windows-related information, can
be found on the:

    a. Toolbar.
    b. Taskbar.
    c. Scroll bar(s).
    d. Formula bar.
    e. None of the above.

True/Make True: If the statement is true, write the word "True" in the
space provided. If the statement is *not* true, write a correct statement in
the space provided. You may refer to the textbook to complete these
questions.

11. Spreadsheets allow users to calculate and correct complicated
problems in a fraction of a second.

_____

_____

12. The Budgeted Income Statement developed in this chapter is for the
first four months of the year.

_____

_____

13. Use the "Redo" button to undelete an item from a cell.

_____

_____

14. You cannot format numeric and alphabetic data on an Excel spreadsheet.

_____

_____

15. Before printing your spreadsheet, you should preview it, and then save your file.

_____

_____

16. From the "Setup" selection, use the "Page" tab to add a header to your spreadsheet.

_____

_____

17. Use "Sheet" tab to change the margins of your spreadsheet.

_____

_____

18. In the first quarter, the utilities are 5.

_____

_____

19. In the first quarter, the rent is 25.

_____

_____

20. In the second quarter the wages are 25.

_____

_____

Exercise 1-1: Follow the instructions below to complete Exercise 1-1.

1. Use the following data to create a spreadsheet for Carol's Surf Shop.

	A	B	C
1	Carol's Surf Shop		
2	Income Statement		
3			
4			
5		January	
6			
7	Revenues		
8	Salaries		
9	Rent		
10	Utiltities		
11	Total Expenses		
12	Net Income		
13			

2. Change "Salaries" to "Wages."

3. AutoFill cells B5 through F5 with months.

4. Replace the data in cell F5 with **Total**.

5. Either save your spreadsheet to drive A, or continue with Exercise 1-2. If you are saving the file, use **Exercise 1-1** as the file name. If you are *not* continuing with Exercise 1-2, save then exit.

Exercise 1-2

If you saved Exercise 1-1 and exited, follow these steps:

- Start Excel.
- Put your disk in drive A.
- Click on the Open [icon] button.
- Select drive A.
- Highlight "Exercise 1-1," then click on Open. Your Exercise 1-1 spreadsheet appears.

1. Add the following data:

    Cell B7:   200
    Cell B8:   50
    Cell B9:   15
    Cell B10:   9

2. Boldface, center, and underline cells B5 through F5.

3. Insert a row between cell B7 and B8.

4. Either continue with Exercise 1-3 or save your spreadsheet. Use **Exercise 1-2** as the file name.

Exercise 1-3

1. If necessary open Exercise 1-2, then continue.

2. In cells A1 and A2, change the font size to 18; boldface; and merge and center over columns A through F.

3. Preview your spreadsheet to make sure that the information is correct.

4. Save or continue. Use **Exercise 1-3** as the file name.

Exercise 1-4

1. If necessary open Exercise 1-3, then continue.

2. Add the following header information:

    Left section: Your Name
    Center section: Exercise 1-4
    Right section: Today's Date

3. Make the selection to horizontally center your spreadsheet.

4. Preview, then save your spreadsheet to a floppy disk in drive A. Use **Exercise 1-4** as the file name.

5. Print your spreadsheet.

The McGraw-Hill Companies, Inc., *Excel Accounting*

CHAPTER 1 INDEX

Chapter 2 — Using Formulas

SOFTWARE OBJECTIVES: In Chapter 2, you will use the software to:

1. Open the budgeted income statement file saved in Chapter 1 on pages 16 and 17.

2. Perform calculations with Excel's math operators.

3. Enter cell references; use AutoSum; learn about Excel's order of preference for calculating formulas; copy formulas within and between worksheets.

4. Link three spreadsheets together.

5. Enter absolute, relative, and mixed cell references.

6. Enter Excel's built-in formulas and financial functions.

7. Complete the exercises and activities in Chapter 2.

WEB OBJECTIVES: In Chapter 2, you will do these Internet activities.

1. Use your Internet browser to go to Excel's Assistance Center at http://office.microsoft.com/assistance/2002/articles/pwExcelMultiWkShts.aspx.[1]

2. Use your Internet browser to go to the book's website.[2]

3. Complete the Internet Activities.

---

[1]Websites are time and date sensitive. The website address shown above may redirect you to another website address. If you cannot access a website shown in the textbook, try this. Go online to http://office.microsoft.com/excel/assistance. In the Search field, select Assistance. Type Multiple Worksheets, then click Go. A list of articles appears; link to one or more articles to complete the web objective.

[2]The book's website is www.mhhe.com/yachtexcel. Steps for setting a website bookmark are in Chapter 1, page 4. You link to the book's Internet Activities from this site.

In this chapter, you will learn to use formulas to make computations. You will also learn to link different spreadsheets together and the significance of absolute and relative cell references.

The first electronic spreadsheet invented was called VisiCalc which stood for visible calculator. The story goes like this—a couple of graduate students were in class watching their accounting professor perform a complicated calculation on the blackboard. When an error was made, the professor would have to correct the error by redoing the entire calculation. The students thought that there must be a better way to do this. They designed an electronic spreadsheet so that if an error was made, only the part that was wrong had to be fixed. Also, if done properly, the entire spreadsheet would recalculate itself.

The ability to change only one part of the spreadsheet and have it recalculate made it possible to perform complicated calculations quicker and with more accuracy. Another important feature is the ability to perform calculations that let you see what will happen if you change part of the spreadsheet. This is called **what-if analysis**.

The key to successfully using Excel is to learn how to setup your spreadsheet and use the appropriate formulas. Although Excel has hundreds of functions, most people use only a few of them. This chapter will introduce Excel's basic functions.

GETTING STARTED

In order to begin Chapter 2, you will need to open the Budgeted Income Stmt file that you saved in Chapter 1 on pages 16 and 17. The quickest way to open a recent file in Windows XP is to click ⚡ *start* , then My Recent Documents. Compare your screen to the one shown on the next page.

From the drop-down list select "Budgeted Income Stmt." This is the file that you saved in Chapter 1 (pages 16 and 17). In Windows XP, the last fifteen files that were opened will be displayed.

Or, follow these steps to open the file called "Budgeted Income Stmt" that you saved on pages 16 and 17. These instructions show you how to open the file from a disk in drive A.

1. Start Windows and Excel.

2. If you saved to a floppy disk in drive A, put that disk in your floppy drive.

3. From Excel's menu bar, click on Eile, Open *or,* click ![icon] on the icon bar.

4. In the Look in field, select the drive where you saved the "Budgeted Income Stmt" file on pages 16 and 17. If you saved to a floppy in drive A, select your floppy drive. If you saved to your hard drive or network location, select that location.

5. Click on Budgeted Income Stmt to highlight it. The textbook instructions show drive A. Your Look in field will show a different location if you saved to a network or hard drive location.

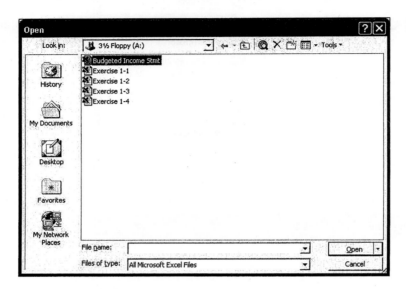

6. Click [Open ▾]. Mike's Surf and Sea Budgeted Income Statement appears on your screen, as shown below.

	A	B	C	D	E	F
1	**Mike's Surf and Sea**					
2	**Budgeted Income Statement**					
3	for the year ended 2002					
4						
5						
6		**Quarter 1**	**Quarter 2**	**Quarter 3**	**Quarter 4**	**Total**
7						
8	Revenues	150				
9						
10	Wages	25				
11	Rent	10				
12	Utilities	5				
13	Total Expenses					
14	Net Income					

USING MATH FUNCTIONS

In order to perform calculations in Excel, you must enter formulas. *Formulas* are mathematical calculations that Excel will perform. All formulas begin with an equal sign (=). The following mathematical signs tell Excel which type of calculation to perform:

Signs	Calculation
+	Add
-	Subtract
*	Multiply
/	Divide
%	Percent
^	Exponentiation

Entering Cell References

Before entering formulas, you should know that there are three ways to enter formulas:

1. Typing in the formulas and cell references.

2. Typing in the formulas then using the arrow keys to point to cell references.

3. Typing in the formulas and using the mouse to point to the cell references.

After you enter the formula, you select [ƒ Function...] from the Insert menu and point to the cell references. You will see how this works later in the chapter.

Using AutoSum

You will begin by using Excel's AutoSum button. This button allows you to add up a group of cells that are connected. We call a group of cells a *range*. In this example, you will add up the amounts in cells B10 through B12 and place the results in cell B13. Cell B13 will then contain the total of all the expenses in cells B10 through B12.

1. Begin by clicking in Cell B13 to make it the active cell.

2. Click on the AutoSum $\boxed{\Sigma}$ button in Excel's standard toolbar.

Comment:

When you click on the AutoSum button, Excel will look at the cells directly above or to the left of the active cell. In this case, Excel knows that the three cells directly above the active cell contains numerical data and assumes that you want to add this data. Excel then highlights the data in cells B10 to B12.

	A	B	C	D	E	F
1		**Mike's Surf and Sea**				
2		**Budgeted Income Statement**				
3		for the year ended 2002				
4						
5						
6		Quarter 1	Quarter 2	Quarter 3	Quarter 4	Total
7						
8	Revenues	150				
9						
10	Wages	25				
11	Rent	10				
12	Utilities	5				
13	Total Expenses	=SUM(B10:B12)				
14	Net Income	SUM(**number1**, [number2], ...)				
15						
16						
17						

3. Press the <Enter> key. Observe that "40" is now in cell B13 for Total Expenses.

4. Your cursor is in cell B14. The next step is to calculate Net Income. In this step, you will type the formula and point to the cell references. All formulas in Excel begin with an equal sign (=). The formula for net income is =B8-B13.

5. To begin the formula for cell B14, enter an equal sign (=).

6. Click on cell B8 and press the minus key (-)

7. Press the up arrow key once

8. Compare your screen to the one shown below.

	A	B	C	D	E	F
1		**Mike's Surf and Sea**				
2		**Budgeted Income Statement**				
3		for the year ended 2002				
4						
5						
6		Quarter 1	Quarter 2	Quarter 3	Quarter 4	Total
7						
8	Revenues	150				
9						
10	Wages	25				
11	Rent	10				
12	Utilities	5				
13	Total Expenses	40				
14	Net Income	=B8-B13				
15						
16						
17						
18						

The McGraw-Hill Companies, Inc., *Excel Accounting*

9. Press the <Enter> key. Observe that "110" is shown in B14.[3]

Now that we have calculated Net Income for the first quarter, we will project net income for the remaining quarters. Before we continue, we will make the following assumptions.

1. Revenues will increase by 5% each quarter.

2. Wages are $20 per quarter plus 3% of revenues.

3. Rent is a fixed cost.

4. Utilities are 3% of revenues.

To increase revenues by 5% each quarter, you must multiply the previous quarter by 105% (1.05). In other words, the revenues in Quarter 2 should be Quarter 1's revenues times 105%.

1. In cell C8, enter the formula =B8*1.05.

	A	B	C	D	E	F
1		**Mike's Surf and Sea**				
2		**Budgeted Income Statement**				
3		**for the year ended 2002**				
4						
5						
6		Quarter 1	Quarter 2	Quarter 3	Quarter 4	Total
7						
8	Revenues	150	=B8*1.05			
9						
10	Wages	25				
11	Rent	10				
12	Utilities	5				
13	Total Expenses	40				
14	Net Income	110				
15						

[3]Formulas may be typed in *either* uppercase or lowercase. In the textbook, uppercase is used.

2. After pressing the <Enter> key, the value in cell C8 is 157.5.

Wages have both a fixed and a variable component. In the example that follows, the fixed component (wages) is $20. The variable component is 3% of revenues. Because this formula will contain more than one operation (multiplication and addition), you must be aware of how Excel computes formulas. The order in which Excel performs calculations is called the ***order of precedence***. Excel performs mathematical calculations in the following order:

1. Percent

2. Exponentiation

3. Multiplication and division

4. Addition and subtraction

For most formulas, Excel performs calculations from left to right. Let's say you have three operations (multiplication, addition, division) that you want to do and that the two operations are in the same order of precedence. Excel will perform the left-most calculation first.

Or, you may manually override the order of precedence by using parenthesis. For example, take a look at the following formulas and the differences in the results.

20+150*3	Result is 470. Excel performs multiplication first (150*3) then addition.
(20+150)*3	Result is 510. Excel performs the functions in the parenthesis first (20+150) then multiplication (170*3).

Remember the order of precedence as you enter formulas. Follow these instructions to enter the formula to calculate wages.

1. In cell C10, enter the formula =C8*.03+20. Compare your screen to the one shown on the next page.

	A	B	C	D	E	F	
1			**Mike's Surf and Sea**				
2			**Budgeted Income Statement**				
3			for the year ended 2002				
4							
5							
6		Quarter 1	Quarter 2	Quarter 3	Quarter 4	Total	
7							
8	Revenues	150	157.5				
9							
10	Wages	25	=C8*.03+20				
11	Rent	10					
12	Utilities	5					
13	Total Expenses	40					
14	Net Income	110					
15							

2. After pressing the <Enter> key, cell C8 shows 24.725.

Now, let's use Excel to calculate rent. Since rent is the same over time, also known as a *fixed cost*, every quarter will be equal. The illustrated spreadsheet shows "10" for rent. To do this, simply make the second quarter equal to the first. Here is what you are going to do:

1. Make cell C11 the active cell.

2. Type the equal sign (=).

3. Press the left arrow to highlight cell C11 and go to cell B11.

4. Press <Enter>. Cell C12 is now the active cell and "10" is shown in cell C11.

Now, let's use Excel to show that Utilities are equal to 3% of revenues.

1. In Cell C12, enter the formula =C8*3%. (Hint: Note that *either* a percent sign or a decimal, .03, can be used in Excel formulas.)

2. Press <Enter>. Cell C13 is now the active cell. Cell C12 shows 4.725.

Copying Formulas

The next step is to copy the formulas from cells B13 and B14 to cells C13 and C14.

1. Highlight cells B13 and B14.

2. Move your cursor over the fill handle until it turns into a cross hair.

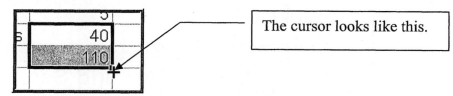

The cursor looks like this.

3. Drag the fill handle until it highlights cells C13 and C14.

	A	B	C	D
1		**Mike's Surf and**		
2		**Budgeted Income Stat**		
3		for the year ended 2002		
4				
5				
6		Quarter 1	Quarter 2	Quarter
7				
8	Revenues	150	157.5	
9				
10	Wages	25	24.725	
11	Rent	10	10	
12	Utilities	5	4.725	
13	Total Expenses	40		
14	Net Income	110	+	
15				

Hold the left mouse button and drag the fill handle to highlight cells C13 and C14.

4. The formulas from cells B13 and B14 are now copied to cells C13 and C14. Observe that cell C13 shows 39.45 and that cell C14 shows 118.05.

Follow these steps to copy the formulas from column C to columns D and E.

1. Highlight the range C8 through C14.

2. Drag the fill handle to cell E14.

After copying the formulas to column E, compare your spreadsheet to the one shown below.

	A	B	C	D	E	F	
1		**Mike's Surf and Sea**					
2		**Budgeted Income Statement**					
3		for the year ended 2002					
4							
5							
6		Quarter 1	Quarter 2	Quarter 3	Quarter 4	Total	
7							
8	Revenues	150	157.5	165.375	173.6438		
9							
10	Wages	25	24.725	24.96125	25.20931		
11	Rent	10	10	10	10		
12	Utilities	5	4.725	4.96125	5.209313		
13	Total Expenses	40	39.45	39.9225	40.41863		
14	Net Income	110	118.05	125.4525	133.2251		
15							
16							

Use the AutoSum button to enter the totals of each quarter in column F.

1. Highlight the range of cells from F8 through F14.

2. Click the AutoSum button.

3. Clear the contents of cell F9 by going to cell F9 and pressing the <Delete> key.

Now you can format the entire spreadsheet so that our numbers appear without decimals.

1. Select the entire spreadsheet by clicking on the blank area above the row 1 header and to the left of the column A header.

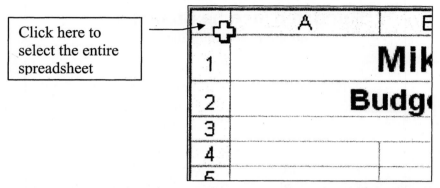

Click here to select the entire spreadsheet

2. To get rid of your decimals, right-click in the highlighted area and select <u>F</u>ormat Cells. If not already selected, select the Number tab then click on Number in the Category box. Set the decimals to zero then click [OK].

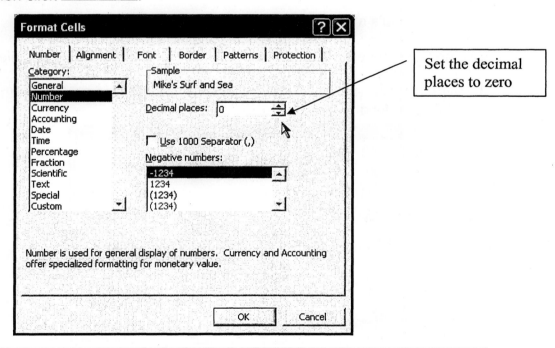

Set the decimal places to zero

The McGraw-Hill Companies, Inc., *Excel Accounting*

3. After formatting the cells, click on your spreadsheet to remove the highlight. Compare your spreadsheet to the one shown below.

	A	B	C	D	E	F
1		**Mike's Surf and Sea**				
2		**Budgeted Income Statement**				
3		**for the year ended 2002**				
4						
5						
6		**Quarter 1**	**Quarter 2**	**Quarter 3**	**Quarter 4**	**Total**
7						
8	Revenues	150	158	165	174	647
9						
10	Wages	25	25	25	25	100
11	Rent	10	10	10	10	40
12	Utilities	5	5	5	5	20
13	Total Expenses	40	39	40	40	160
14	Net Income	110	118	125	133	487

Follow these steps to save your spreadsheet.

1. From Excel's menu bar, select <u>F</u>ile, Save <u>A</u>s.

2. The Save <u>i</u>n field shows the location where you are saving this file.

3. Type a space and the number **2** after Budgeted Income Stmt in the File <u>n</u>ame field.

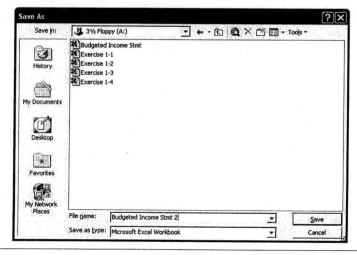

4. Click .

COPYING BETWEEN WORKSHEETS

We will now use the data from the budgeted income statement you just prepared to complete a statement for one of the departments of Mike's Surf and Sea.

Before you begin, follow these steps to change the header on this spreadsheet to indicate that it is for the Retail Department.

1. Put your cursor on the row 3 header ("for the year ended 2002"). Right-click to insert a row between rows 2 and 3.

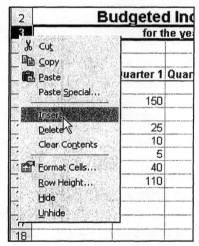

2. Select I<u>n</u>sert. When the Insert pop-up window appears, accept the default for Shift cells <u>d</u>own by clicking OK.

3. In the blank row, type **Retail Department** and press <Enter>.

4. Center and merge between columns A and F. (*Hint:* Highlight the range A3:F3 and click the Merge and Center button 🖾 .)

Compare your spreadsheet to the one shown on the next page.

	A	B	C	D	E	F
1	**Mike's Surf and Sea**					
2	**Budgeted Income Statement**					
3	**Retail Department**					
4	for the year ended 2002					
5						
6						
7		Quarter 1	Quarter 2	Quarter 3	Quarter 4	Total
8						
9	Revenues	150	158	165	174	647
10						
11	Wages	25	25	25	25	100
12	Rent	10	10	10	10	40
13	Utilities	5	5	5	5	20
14	Total Expenses	40	39	40	40	160
15	Net Income	110	118	125	133	487
16						
17						

Next, we will copy the data from this spreadsheet onto another spreadsheet.

1. Begin by highlighting the range of cells A1 through F15.

2. Right-click in the highlighted area and select Copy.

3. Make sheet 2 the active sheet by clicking on the Sheet2 tab.

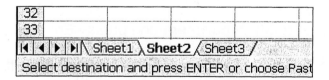

4. Right-click in cell A1 and select Paste.

You have just copied the data from Sheet1 onto Sheet2. Now, you will change the heading and the data in sheet 2 to show that it is for the Wholesale Department.

1. Click in A3 and type **Wholesale Department**. Press <Enter>.

2. Change the revenues in Quarter 1 to **250** (cell B9). Press <Enter>.

3. Double-click the border between columns A and B to resize column A. Compare your spreadsheet with the one below.

	A	B	C	D	E	F
1	**Mike's Surf and Sea**					
2	**Budgeted Income Statement**					
3	**Wholesale Department**					
4	for the year ended 2002					
5						
6						
7		Quarter 1	Quarter 2	Quarter 3	Quarter 4	Total
8						
9	Revenues	250	263	276	289	1078
10						
11	Wages	25	28	28	29	110
12	Rent	10	10	10	10	40
13	Utilities	5	8	8	9	30
14	Total Expenses	40	46	47	47	180
15	Net Income	210	217	229	242	898
16						

When using more than one sheet in a workbook, it is usually a good idea to change the sheet tab labels as well.

1. Double-click on the Sheet1 tab. In place of the highlighted Sheet1, type **Retail**.

2. Double-click on the Sheet2 tab and type **Wholesale**.

3. Double-click on the Sheet3 tab and type **Total**.

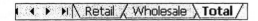

Retail / Wholesale \ **Total** /

You have just renamed the sheet tabs. Now you will prepare a final sheet that will consolidate all of the data in the retail (sheet 1) and wholesale (sheet 2) departments. This time, we will use AutoFill to copy the data from one worksheet to another.

1. Click on the Wholesale tab. With the Wholesale sheet active, select the range from A1 through F15.

2. Hold the <Ctrl> key down and click on the Total tab.

3. From the Edit menu, select Fill then Across Worksheets...

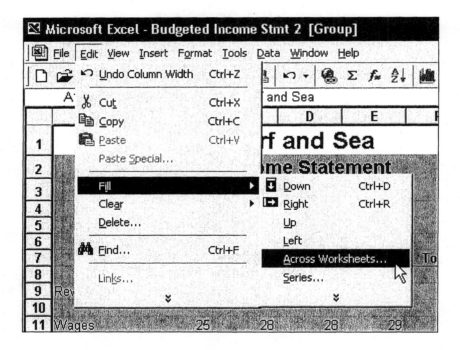

4. When the Fill Across Work... dialog box pops-up, click [OK].

5. Hold down the CTRL key and click on the Total tab to ungroup it.

You have just copied the data from the Wholesale spreadsheet to the Total spreadsheet. The new spreadsheet (Total) will occupy the same cells as the spreadsheet (Wholesale) you copied from.

LINKING WORKSHEETS

Now that you have copied the data, you can modify the heading in the Total spreadsheet to indicate that it is for all departments. You will also change the formulas to consolidate the numbers from the two departments.

1. If necessary, make the Total spreadsheet the active sheet by clicking on the Total tab.

2. Change row 3 to **All Departments**.

3. Double-click the border between columns A and B to resize column A.

At this point, you are ready to consolidate your data. Since all three spreadsheets are laid out exactly the same way, you will use Excel's AutoSum feature combined with the Multi-sheet selector.

1. If necessary, activate the Total spreadsheet by clicking on the Total tab. The budgeted income statement for all departments is displayed.

2. Select the cell B9. (Quarter 1 revenues.)

3. Click on the AutoSum button Σ ▼ .

4. Click the Retail sheet, then select cell B9.

5. Hold the <Shift> key down and click on the Wholesale sheet tab. This does an AutoSum between cell B9 of the Retail sheet and cell B9 of the Wholesale sheet. It is as if you are adding numbers three dimensionally. Observe that the formula row shows =sum('Retail:Wholesale'!B9). (*Hint: If you are using Windows 98, these steps will differ.*)

6. Press<Ctrl> + <Enter>. This has the effect of entering the formula without moving the cursor. You can do the same by clicking on the green check mark in the formula bar.

7. Using the fill handle, copy the data to column E. (*Hint:* Copy data from cells B9 to E9.)

8. Highlight the range B9:E15.

9. From the Edit menu, select F̲ill then R̲ight.

10. From the Edit menu, select Fill then D̲own.

11. Clear the contents in cells B10 through E10 by highlighting the range and pressing the <Delete> key.

Now that you have created a consolidated sheet, we can format all of the sheets to use the comma format without decimals.

1. If the Total sheet is not active, make it active by clicking on the Total sheet tab.

2. Select the range B9:F15.

3. Hold the <Shift> key down and select the Retail sheet tab. This selects all of the sheets and puts you in group mode (see the title bar). Anything you do now will be done on all of the selected sheets.

4. Click on the Comma Style button [,].

5. Click on the Decrease Decimal button [.00/+.0] twice.

6. Hold down the <Shift> key and click on the Total sheet tab. This will take you out of group mode and make the Total sheet the active sheet. Compare your spreadsheet with the one shown on the next page.

	A	B	C	D	E	F
1	Mike's Surf and Sea					
2	Budgeted Income Statement					
3	All Departments					
4	for the year ended 2002					
5						
6						
7		Quarter 1	Quarter 2	Quarter 3	Quarter 4	Total
8						
9	Revenues	400	420	441	463	1,724
10						
11	Wages	50	53	53	54	210
12	Rent	20	20	20	20	80
13	Utilities	10	13	13	14	50
14	Total Expenses	80	85	86	88	339
15	Net Income	320	335	355	375	1,385

7. Save your workbook as **Budgeted Income Stmt Consol**.

8. You have now applied the Comma style with no decimals to all of the spreadsheets. Click on the other sheets to be sure the formatting is consistent. Observe that the Retail sheet's amounts are added to the Wholesale sheet's amount to create the Total sheet. For example, click on the Retail tab. In cell B9 for Quarter 1, the revenue amount shown is 150; click on the Wholesale tab, revenues for Quarter 1 are 250. Now click on the Total sheet. Observe that cell B9 (revenues for Quarter 1) are 400 (150+250=400). The rest of the Total sheet reflects the amounts from the Retail sheet being added together with the Wholesale sheet's amounts.

9. Close the workbook.

USING RELATIVE AND ABSOLUTE REFERENCES

When a spreadsheet is designed properly, you should be able to change the data in one cell and any related information should also change. This is made possible through the use of formulas. Almost all formulas reference other cells. In other words, if the formula in cell B1 refers to cell A1, any change in cell A1 should result in a change in cell B1.

When you refer to another cell in a formula, this is called a ***cell reference***. For example, if you enter the formula =A1 in cell B1, A1 is called the cell reference. You can also make a range reference in a formula such as =sum(A1:B1). The range A1 to B1 is the range reference.

There are three types of references you can use:

Relative reference: When you use a relative reference, the formula will change if you copy the formula to another cell. Any references are made *relative* to the cell containing the formula. For example, if cell B1 contains the formula =A1 you are really telling Excel to make cell B1 equal to the cell one column to the left. If you copy this formula to cell D5, the formula will change to =C5 (equal to one cell to the left).

 Read Me

The steps that follow were written with Windows XP. If you are using a different version of Windows; for example, Windows 98, the steps will differ.

The following steps will illustrate this example:

1. Open a blank spreadsheet and enter the formula =A1 in cell B1.

2. Copy this formula to cell D5.

3. Make cell D5 the active cell.

4. From the menu bar, select <u>T</u>ools, then <u>O</u>ptions.

5. In the General tab, make sure the R1C1 reference style is checked.

6. Click OK. The formula in the formula bar changes to =RC[-1].

7. Click on cell B1. Notice that the formula is exactly the same as the formula in cell D5. This formula is referring to the cell in the same row but one cell to the left [-1].

8. Remove the R1C1 reference style from the Options dialog box. (*Hint:* Uncheck the box next to R1C1 reference style.)

Absolute reference: When using absolute references, the cell or range references never change. In other words, when you use an absolute cell reference, you are telling Excel to absolutely go to this cell all the time. Even if you copy this formula to another cell, it will still refer to the same cell. You can make a reference absolute by pressing the <F4> function key. We will now change our spreadsheet to make our reference absolute.

1. Double-click on cell B1 to make it the active cell.

2. Press the <F4> function key. The cell reference should change to =$A$1. Press <Enter>.

3. Copy the formula in cell B1 to cell D5. Notice that the formula did not change. It still refers to cell A1.

Mixed reference: A mixed reference will contain both a relative and an absolute component. You can have either a relative column with an absolute row or an absolute column with a relative row. The dollar sign in the formula will indicate which component is absolute. For example the formula =$A1 indicates that the column is absolute and the row is relative. On the other hand, the formula =A$1 indicates that the column is relative and the row is absolute. Again, the <F4> function key will allow you to toggle through your options.

1. Double-click on cell B1 to make it active.

2. Press the <F4> function key. The formula should change to =A$1 (relative column, absolute row). When you copy this formula to any other cell, the column may change but the row will always be the same.

3. Press the <F4> function key again. The formula should change to =$A1 (absolute column, relative row). When you copy this formula to any other cell, the column will always be the same but the row may change.

4. Press the <F4> function key again and the formula changes to relative.

5. Press the <F4> function key two more times. The formula should be =A$1.

6. Press the <Enter> key.

7. Copy the formula to cell D5. The formula should change to =C$1. The column is relative but the row is absolute.

8. Double-click on cell B1 to make it the active cell.

9. Press the <F4> function key. The formula will change to =$A1.

10. Copy the formula to cell D5. The formula changes to =$A5. The column is absolute and the row is relative.

11. Close the workbook without saving.

USING BASIC FUNCTIONS

Excel has some built-in formulas that you can use to perform certain tasks quickly and easily. These built-in formulas are called functions. This section explains some of the more common functions.

Go to a blank worksheet. Enter the data shown in cells A1 through A12 from the worksheet on the next page. Then follow steps 1 through 6 to add formulas in cells C1 through C12. (Hint: The data shown in column C is *after* the formulas are entered. Remember to enter data in column A only, then follow the steps to enter formulas in column C.)

	A	B	C	
1	5		539	
2	15		44.91667	
3	36		5	
4	95		95	
5	45		12	
6	75			
7	33			
8	57			
9	12			
10	89			
11	64			
12	13			
13				
14				

1.   In cell C1, enter the formula **=sum(A1:A12)**. This can also be done using the AutoSum button.

2.   In cell C2, enter the formula **=average(A1:A12)**. This will calculate the average in the range A1:A12.

3.   In cell C3, enter the formula **=min(A1:A12)**. This will return the lowest number in the range.

4.   In cell C4, enter the formula **=max(A1:A12)**. This will return the highest number in the range.

5.   In cell C5, enter the formula **=count(A1:A12)**. This will return the number of cells containing data.

6.   After checking your data, close the workbook without saving.

A conditional formula is one of the most useful functions. With conditional formulas, if a certain condition is met, then Excel will perform a certain action, but if it is not met, Excel will perform another action. An easy way to think of this is to use the phrase "if, then, else." In other words, **if** a condition is met, **then** perform action A, **else** perform action B.

To illustrate this, we will assume that a sales clerk will earn commissions based on the amount of sales he or she generates. **If** the clerk's sales exceed $1,000, **then** he or she will earn 5% in commissions, **else** he or she will only earn 3%.

1.   Open a blank workbook.

2.   Type **Sales** in cell A1.

3.   Type **Commission** in cell A2.

4.   In cell B2, enter the formula **=if(B1>1000,B1*5%,B1*3%)**. Think of the formula like this,

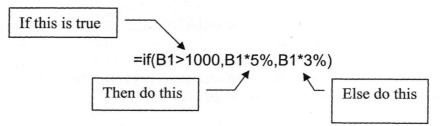

The formula can be read "if B1 is greater than 1,000 then B1 times 5% else B1 times 3%."

5.   Type **5000** in cell B1. The formula will calculate 5% of this amount in, which is 250 (cell B2).

6.   Type **900** in cell B1. The formula will calculate 3% of this amount, which is 900 (cell B2).

You can also have a conditional function within a conditional function. This is called a ***nested conditional function***. For example, using the same example above, we can add another level of commissions. Let's say that the sales clerk will earn a commission based on the following:

Sales	Commission
Greater than $1,000	5%
500 – 900	4%
Less than 500	3%

The formula would be written like this:

=if(A2>1000,A2*5%,if(A2>500,A2*4%,A2*3%)).

Since A2 represents sales, we can say that if sales are greater than 1,000 then multiply sales times 5%. The second IF occurs if sales are not more than 1,000. In this case, if sales are more than 500, then multiply sales by 4%, else multiply sales by 3%.

USING FINANCIAL FUNCTIONS[4]

Excel offers sixteen different financial functions. This category includes everything from depreciation to loan interest payments. To illustrate, lets assume you want to purchase a new car. The car costs $28,000 and the bank is offering a rate of 6% a year for five years. How much will you have to pay each month? You can use Excel's payment function to calculate your monthly payments as follows:

1. Activate Sheet 3.

2. Type **Loan amount** in cell A1.

3. Type **Interest rate** in cell A2.

4. Type **Months** in cell A3.

5. Type **Payment** in cell A4.

6. Resize column A.

---

[4]The steps on this page and page 66 were written with Windows XP. If you are using a different version of Windows, your steps will differ. Your result should be the same.

7. Enter **28000** in cell B1 and format with the Currency style 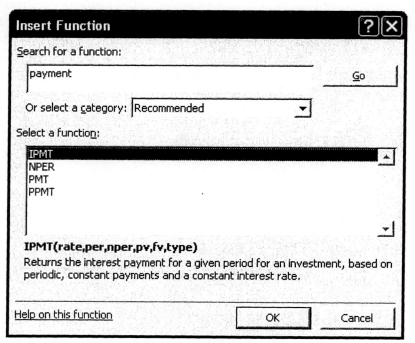 and no decimals.

8. Enter **6%** in cell B2 and format with the percent style %.

9. Enter the formula **=5*12** in cell B3. This formula will convert five years into months (60 months). Format with the Comma style and no decimals , .

10. Make cell B4 the active cell.

11. Click on the Paste Function button *fx*. This will display the Insert Function dialog box.

12. Type **Payment** in the Search for function dialog box and click the Go button.

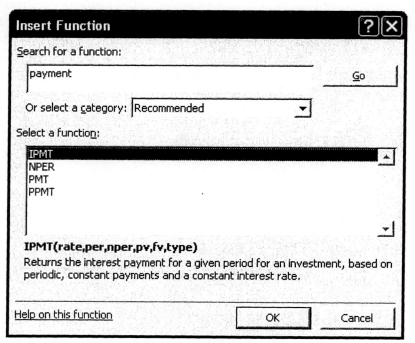

13. Double-click on "PMT" and the following will appear. This is called a Formula Palette. This will display the name of the formula and

each of its arguments (blank boxes). Clicking in one of the boxes
will display the function of the argument.

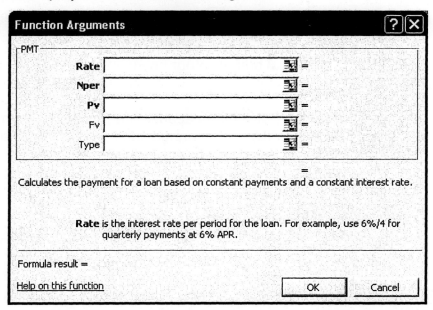

14.   Click in the **Rate** box and see the description of the argument at
       the bottom of the Formula Palette.

15.   To enter a reference, click on the ⬛ to hide the dialog box. (*Hint:*
       These icons are consistent with Office XP and Excel 2002; if you
       are using a different version, your icons may differ.)

16.   Click on the interest rate in cell B2.

17.   Click on the ⬛ to go back to the Formula Palette.

18.   Click in the **Nper** box. Notice the description at the bottom.

19.   Click on the ⬛ and click on B3.

20.   Click on the ⬛ to go back to the Formula Palette.

21.   Press the <Tab> key to go to the **Pv** field.

22.   Read the description at the bottom and click ▦.

23.   Click on cell B1 and click the ▦ to go back to the Function Palette.

24.   Click on the [OK] button. Your payment should be ($1,732.52).

Why is this amount so high? It is high because the payments are made monthly but the interest rate (6%) is an annual interest rate. We have to modify the formula to convert the annual interest rate into a monthly interest rate.

1. Click on cell B4 to make it active.

2. Click on the Paste Function button.

3. Click in the Rate box.

4. Type **/12** after the cell reference. Dividing the amount in cell B2 by 12 will convert it into a monthly rate.

5. Click [OK]. Your payment should now be ($541.32).

6. Close the workbook without saving.

INTERNET ACTIVITIES	
The Excel websites offer many tips for using the program. Follow the steps below to learn about Excel's Assistance Center.	
1.	From your Internet browser, go to the textbook's website at http://www.mhhe.com/yachtexcel. Go to the Student link.
2.	Link to Internet Activities, then WEB EXERCISES, PART 1 – Chapter 2.
3.	Access this website: http://office.microsoft.com/assistance/2002/articles/pwExcelMultiWkShts.aspx.
4.	Read the article "5 Tips for Working with Multiple Worksheets in Excel." Complete the exercise shown on this website.
5.	Go to the American Accounting Association website at (http://aaahq.org/index.cfm). Link to Links & Organizations. From this site, select three areas to explore.
5.	Write three brief essays (minimum length 50 words; maximum length 100 words).

SUMMARY AND REVIEW

SOFTWARE OBJECTIVES: In Chapter 2, you used the software to:

1. Open the budgeted income statement file saved in Chapter 1 on pages 16 and 17.

2. Perform calculations with Excel's math operators.

3. Enter cell references; use AutoSum; learn about Excel's order of preference; copy formulas within and between worksheets.

4. Link three spreadsheets together.

5. Enter absolute, relative, and mixed cell references.

6. Enter Excel's built-in formulas and financial functions.

7. Complete the exercises and activities in Chapter 2.

WEB OBJECTIVES: In Chapter 2, you did these Internet activities.

1. Used your Internet browser to go to Excel's Assistance Center at http://office.microsoft.com/assistance/2002/articles/pwExcelMultiWkShts.aspx. [5]

2. Used your Internet browser to go the book's website.

3. Completed the Internet Activities.

---

[5]Websites are time and date sensitive. If you cannot access a website shown in the textbook, try this. Go online to http://office.microsoft.com/excel/assistance. In the Search field, select Assistance. Type Multiple Worksheets, then click Go. A list of articles appears; link to one or more articles to complete the web objective.

Multiple-Choice Questions: In the space provided, write the letter that best answers each question.

_____1. The first spreadsheet software was called:

   a. Excel.
   b. Calculator.
   c. VisiCalc.
   d. Word Perfect.
   e. None of the above.

_____2. The ability to perform calculations that let you see what will happen if you change part of the spreadsheet is called:

   a. Budgeting.
   b. Functions.
   c. Complicated features.
   d. What-if analysis.
   e. None of the above.

_____3. The mathematic calculations that Excel performs are called:

   a. Formulas.
   b. Cell references.
   c. Paste command.
   d. Insert command.
   e. None of the above.

_____4. Excel will look at the cells directly above and to the left of the active cell when you use this feature:

   a. Paste command.
   b. Copy command.
   c. Range reference.
   d. AutoSum.
   e. None of the above.

_____5. The sequence in which Excel performs calculations is called:

    a. Preferential treatment.
    b. Order of precedence.
    c. Fixed costs.
    d. Variable costs.
    e. None of the above.

_____6. In what order does Excel calculate this formula, =25+140*4, and what is the result.

    a. 140*4; then add 25; result is 585.
    b. 25+140, then multiply by 4; result is 660.
    c. Excel does not calculate formulas without parentheses.
    d. Excel computes addition first.
    e. None of the above.

_____7. In what order does Excel calculate this formula, =(20+175)*4, and what is the result.

    a. Excel does not calculate formulas with parentheses.
    b. 4*175+20; the result is 700.
    c. (20+175)*4; the result is 780.
    d. Excel performs percentage calculations only.
    e. None of the above.

_____8. Costs that are the same over time are called:

    a. Variable costs.
    b. Temporary costs.
    c. Nominal costs.
    d. Fixed costs.
    e. None of the above.

_____9. If you copy a formula from one cell to another and the cell references change, you are using

   a. Absolute reference.
   b. Relative reference.
   c. Functions.
   d. Range reference.
   e. None of the above.

_____10. A reference to a cell or range of cells that never changes is called a(n):

   a. Absolute reference.
   b. Relative reference.
   c. Range reference.
   d. Mixed reference.
   e. None of the above.

True/Make True: If the statement is true, write the word "True" in the space provided. If the statement is *not* true, write the correct answer in the space provided.

11. Built-in formulas that can be used to perform tasks efficiently are called functions.

_____

_____

12. Another way to explain conditional formatting is to call it, IF, THEN, ELSE.

_____

_____

13.   Excel is an example of the first calculator.

_____

_____

14.   The only way to enter formulas in Excel is by typing in the formulas and cell references.

_____

_____

15.   A group of cells is called a range.

_____

_____

16.   The AutoSum feature is identified by the *fx* button.

_____

_____

17.   All formulas in Excel must be preceded by an equal (=) sign.

_____

_____

18. In this chapter, wages have both a fixed and a variable component.

_____

_____

19. If something has a fixed cost that means the amount will probably change each month.

_____

_____

20. To copy a formula, use Excel's fill handle.

_____

_____

Exercise 2-1

1. Open the Exercise 1-4 spreadsheet file. You saved this file on page 37.

2. Insert a third heading line called January through April. Center the heading across columns A through F.

3. Increase the width of column A.

4. Use AutoSum to calculate total expenses.

5. Calculate net income.

6. Increase revenues by 6% each month.

7.   Wages are $44 a month plus 3% of revenues.

8.   Rent is fixed.

9.   February through April's utilities are 4% of revenues.

10.   Copy the formulas from the range B12:B13 to cells C12:C13

11.   Copy the formula from the range C7:C13 to cells E7:E13.

12.   Calculate the Total column. Clear the contents of any cell that shows a zero.

13.   Use number format and no decimal places.

14.   The spreadsheet's header should show your name (left section), the exercise number (center section), and today's date (right section).

15.   Save your spreadsheet as Exercise 2-1.

16.   Print your spreadsheet.

Exercise 2-2

1.   Open Exercise 2-1. Using the data in Exercise 2-1, copy the information to Sheet2 and Sheet3.

2.   On Sheet1, add Men's Department as the third line header. Center the heading. Change the monthly columns to Quarter 1, Quarter 2, Quarter 3, and Quarter 4.

3.   On Sheet2, change the third heading line to Women's Department. (Make sure that columns B, C, D, and E show Quarter 1, Quarter 2, Quarter 3, and Quarter 4.)

4. On Sheet3, change the third heading line to Both Departments. (Make sure that columns B, C, D, and E show Quarter 1, Quarter 2, Quarter 3, and Quarter 4.)

5. Rename the sheet tabs, Men's, Women's, and Total.

6. Link the three spreadsheets so that the Total sheet represents the information from the Men's and Women's sheets. Clear any cell contents that show zeroes.

7. Use the Comma style and no decimal places to format your spreadsheet. Check each spreadsheet and when necessary, widen columns

8. The spreadsheet's header should show your name, exercise number and spreadsheet name, and today's date.

9. Add the appropriate header to each spreadsheet. Save your spreadsheets as Exercise 2-2.

10. Print the three spreadsheets.

11. Close the workbook.

Exercise 2-3

1. Open a blank spreadsheet. Enter the following amounts on a spreadsheet.

	A	B	C
1	6		
2	15		
3	37		
4	95		
5	46		
6	70		
7	33		
8	57		
9	12		
10	89		
11	64		
12	12		

2. In cell C1 compute the sum of the amounts shown in cells A1 through A12. Continue to use column C to show the amounts in steps 2 through 7.

3. Compute the average number in cells A1 through A12.

4. Compute the smallest number in cells A1 through A12.

5. Compute the largest number in cells A1 through A12.

6. How many different numbers are shown cells A1 through A12.

7. The spreadsheet's header should show your name, the exercise number, and today's date. Save your file as Exercise 2-3.

8. Print your spreadsheet.

9. Close the workbook.

Exercise 2-4

1. Set up a spreadsheet to calculate a car payment based on the following facts.

    A car costs $25,000 and the bank is offering an interest rate of 5% for five years. How much will you have to pay each month?

2. Use proper formatting and number of decimal places for each amount.

3. The spreadsheet's header should show your name, the exercise number, and today's date. Save your file as Exercise 2-4.

4. Print your spreadsheet.

5. Close the workbook.

CHAPTER 2 INDEX

Chapter 3 Formatting

SOFTWARE OBJECTIVES: In Chapter 3, you will use the software to:

1. Format spreadsheets using various Excel features.

2. Set up Excel's standard and formatting toolbars so that they display on two lines.

3. Merge cells and use the format painter.

4. Apply fonts, number formats, and borders and shading.

5. Complete the exercises and activities in Chapter 3.

WEB OBJECTIVES: In Chapter 3, you will do these Internet activities.

1. Use your Internet browser to go the book's website.

2. Complete the Internet Activities.

In Chapter 3, you will practice formatting data in a spreadsheet. *Formatting* refers to the ways you can change the appearance of your Excel spreadsheet. You will change how the spreadsheet looks on the screen as well as how it looks when it is printed. In this chapter you will learn how to change fonts, use various alignments, format both text and numeric data, and add borders. Before you begin, you should be familiar with the basic tools on the formatting toolbar.

GETTING STARTED

When you open Excel for the first time, the standard toolbar and the formatting toolbar appear on one line similar to the screen illustration shown on the next page.

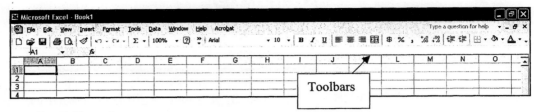

1. Start Excel.

2. To verify that the formatting toolbar is being displayed, right click on the toolbar and the toolbar shortcut menu will appear. The option for "Formatting" should be checked. If there is not check mark in front of the Formatting option, click on the Formatting option.

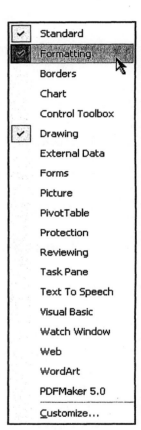

3. To view both the standard toolbar and the formatting toolbar, you should display both the toolbars in two rows. To do this, click on the Toolbars dropdown arrow 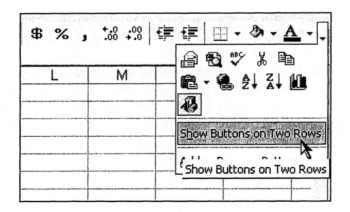 and select "Show Buttons on Two Rows." The Toolbars dropdown arrow is the last down arrow on your toolbar.

4. Observe that this selection displays the standard toolbar on the top row and the formatting toolbar on the bottom row.

The formatting toolbar will allow you to change the way text and numbers appear on the spreadsheet. To see what each button on the toolbar does, simply move your mouse pointer over a tool on the toolbar and a description will appear. These descriptions are known as ***screen tips.*** Excel uses a method called ***select-to-do*** meaning that you must highlight the data you want to apply the formatting to before the tool will show what it does. Follow these steps to see what some of the tools represent.

1. Click on cell A1.

2. Move your mouse pointer over the Fill Color tool [image]. Below the tool, it says "Fill Color (Yellow)." Your tool might show a different color.

3. Move your mouse pointer over the Font Color tool [image].

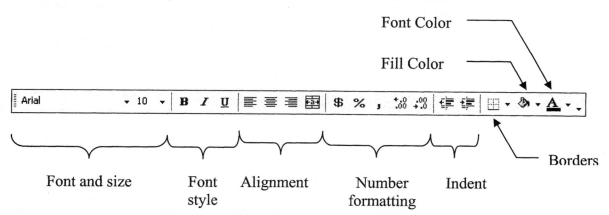

The descriptions below the formatting toolbar describe what tasks you can perform. The rest of the chapter will show you how to use these features.

Another way to format data is to right click the cell containing the data you want to format, then select Format Cells from the shortcut menu. When you do that, the Format Cells dialog box appears. This dialog box will allow you to control the way text and numbers appear on your spreadsheet. It also allows you to control the borders, colors and patterns on the spreadsheet. To see the dialog box, follow these steps.

1. Go to cell B5. Right-click on B5.

2. Observe that there is a Format Cells option.

3. When you click on Format Cells, this Format Cells dialog box appears.

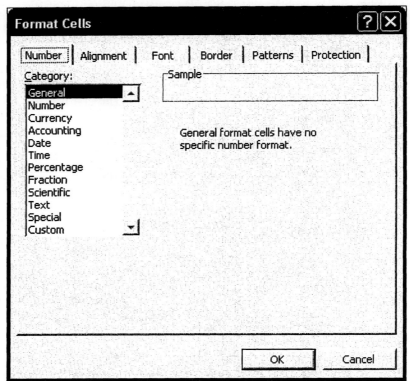

4.   Click [Cancel] to close the Format Cells screen.

MERGING CELLS

In Chapter 1 you created a Budgeted Income Statement for Mike's Surf and Sea. Now you will create the actual income statement. Although you learned some formatting techniques in Chapter 1, you will use other techniques in this chapter. You should follow the steps carefully.

1. If necessary, start a new workbook.

2. Enter the following data in column A.

	A	B	C	D
1	Mike's Surf and Sea			
2	Income Statement			
3	for the year ended 12/31/02			
4				
5	Revenues			
6				
7	Expenses			
8	Wages			
9	Rent			
10	Utilities			
11	Total expenses			
12				
13	Net Income			
14				
15				
16				

3. Highlight the range A1:C1.

4. Click the Merge and Center tool 🔲. This will center the data across the highlighted range and merge it into one cell.

5. Right-click in the highlighted area and select Format Cells. This will display the Format Cells dialog box.

6. Select the Alignment tab. It should appear similar to the screen shown on the next page.

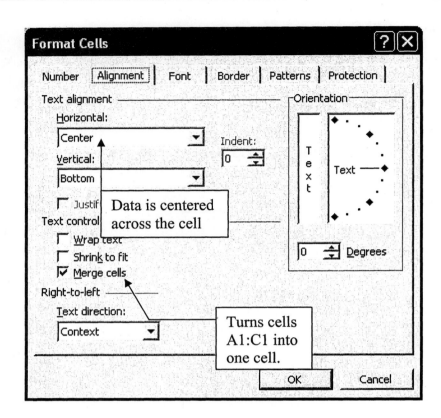

7. Click [Cancel].

USING THE FORMAT PAINTER

1. With the range A1:C1 still highlighted and centered, click on the Format Painter tool [icon] on the standard toolbar. This will copy the cell's formatting onto the clipboard.

2. Click on cell A2. This will paste the formatting from the clipboard to the range A2:C2 (merge and center).

3. Click on the Format Painter tool.

4. Click cell A3. Notice that the range A3:C3 is highlighted.

APPLYING FONT STYLES

1. Click on cell A1. Change the font size to 14 and click on the Bold tool **B** .

2. Select cell A2.

3. Change the font size to 12 points and bold style.

4. Select cell A3.

5. Change the font style to bold. Your worksheet should now be similar to the following:

	A	B	C	D
1	**Mike's Surf and Sea**			
2	**Income Statement**			
3	**for the year ended 12/31/02**			
4				
5	Revenues			
6				
7	Expenses			
8	Wages			
9	Rent			
10	Utilities			
11	Total expenses			
12				
13	Net Income			
14				

6. Save your workbook as **Income Stmt**.

APPLYING NUMBER FORMATS

1. Enter the following data in the range C5:C10.

	A	B	C	D
1	**Mike's Surf and Sea**			
2	Income Statement			
3	for the year ended 12/31/02			
4				
5	Revenues		100	
6				
7	Expenses			
8	Wages		25	
9	Rent		10	
10	Utilities		5	
11	Total expenses			
12				
13	Net Income			
14				

2. Highlight the data in cells C8:C10.

3. Move the cursor to the border of the highlighted range until you see the cursor turn into an arrow with a cross hair like the one in the following image.

4. Drag the box to the range B8:B10. Compare your spreadsheet to the one shown on the next page.

	A	B	C	D
1	**Mike's Surf and Sea**			
2	**Income Statement**			
3	**for the year ended 12/31/02**			
4				
5	Revenues		100	
6				
7	Expenses			
8	Wages	25		
9	Rent	10		
10	Utilities	5		
11	Total expenses			
12				
13	Net Income			
14				

5. Make cell C11 the active cell.

6. Click on the AutoSum button $\boxed{\Sigma \ \blacktriangledown}$.

7. Highlight the range B8:B10.

8. Press the <Enter> key twice. This will make cell C13 the active cell.

9. Type the equal sign (=).

10. Click on cell C5.

11. Type the minus sign (-).

12. Press the up arrow twice. This will highlight cell C11.

13. Press the <Enter> key. Compare your spreadsheet with the one shown on the next page.

	A	B	C	D
1	**Mike's Surf and Sea**			
2	**Income Statement**			
3	**for the year ended 12/31/02**			
4				
5	Revenues		100	
6				
7	Expenses			
8	Wages	25		
9	Rent	10		
10	Utilities	5		
11	Total expenses		40	
12				
13	Net Income		60	
14				

14.   Save your workbook.

15.   Highlight columns B and C.

16.   Click on the Comma Style button 〔 ﹐ 〕. Using the comma style will help to align all of the numbers later when you apply the currency style.

17.   Click the Decrease Decimal button 〔 .00 →.0 〕 twice. This will show the numbers without decimals.

18.   Click on cell C5.

19.   While holding the <Ctrl> key down, click on cells B8 and C13. Cells C5, B8 and C13 should now be highlighted. Holding down the <Ctrl> key will allow you to highlight noncontiguous cells and ranges.

20.   Right-click in one of the highlighted cells.

21.   Select Format Cells from the shortcut menu.

22. Select the Number tab, if necessary.

23. Click on Accounting in the Category box.

24. Set Decimal places to zero (0).

25. Set the Symbol to the dollar sign "$." This will format the highlighted cells with a dollar sign and no decimals. Compare your screen to the illustration below.

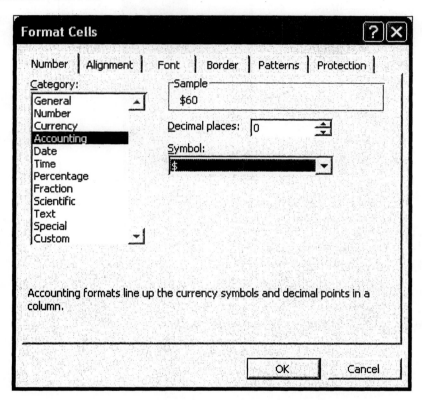

26. Click OK.

27. Click on the column B and C headers to highlight the columns.

28. If necessary, click the Decrease Decimal button twice. This will decrease the decimals so that no decimals are shown. Compare your screen with the one shown below.

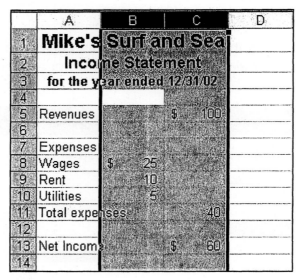

29. Save the workbook.

APPLYING BORDERS

1. Make cell B10 the active cell.

2. Click the drop down arrow on the Borders tool.

3. Select the Bottom Border tool from the menu.

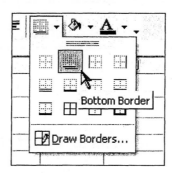

4. Make cell C13 the active cell.

5.   Select the drop down arrow on the Borders tool.

6.   Select the Top and Double Bottom Border tool.

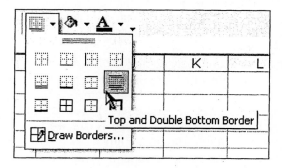

7.   Highlight the range A8:A10.

8.   Click the Increase Indent button. This will indent the highlighted data. Indenting the detailed expenses sets it apart from the category header (Expenses).

9.   Adjust column width of column A so that all of the data in the column fits.

10.   Save your work. The spreadsheet should be similar to the one shown below.

	A	B	C	D
1	**Mike's Surf and Sea**			
2	**Income Statement**			
3	**for the year ended 12/31/02**			
4				
5	Revenues		$ 100	
6				
7	Expenses			
8	Wages	$ 25		
9	Rent	10		
10	Utilities	5		
11	Total expenses		40	
12				
13	Net Income		$ 60	
14				

INTERNET ACTIVITIES	
The Excel websites offer many tips for using the program. Follow the steps below to learn more about Excel's Assistance Center.	
1.	From your Internet browser, go to the textbook's website at www.mhhe.com/yachtexcel. Go to the student link. Link to Internet Activities, then WEB EXERCISES, PART 1-Chapter 3.
2.	Access this website. http://office.microsoft.com/assistance/2002/articles/oAddNewFonts.aspx.[1]
3.	Read the article "Add New Fonts to use with Office XP." Write a review of this article—maximum length 100 words; minimum length, 75 words. If necessary, include the appropriate website address(es) used to write your essay.
4.	Go to the Encyclopedia of Business Case Terms website at www.solutionmatrix.com/encyclopedia.html.
5.	Look up three words related to accounting. Write the definition of each word and include the appropriate website addresses.
6.	Link to other related words (hyperlinks within the word(s) you defined.) Write the definition of each word and include the appropriate website addresses.

SUMMARY AND REVIEW:

SOFWARE OBJECTIVES: In Chapter 3, you used to software to:

1. Format spreadsheets using various Excel features.

2. Set up Excel's standard and formatting toolbars so that they display on two lines.

3. Merge cells and use the format painter.

4. Apply fonts, number formats, and borders and shading.

5. Complete the exercises and activities in Chapter 3.

WEB OBJECTIVES: In Chapter 3, you did these Internet activities:

1. Used your Internet browser to go the book's website.

---

[1]Since website addresses are time and date sensitive, they will change. If a website address shown in the textbook does *not* work, try this to access Excel's assistance center. Go online to http://office.microsoft.com/excel/assistance. In the Search field, select Assistance. Type **Facts About Fonts**; click Go. Link to Facts About Fonts.

2. Completed the Internet Activities.

Multiple-Choice Questions: In the space provided, write the letter that best answers each question.

_____1.   Formatting refers to the ways you can change the appearance of your spreadsheet in which of the following ways:

a. Change the fonts.
b. Change numeric alignments.
c. Add borders.
d. All of the above.
e. None of the above.

_____2.   Most of the formatting features in Excel, can be found on the:

a. Customize tool.
b. Forms options.
c. Toolbars.
d. Command lines.
e. None of the above.

_____3.   If your screen defaults to one toolbar, to view both the standard and the formatting toolbars, select:

a. Show buttons on one row.
b. Show buttons on two rows.
c. Show buttons on three rows.
d. Show button on four rows.
e. None of the above.

_____4. To see which toolbars are being displayed:

    a. Click on the standard toolbar.
    b. Right-click on the toolbar to see the shortcut menu.
    c. Click on the toolbar to see the drop-down menu.
    d. Click on any tool on the toolbar.
    e. All of the above.

_____5. You must highlight the data or cell that you want to apply formatting to because Excel uses _____ to identify toolbar selections.

    a. What-you-see-is-what-you-get (WYSIWYG).
    b. Graphical user interface (GUI).
    c. Select-to-do.
    d. Ready-to-change.
    e. All of the above.

_____6. The Format Cells dialog box allows you to do the following:

    a. Control the way text and numbers appear.
    b. Change colors and patterns.
    c. Align data.
    d. All of the above.
    e. None of the above.

_____7. The Merge and Center tool is identified by the following icon.

    a.
    b.
    c.
    d.
    e. None of the above.

_____8. The Format Painter tool is identified by the following icon.

    a.

    b.

    c.

    d.

    e. None of the above.

_____9. In order to apply borders, select the following tool.

    a.

    b.

    c.

    d.

    e. None of the above.

_____10. To increase an indentation, select the following tool.

    a.

    b.

    c.

    d.

    e. None of the above.

True/Make True: If the statement is true, write the word "True" in the space provided. If the statement is *not* true, write the correct answer in the space provided.

11. Formatting refers to the way you save your spreadsheets.

_____

_____

12. The default for the standard and formatting toolbar is to display on one row.

_____

_____

13. In this chapter the toolbars are shown on two rows.

_____

_____

14. The standardized toolbar allows you to change the way text and numbers appear on the spreadsheet.

_____

_____

15. The descriptions below the toolbar tools describe what tasks you can perform.

   _____

   _____

16. The Format Cells dialog box allows you to control such things as the borders, colors, and patterns on your spreadsheet.

   _____

   _____

17. When changing font size and using boldface, you need to change the point size first.

   _____

   _____

18. In this chapter, the balance sheet is used to show revenue and expense data.

   _____

   _____

19. The total expenses on your worksheet are $100.

   _____

   _____

20. The net income on your spreadsheet is $60.

_____

_____

Exercise 3-1

1.   Start Excel.

2.   Enter the following data in column A.

	A	B	C	D
1	Carol's Surf Shop			
2	Income Statement			
3	for the year ended 12/31/03			
4				
5	Revenues			
6				
7	Expenses			
8	Wages			
9	Rent			
10	Utilities			
11	Total expenses			
12				
13	Net Income			
14				

3.   The spreadsheet's header should show your name, the file name (Exercise 3-1), and today's date.

4.   Save your spreadsheet as **Exercise 3-1**.

Exercise 3-2

1. If necessary, start Excel and open Exercise 3-1.

2. Use the Merge and Center tool to center the first line of the heading (cells A1:C1).

3. Use the format painter to center lines 2 and 3 of the heading (cells A2:C2 and A3:C3).

4. Boldface the first heading line and change the font to 14.

5. Boldface the second header line and change the font size to 12.

6. Boldface the third header line. Do *not* change the font size.

7. Indent cells A8:A10 (Wages, Rent, and Utilities).

8. The spreadsheet's header should show your name, file name (Exercise 3-2), and today's date.

9. Save your spreadsheet as **Exercise 3-2**.

Exercise 3-3

1. If necessary, start Excel and open Exercise 3-2.

2. Add the following information to cells C5 through C10.

   C5:   200
   C8:   25
   C9:   10
   C10:   5

3. Move cells C8:C10 to B8:B10.

4. Compute total expenses and net income.

5. The spreadsheet's header should show your name, file name (Exercise 3-3), and today's date.

6. Save your spreadsheet as **Exercise 3-3**.

Exercise 3-4

1. If necessary, start Excel and open Exercise 3-3.

2. Apply the Comma Style to columns B and C. to align the numbers.

3. Format the numbers in cells C5, B8, and C13 for "Accounting," zero decimal places, and dollar signs. (revenues, wages, and net income should now appear with dollar signs.)

4. Widen column A.

5. Add single and double borders where necessary.

6. The spreadsheet's header should show your name, file name (Exercise 3-4), and today's date.

7. Setup your spreadsheet so that it is centered horizontally on the page.

8. Save your spreadsheet as **Exercise 3-4**.

9. Print the spreadsheet.

CHAPTER 3 INDEX

Part 2   Accounting Projects

In Part 2, you apply what you have learned in Part 1 (Chapters 1, 2, and 3) to using Excel for accounting projects. Additionally, you also learn how to use the template files that are included on the CD that accompanies this textbook. There are three chapters in Part 2.

Chapter 4: Template Tutorial

Chapter 5: Financial Accounting

Chapter 6: Managerial Accounting

In Chapter 4, Template Tutorial, you apply the skills that you learned in Chapters 1, 2, and 3 to complete accounting projects. First, you open the appropriate template file included on the CD that accompanies this textbook. Then, you record transactions to change the spreadsheets. After recording the transactions, you analyze the data.

In Chapter 5, Financial Accounting, you use preformatted templates for inventory valuation; recording transactions in the cash receipts journal; completing bank reconciliation; computing an accounts receivable aging schedule; determining depreciation; completing a payroll register; doing a percentage of completion spreadsheet; doing bond amortization; and financial statement analysis.

In Chapter 6, Managerial Accounting, you use preformatted templates to complete a schedule of the cost of goods manufactured; determine the total cost and unit cost of a job; prepare production cost reports; complete break-even analysis; prepare flexible budgets; calculate the price, quantity and total variance for direct materials; and determine make and buy decisions.

The table on the pages 104 and 105 shows the chapter, file name, and page numbers where you saved Excel files.

Chapter	File Name	Page Nos.
4	Chapter 4-1 answer.xls	112
	Chapter 4-2_adjusted.xls	116
	Chapter 4-2 answer.xls	117-118
	Chapter 4-3.xls	119
	Chapter 4-3_Income Statement.xls	122-123
	Chapter 4-3_Owner's Equity.xls	124-125
	Chapter 4-3_Balance Sheet.xls	127
	Chapter 4-3_whatif.xls	128
	Exercise 4-1_answer.xls	136
	Exercise 4-2_adjusted.xls	137
	Exercise 4-3_answer.xls	138
	Exercise 4-4_whatif.xls	139
5	Chapter 5-1 answer.xls	145
	Chapter 5-2 answer.xls	146-147
	Chapter 5-3 answer.xls	148
	Chapter 5-4 answer.xls	149
	Chapter 5-5 answer.xls	151
	Chapter 5-6 answer.xls	152
	Chapter 5-7 answer.xls	155
	Chapter 5-8 answer.xls	156
	Chapter 5-9 answer.xls	157
	Chapter 5-10 answer.xls	158
	Chapter 5-11 answer.xls	160
	Chapter 5-12 answer.xls	161
	Chapter 5-13 answer.xls	162
	Chapter 5-14 answer.xls	163
	Chapter 5-15 answer.xls	164
	Chapter 5-16 answer.xls	165
	Chapter 5-17 answer	166-167
	Chapter 5-18 answer	167-168
	Chapter 5-19 answer	169-171
	Exercise 5-1_inventory.xls	178
	Exercise 5-2_gross profit.xls	179
	Exercise 5-2_whatif.xls	179
	Exercise 5-3_cash receipts.xls	180
	Exercise 5-4_aging schedule.xls	181
	Exercise 5-4_whatif.xls	181
	Exercise 5-5_bond amortization	181
6	Chapter 6-1 answer.xls	185-186
	Chapter 6-2 answer.xls	187-188
	Chapter 6-3 answer.xls	188-189

Chapter	Filename	Page Nos.
	Chapter 6-4 answer.xls	189-190
6	Chapter 6-5 answer.xls	191-192
	Chapter 6-6 answer.xls	193
	Chapter 6-7 answer.xls	194
	Chapter 6-8 answer.xls	194-195
	Chapter 6-8a answer	195
	Chapter 6-8b answer	195-196
	Chapter 6-8c answer	196
	Chapter 6-9 answer.xls	197
	Chapter 6-10 answer.xls	198
	Chapter 6-11 answer.xls	199
	Chapter 6-12 answer.xls	200
	Chapter 6-13 answer.xls	201
	Chapter 6-14 answer.xls	201
	Exercise 6-1_answer.xls	208
	Exercise 6-1_whatif.xls	208
	Exercise 6-2_answer.xls	208
	Exercise 6-2_whatif.xls	209
	Exercise 6-3_answer.xls	209
	Exercise 6-4_answer.xls	210

Chapter 4

Template Tutorial

SOFTWARE OBJECTIVES: In Chapter 4, you will use the software to:

1. Open template files from the CD that accompanies this book.[1]

2. Enter transactions in a tabular format and use tabular analysis.

3. Apply what-if analysis scenarios.

4. Create an accounting worksheet.

5. Prepare financial statements.

6. Complete the exercises and activities in Chapter 4.

WEB OBJECTIVES: In Chapter 4, you will do these Internet activities.

1. Use your Internet browser to go the book's website.

2. Complete the Internet Activities for Part 2, Chapter 4.

In Chapters 1, 2 and 3, you learned about Excel's basic features and functions. You should be familiar with the basic terminology used to describe actions used in Excel. You should also know how to input, format, copy and move text, change data, and use formulas.
In Chapter 4, you will apply your newly acquired Excel skills to complete various accounting projects. In this section, the spreadsheets are partially completed for you. Files that are partially completed and saved as Excel files (.xls extensions) are called templates. Think of templates

---

[1]The CD that accompanies this book contains template files. These files are called "student data files" in this textbook. Your instructor may have saved these files to a network or hard drive location. Ask your instructor if you should open the files from the CD that accompanies this book or if the template files are stored on the classroom computer.

---

as files that can be used over and over again. The template files can be used with Microsoft Excel 97 and higher. In this book, Windows XP and Excel 2002 are used for the illustrations.

This textbook often makes reference to templates. A template is a preformatted Excel file. In this chapter you will use a preformatted template to begin your work, and then add additional information.

Once you complete a spreadsheet, you can analyze the data. This chapter will walk you through how to do that. In Chapters 5 and 6, you will also use template data to complete spreadsheets.

GETTING STARTED

This chapter will show you how to work with data that already exists on templates. After opening the template file, you complete the spreadsheet and analyze the data.

The templates used in this chapter are on the CD that accompanies this text. The sections that follow explain how to use these templates.

The names of the template files are: Chapter 4-1.xls and Chapter 4-2.xls.

ENTERING TRANSACTIONS IN A TABULAR FORMAT

In the steps that follow you will open a workbook that is in *tabular format*. In Excel, data tables are usually arranged in tabular format. Data tables are a range of cells that show how changing certain values in your formulas affect the results of the formulas. Data tables often provide shortcuts for calculating multiple versions in one operation, and are a way to view and compare the results of different variations. Both of the templates for this chapter use tabular formats that will allow you to apply tabular analysis.

Follow these steps to open the Chapter 4-1 template file. The title that appears on the worksheet is Mike's Surf & Sea, Tabular Analysis.

1.   Start Excel.

2. Put the CD included with this textbook in your CD drive. *Or, if your instructor has copied these files to a network or hard drive location, open the template file from that location.*

3. From Excel's menu bar, click on File, Open.

4. In the Look in field, open the appropriate drive location for your template data. Click on the Chapter 4-1 Excel file to highlight it.

5. Click [Open ▾]. Compare your screen to the one shown below.

	A	B	C	D	E	F	G	H
1					Mike's Surf Shop			
2					Tabular Analysis			
3								
4								
5			Assets		Liabilities	Owner's Equity		
6	Date	Cash	Accounts Receivable	Supplies	Accounts Payable	Capital	Notes	Cash Balance
7								
8	1/1/03	10,000				10,000	Investment	10,000
9	1/2/03							10,000
10	1/3/03							10,000
11	1/5/03							10,000
12	1/7/03							10,000
13	1/8/03							10,000
14	1/9/03							10,000
15	1/16/03							10,000
16	1/23/03							10,000
17	1/25/03							10,000
18	1/30/03							10,000
19								
20		10,000	-	-	-	10,000		
21								
22						10,000	Total Assets	
23								
24						-	Liabilities	
25						10,000	Owner's Equity	
26						10,000	Total Liabilities and Owner's Equity	
27								
28						-	Difference	

Before you start, go to cell F28.

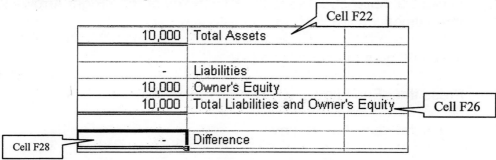

10,000	Total Assets	← Cell F22
-	Liabilities	
10,000	Owner's Equity	
10,000	Total Liabilities and Owner's Equity	← Cell F26
Cell F28 → -	Difference	

Observe that cell F28 compares the difference between Total Assets (cell F22) and Total Liabilities and Owner's Equity (cell F26). As you know from your study of accounting, the amount shown for Total Assets should be the same as the amount shown for Total Liabilities and Owner's Equity. You need to keep an eye on this cell because the balance should always be zero, which will be shown as a - (dash). If you ever have a difference in this cell, your data is out of balance.

When entering the data into this type of spreadsheet, you should enter an amount in one column and enter a formula in the second column that will make it equal to the first column.

6.   Click in cell F8 to view the formula. Notice that the formula makes this cell equal to cell B8 (=B8). This shows that if the amount in cell B8 needs to be changed, cell F8 will also change and your data will remain in balance.

To illustrate, let's complete the following transaction.

Date   *Transaction*

Jan 2   Mike gave a surfing lesson to guests of the Waikiki Hotel on account for $500.

Follow these steps to enter the January 2 transaction.

1.   In cell C9, enter 500. Press the <Tab> key or the <Right Arrow> key three times.

2.   In cell F9 type the equal sign (=).

3.   Press the <End> key.

4.   Press the <Left Arrow> key.

| 9 | 1/2/03 | 500 | | =C9 | |

If you are in an empty cell, the <End> key followed by an arrow key will move the cursor in the direction of the arrow key to the next cell with data in it.

5.   Press <Enter>.

6.   Type **Service revenue** in cell G9. Remember to check cell F28; the "Difference" remains zero.

Enter the following transactions into the appropriate cells using the technique just described. For any data in the Owner's Equity column, indicate the account that should be charged.

Additional Transactions

Date   *Transactions*

Jan. 3   Purchased $1,000 of wax, leashes and sun screen (supplies) on account.

5   Paid $600 for surfboard locker rent. (Hint: Use a minus sign to indicate subtraction.)

7   Paid $300 on amount due for supplies purchased on Jan. 3.

8   Received $500 from Waikiki Hotel for surf lessons given on Jan. 2. (Hint: Remember to use a minus sign in cell C13.)

9   Gave surf lessons to tourists for $800. The tourists paid in cash.

15   Received a utility bill for $100 due at the end of the month.

23   Gave lessons to guests of the Waikiki Hotel for $300 on account.

25   Paid the remaining amount owed for the supplies purchased on January 3.

30   After doing a physical count, determined that $250 of supplies were on hand.

After completing all of the transactions, your total assets should be $10,250. Follow these steps to display your spreadsheet.

1. Click on Print Preview to view your document.

2. Change the setup so that the document prints in landscape.

3. Change the margins so that the document is centered horizontally.

4. Format the Header so that your name is left aligned; the file name, Chapter 4-1 answer; is centered and today's date is right aligned.

5. Click on the sheet tab and select gridlines. This will format the sheet so that the gridlines will print on the document.

6. Save your spreadsheet. Use Chapter 4-1 answer.xls as the filename. Compare your spreadsheet to the one shown below.

Student Name					Chapter 4-1 answer			Today's Date
					Mike's Surf and Sea			
					Tabular Analysis			
		Assets		**Liabilities**	**Owners' Equity**			
		Accounts		**Accounts**				**Cash**
Date	**Cash**	**Receivable**	**Supplies**	**Payable**	**Capital**		**Notes**	**Balance**
1/1/03	10,000				10,000		Investment	10,000
1/2/03		500			500		Service revenue	10,000
1/3/03			1,000	1,000				10,000
1/5/03	(600)				(600)		Rent expense	9,400
1/7/03	(300)			(300)				9,100
1/8/03	500	(500)						9,600
1/9/03	800				800		Service revenue	10,400
1/15/03				100	(100)		Utilities expense	10,400
1/23/03		300			300		Service revenue	10,400
1/25/03	(700)			(700)				9,700
1/30/03			(750)		(750)		Supplies expense	9,700
	9,700	300	250	100	10,150			
					10,250		Total Assets	
					100		Liabilities	
					10,150		Owners' Equity	
					10,250			
					-		Difference	

WHAT-IF ANALYSIS: FIRST SCENARIO

When you change the conditions of a spreadsheet, this is called what-if analysis. Here is an example of how to apply what-if analysis:

What if   Since Mike does not have a lot of cash on hand, he would

analysis   like to invest as little cash as possible. Analyze your data to determine how much Mike would have to invest without ever having his cash balance fall below zero and also have at least $500 cash at the end of the month.

Answer: Did you change B8 (initial investment to $1,400)? Observe that the cash balance never drops below $500. Compare your spreadsheet to the one shown on page 112.

The best way to find your answer is to use Excel's Goal Seek command. *Goal Seek* is part of a group of commands that are also called what-if analysis tools. When you know the desired result of a single formula but not the input value the formula needs to determine the result, you can use the Goal Seek feature. To use Goal Seek, follow these steps:

1.   Highlight the lowest amount in column H (H12).

2.   Click on Tools, Goal Seek.

3.   Cell H12 should already be entered in the Set Cell box. If it is not entered, click in the box to select it then click on cell H12.

4.   Type **500** in the "To value" box. This is the value that we want cell H12 to become.

5.   Click in the "By changing cell" box to select it.

6.   Click in cell B8 to enter the cell reference into the "By changing cell" box.

7.   Compare your Goal Seek screen to the one shown below. The information shown is asking Excel to compute the amount that should be in cell B8 to make the amount in cell H12 equal to $500.

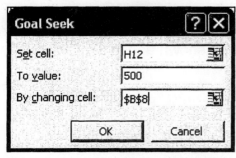

8. Click [OK]. When the Goal Seek Status screen appears, click
[OK]. Compare your screen to the one shown below.

	A	B	C	D	E	F	G	H
1				**Mike's Surf Shop**				
2				**Tabular Analysis**				
3								
4								
5			**Assets**		**Liabilities**	**Owner's Equity**		
6	**Date**	**Cash**	**Accounts Receivable**	**Supplies**	**Accounts Payable**	**Capital**	**Notes**	**Cash Balance**
7								
8	1/1/03	1,400				1,400	Investment	1,400
9	1/2/03		500			500	Service revenue	1,400
10	1/3/03			1,000	1,000			1,400
11	1/5/03	(600)				(600)	Rent expense	800
12	1/7/03	(300)			(300)			500
13	1/8/03	500	(500)					1,000
14	1/9/03	800				800	Service revenue	1,800
15	1/15/03				100	(100)	Utilities expense	1,800
16	1/23/03		300			300	Service revenue	1,800
17	1/25/03	(700)			(700)			1,100
18	1/30/03			(750)		(750)	Supplies expense	1,100
19								
20		1,100	300	250	100	1,550		
21								
22						1,650	Total Assets	
23								
24						100	Liabilities	
25						1,550	Owner's Equity	
26						1,650		
27								
28						-	Difference	
29								
30								
31								
32								
33								
34								
35								
36								
37								
38								
39								
40								
41								
42								
43								

You will use the Chapter 4-2 template in the next section. You do *not* need to save the spreadsheet shown above. Follow these steps to close your spreadsheet.

1. From the menu bar, select File, Exit.

2. When the screen pops up that says do you want to save changes, click No .

USING AN ACCOUNTING WORKSHEET FOR ADJUSTING ENTRIES

The Chapter 4-2 template file contains worksheet data for recording adjusting entries. You will begin by entering data in the adjustments column. Remember to enter the adjustment amount in one cell, and then make the related debit or credit equal to it. The first adjusting entry is shown below.

Date   *Transaction*

Jan 31   Record the adjusting entry for $5,000 of depreciation expense.

Follow these steps to record an adjusting entry for depreciation.

1. Open the Chapter 4-2 Excel file.

2. In cell D24, type the reference **a** and press the Tab key to move the cell E24.

3. Type **5,000**. Press <Enter>. The next step is to enter a formula to make the corresponding credit to Accumulated depreciation equal to the Depreciation expense debit.

4. Make cell F13 equal to cell D24 by entering the formula **=D24** in cell F13.

5. Use the fill handle to copy the formula in cell F13 to cell G13. Cells F13:G13 should now look the same as cells D24:E24.

6. In the same manner, make the following adjustments.

   Adjustment b: $200 of prepaid insurance has expired.

   Adjustment c: You have $575 in supplies on hand.

   Adjustment d: Accrued salaries are $700.

7. Save your spreadsheet. Use Chapter 4-2_adjusted as the filename. After making adjustments, your total debits and credits in the adjustments column should be $6,825. In this example, the Adjusted Trial Balance columns should be automatically calculated for you. Compare your spreadsheet to the one below.

	A	B	C	D	E	F	G	H	I
1					**Mike's Surf Shop**				
2					Worksheet				
3									
4									
5		Trial Balance			Adjustments			Adj. Trial Balance	
6	Account	Debit	Credit		Debit		Credit	Debit	Credit
7									
8	Cash	5,600						5,600	
9	Accounts receivable	2,000						2,000	
10	Supplies	1,500				c	925	575	
11	Prepaid insurance	2,400				b	200	2,200	
12	Equipment	50,000						50,000	
13	Accumulated depreciation-Equipment		20,000			a	5,000		25,000
14	Accounts payable		2,300						2,300
15	Notes payable		7,000						7,000
16	MF, Capital		9,700						9,700
17	MF, Drawing	2,000						2,000	
18	Service revenue		35,000						35,000
19	Salaries expense	8,000			d	700		8,700	
20	Rent expense	1,200						1,200	
21	Utilities expense	800						800	
22	Advertising expense	300						300	
23	Insurance expense	200			b	200		400	
24	Depreciation expense				a	5,000		5,000	
25									
26		74,000	74,000						
27									
28	Supplies expense				c	925		925	
29	Salaries payable						d	700		700
30									
31	Totals					6,825		6,825	79,700	79,700
32	Net Income/Loss								
33	Totals								

Next, you will enter a conditional formula in the Balance Sheet and Income Statement columns to automatically fill these cells.

1. Make cell L8 the active cell.

2. Enter the formula =IF(H8>0,H8,""). If there is data in the debit column of the adjusted trial balance, (H8), this formula will enter the same amount into the debit column of the Balance Sheet.

3. Highlight the range L8:M8 and, using the fill handle, copy the data down to row 17.

4. Enter a formula into cell J18 that will perform the same function as the formula you entered in cell L8 in step 2 above. (Hint: Use cell H18 in your formula.)

5. Copy the formula to cell K18.

6. Using the fill handle, copy the formulas to row 28.

7. Enter the appropriate formula in the Balance Sheet column of row 29.

8. Format the spreadsheet so that it prints in landscape and on one page. (Hint: On the Page Setup/Page tab, select Fit to 1 page.)

9. The spreadsheet should be centered horizontally.

10. The header should have your name left aligned, the file name (Chapter 4-2 answer) centered, and the date right aligned.

11. Setup the spreadsheet so that the gridlines will print when you print the spreadsheet.

12. Save the spreadsheet. Use Chapter 4-2 answer as the file name. If everything is done correctly, Net Income should be $17,675 and the debits and credits in the Income Statement and Balance Sheet columns of row 33 should be equal to each other.

13. Print the spreadsheet. Compare your spreadsheet to the one shown on the next page.

Student Name   Chapter 4-2 answer   Today's Date

Mike's Surf Shop
Worksheet

Account	Trial Balance Debit	Trial Balance Credit	Adj. ref	Adjustments Debit	Adj. ref	Adjustments Credit	Adj. Trial Balance Debit	Adj. Trial Balance Credit	Income Statement Debit	Income Statement Credit	Balance Sheet Debit	Balance Sheet Credit
Cash	5,600						5,600				5,600	
Accounts receivable	2,000						2,000				2,000	
Supplies	1,500				c	925	575				575	
Prepaid insurance	2,400				b	200	2,200				2,200	
Equipment	50,000						50,000				50,000	
Accumulated depreciation-Equipment		20,000			a	5,000		25,000				25,000
Accounts payable		2,300						2,300				2,300
Notes payable		7,000						7,000				7,000
MF, Capital		9,700						9,700				9,700
MF, Drawing	2,000						2,000				2,000	
Service revenue		35,000						35,000		35,000		
Salaries expense	8,000		d	700			8,700		8,700			
Rent expense	1,200						1,200		1,200			
Utilities expense	800						800		800			
Advertising expense	300						300		300			
Insurance expense	200		b	200			400		400			
Depreciation expense			a	5,000			5,000		5,000			
	74,000	74,000										
Supplies expense			c	925			925		925			
Salaries payable					d	700		700				700
Totals				6,825		6,825	79,700	79,700	17,325	35,000	62,375	44,700
Net Income/Loss									17,675			17,675
Totals									35,000	35,000	62,375	62,375

PREPARING FINANCIAL STATEMENTS

The purpose of using the accounting worksheet is to help you prepare your financial statements. In this exercise, you will use the worksheet you just prepared to create a set of financial statements. This will require you to rename the sheets in the workbook and link worksheets together.

1. If it is not already open, open the Chapter 4-2 answer.xls file.

2. Rename Sheet1 to Worksheet. (Double-click on the sheet tab, type "Worksheet" and press <Enter>.)

3. Rename Sheet2 to Income Statement.

4. Rename Sheet3 to Owner's Equity.

5. Insert another worksheet. (Right-click on the sheet tab, select Insert..., click <OK>.)

6. Rename the inserted worksheet Balance Sheet.

7. Move (drag) the Balance Sheet sheet tab so that it is the last tab.

8.   Make the Worksheet your active spreadsheet.

9.   Change the header so that the centered header prints the file name (Chapter 4-3) on the top line and the sheet name on the second line.

10.   Save your workbook as Chapter 4-3.

Student Name	Chapter 4-3 Worksheet	Today's Date
	Mike's Surf Shop	
	Worksheet	

11.   Reposition the worksheet so that cell A5 is the top left cell showing on the spreadsheet.

12.   Make cell B7 the active cell.

13.   From the menu bar, select Window, Freeze Panes. This will freeze column A and rows 5 and 6 so that they are always displayed on the page.

14.   Save your spreadsheet.

15.   Make the Income Statement the active sheet.

16.   Make cell A1 the active cell

17.   While holding down the Shift key, click on the Balance Sheet tab. This will highlight the Income statement, Owner's Equity and Balance Sheet tabs.

18.   Type **Mike's Surf Shop** in cell A1. Format the font to be bold and 18 points.

19.   Type **for the year ended 12/31/03** in Cell A3. Format the font to be bold and 12 points.

20.   Hold down the Ctrl key and click on the Owner's Equity and Balance Sheet tabs to deselect them.

21.   Make sure the Income Statement is the active sheet.

22.   Type **Income Statement** in cell A2. Format the font so that it is bold and 14 points.

23.   Make the Worksheet the active sheet

24.   Highlight the range A18:A28.

25.   Right click in the highlighted area and select <u>C</u>opy.

26.   Make Income Statement the active sheet.

27.   Right click in cell A7.

28.   Select Paste <u>S</u>pecial.

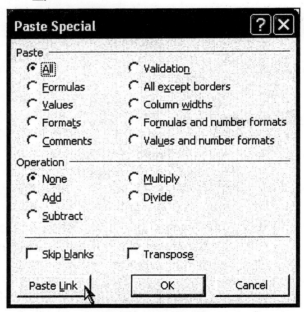

29.   Click on the Paste <u>L</u>ink button at the bottom of the screen. This will link the data from the worksheet to the Income Statement sheet so that any changes made to the worksheet will also be changed on the Income Statement.

30.   Highlight rows 14, 15 and 16.

31.   Right click in the highlighted area and select <u>D</u>elete. This will delete the rows and move the data in row 17 to row 14.

Income Statement

Now you are going to use the Worksheet to complete the Income Statement. Follow these steps to complete the Income Statement.

1.   Make the Worksheet your active sheet.

2.   Highlight the range J18:K28.

3.   Press <Ctrl>+<C>. This will copy the highlighted data.

4.   Make the Income Statement the active sheet.

5.   Make cell C7 the active cell. Paste Link the data the same way you did in steps 28 and 29 on page 120.

6.   Delete the range C14:D16. In the Delete dialog box, select Shift cells up, then click <OK>.

7.   Format the entire spreadsheet so that the numbers are displayed as Comma Style with no decimals.

8.   Highlight rows 8 and 9 by clicking on the row headers.

9.   Right click in the highlighted area and select Insert.

10.   Type **Revenues** in cell A6. Format the font so that it is bold.

11.   Indent the data in cell A7.

12.   Type **Expenses** in cell A9. Format the font so that it is bold.

13.   Indent the data in the range A10:A16.

14.   Type **Total Expenses** in cell A17.

15.   Type **Net Income** in cell A19.

16. Use the AutoSum function in cell D17 to get a total of the expenses.

17. Enter the appropriate formula in cell D19.

18. Hold the <Ctrl> key down and click on cells D7, C10 and D19.

19. Format with the currency style and no decimals.

20. Put a bottom border in cell C16.

21. Put a top and double bottom border in cell D19.

22. Merge and center rows 1, 2 and 3.

23. AutoFit column A by double clicking the border between the column A and column B headers.

24. Delete column B.

25. Save the workbook as Chapter 4-3_Income Statement. Compare your spreadsheet to the one shown below.

	A	B	C
1	**Mike's Surf Shop**		
2	**Income Statement**		
3	**for the year ended 12/31/03**		
4			
5			
6	**Revenues**		
7	Service revenue		$ 35,000
8			
9	**Expenses**		
10	Salaries expense	$ 8,700	
11	Rent expense	1,200	
12	Utilities expense	800	
13	Advertising expense	300	
14	Insurance expense	400	
15	Depreciation expense	5,000	
16	Supplies expense	925	
17	Total Expenses		17,325
18			
19	Net Income		$ 17,675

26. Setup the page so that it prints in portrait and on one page, is centered horizontally, left align your name and right align the date in the header and do not print gridlines.

27. Save and print the Income Statement. Compare your Income Statement to the one shown below.

Student Name			Today's Date
	Mike's Surf Shop		
	Income Statement		
	for the year ended 12/31/03		
	Revenues		
	Service revenue		$ 35,000
	Expenses		
	Salaries expense	$ 8,700	
	Rent expense	1,200	
	Utilities expense	800	
	Advertising expense	300	
	Insurance expense	400	
	Depreciation expense	5,000	
	Supplies expense	925	
	Total Expenses		17,325
	Net Income		$ 17,675

Statement of Owner's Equity

Next, you will use the data from both the Worksheet and the Income Statement to create an Owner's Equity Statement.

1. Click on the Owner's Equity tab to make it the active sheet.

2. Type **Statement of Owner's Equity** in cell A2. Format the font so that it is bold and 14 points.

3. Type **Beginning Capital** in cell A6. Press <Tab> two times to go to cell C6.

4. Type the equal sign (=).

5. Make the Worksheet the active sheet.

6.   Click on cell M16. Press the <Enter> key. You are returned to the Statement of Owner's Equity. Observe that 9700 is in cell C6.

7.   Make cell A7 the active cell. Type **Net Income**. Press <Tab> two times to go to cell C7.

8.   Type the equal sign (=).

9.   Make the Income Statement the active sheet.

10. Click on cell C19. Press <Enter>. The net income amount (17675) is shown on cell C7 of the Owner's Equity sheet.

11. Use the AutoSum function in cell C8.

12. Type **Less: Drawing** in cell A9.

13. Make cell C9 equal to cell L17 on the worksheet.

14. Type **Ending Capital** in cell A10.

15. Enter the appropriate formula in cell C10.

16. Save the workbook as Chapter 4-3_Owner's Equity.

17. Merge and center rows 1, 2, and 3.

18. Format the spreadsheet so that all of the numbers use the comma style with no decimals.

19. Resize column A.

20. Use currency style with no decimals in cells C6 and C10.

21. Format the applicable cells with appropriate borders.

22. Use the same page setup as was used in the Income Statement.

23. Save and print the spreadsheet. Compare your owner's equity statement with the one shown on the next page.

Student Name   Today's Date

Mike's Surf Shop
Statement of Owner's Equity
for the year ended 12/31/03

Beginning Capital	$	9,700
Net Income		17,675
		27,375
Less: Drawing		2,000
	$	25,375

Balance Sheet

Once the Income Statement and Statement of Owner's Equity are completed, you can enter the data to complete the Balance Sheet.

1. Make Balance Sheet the active sheet. Type **Balance Sheet** In cell A2. Format the font so that it is bold and 14 point.

2. Change cell A3 to **As of 12/31/03**.

3. Make Worksheet the active sheet.

4. Highlight the range A8:A15 and A29 (use the Ctrl key).

5. Right click in the highlighted area and select copy.

6. Make Balance Sheet the active sheet.

7. Paste link the data into cell A7.

8. Make Worksheet the active sheet.

9. Highlight the range L8:M15 and L29:M29. Copy the data.

10. Make Balance Sheet the active sheet.

11. Paste link the data into cell C7.

12. Move the data from the range C7:C11 to D7:D11.

13. Merge and center rows 1, 2 and 3.

14. Type **Assets** in cell A6. Make the data in cell A6 bold.

15. Indent the range A7:A12.

16. Indent the range A11:A12 again.

17. Move the data from the range D11:D12 to C11:C12.

18. Highlight rows 13 through 16.

19. Insert new rows.

20. Enter a formula in D13 to subtract C12 from C11.

21. Type **Total Assets** in cell A14.

22. Use the AutoSum in cell D14 to sum up the appropriate data.

23. Type **Liabilities** in cell A16. Make the data in cell A16 bold. Remove the indent on this cell.

24. Type **Total Liabilities** in cell A20.

25. Use AutoSum or type the appropriate formula in cell D20.

26. Type **Owner's Equity** in cell A22. Make the cell A22 bold.

27. Type **Capital** in cell A23.

28. Make cell D23 the active cell.

29. Link cell D23 to the appropriate cell on the Owner's Equity sheet.

30. Type **Total Liabilities and Owner's Equity** in cell A25.

31. Use AutoSum in D25.

32. Indent cells A17:A19 and cell A23.

33.   Use the appropriate borders in all of the necessary cells. If necessary, delete any zeroes in cells.

34.   Format the spreadsheet so that all of the numbers are formatted with the comma style and no decimals.

35.   Widen column A.

36.   Format the appropriate cells with currency style and no decimals.

37.   Delete column B.

38.   Setup the page the same as the Income Statement.

39.   Save the workbook as Chapter 4-3_Balance Sheet. Print the workbook. Compare your Balance Sheet with the one shown below.

Student Name			Today's Date
Mike's Surf Shop			
Balance Sheet			
As of 12/31/03			
Assets			
Cash		$	5,600
Accounts receivable			2,000
Supplies			575
Prepaid insurance			2,200
Equipment	$	50,000	
Accumulated depreciation-Equipment		25,000	
			25,000
Total Assets		$	35,375
Liabilities			
Accounts payable		$	2,300.0
Notes payable			7,000
Salaries payable			700
Total Liabilities		$	10,000
Owner's Equity			
Capital			25,375
Total Liabilities and Owner's Equity		$	35,375

WHAT-IF ANALYSIS: SECOND SCENARIO

Mike is considering buying new equipment for his business. The equipment would cost $10,000 and would be purchased on account. Change the data in the trial balance column to reflect this.

The purchase would also affect depreciation and interest. Depreciation expense will increase $2,000 and Interest expense will be $500. Make these adjustments in the Adjustments column.

Update the Worksheet and any financial statements that need adjusting.

Save the workbook as Chapter 4-3_whatif. Print the new financial statements reflecting these changes. What affect did these changes have on the financial statements?

The questions that follow apply to the Chapter 4-3_whatif.xls file. Compare the amounts with your Chapter 4-3 financial statement files.

1. On the Income Statement, what is the amount of depreciation expense? Does this increase or decrease deprecation? Indicate the amount of the increase or decrease.

   _____

   _____

2. What is the amount of net income? Did net income increase or decrease?

   _____

   _____

3. What is the ending capital amount?

    _____

    _____

4. What changes occurred on the Balance Sheet? Indicate the dollar
    amount of the increases or decreases.

    _____

    _____

    _____

    _____

    _____

	INTERNET ACTIVITIES
1.	From your Internet browser, go to the textbook's website at http://www.mhhe.com/yacht2004. Go to the Student link.
2.	Link to Internet Activities, then WEB EXERCISES, PART 2-Chapter 4.
3.	Access this website. http://office.microsoft.com/excel/assistance. In the Search field, select Assistance. Type **Template**; then click Go.
4.	Go to two Excel-related links from this website. Write two brief essays (maximum length 150 words; minimum length 125 words.) Include the appropriate website address or **URL** (Uniform Resource Locator) with each essay. The URL identifies the global address of documents and other resources on the World Wide Web.
6.	Go to this website http://www.moneywords.com. Explore three links on this site. Write up a summary of what you have seen. Your summary should have no more than 75 words or less than 50 words. Include the appropriate website addresses.

SUMMARY AND REVIEW

SOFWARE OBJECTIVES: In Chapter 4, you used to software to:

1. Open template files from the CD that accompanies this book.

2. Enter transactions in a tabular format.

3. Apply what-if analysis scenarios.

4. Create an accounting worksheet.

5. Prepare financial statements.

6. Complete the exercises and activities in Chapter 4.

WEB OBJECTIVES: In Chapter 4, you did these Internet activities:

1. Used your Internet browser to go the book's website.

2. Completed the Internet Activities for Part 2, Chapter 4.

Multiple-Choice Questions: In the space provided, write the letter that best answers each question.

_____1. Files that are partially completed and saved with an .xls extension are called:

    a. Word files.
    b. PowerPoint files.
    c. Templates.
    d. All of the above.
    e. None of the above.

_____2. The two files that you open to complete work in this chapter are:

    a. Budgeted Income Stmt.
    b. Budgeted Income Stmt2.
    c. Chapter 4-1.xls and Chapter 4-2.xls.
    d. None of the above.
    e. All of the above.

_____3. The spreadsheet that shows the worksheet is arranged in what format?

    a. Headers and Footers.
    b. Tabular.
    c. Rows only.
    d. Columns only.
    e. All of the above.

_____4. To make sure that your debit columns and credit columns are in balance, you check which of the following worksheet cells:

    a. Total Assets.
    b. Owner's Equity.
    c. Total Liabilities and Owner's Equity.
    d. Difference.
    e. None of the above.

_____5. After completing the January 3 through January 30 transactions, your total assets are:

    a. $10,250.
    b. $10,150.
    c. $19,700.
    d. $13,000.
    e. None of the above.

_____6. What Excel command can be used to perform what-if analysis?

    a. There are no commands to perform what-if analysis.
    b. AutoSum.
    c. Scenarios.
    d. Goal seek.
    e. All of the above.

_____7. On the Chapter 4-2_adjusted worksheet, the total adjustments are:

    a. $7,400.
    b. $9,700.
    c. $6,825.
    d. $9,500.
    e. None of the above.

_____8. On the Chapter 4-2 answer worksheet, the Net Income/Loss is:

    a. $18,675.
    b. $17,675.
    c. $17,375.
    d. ($6,825).
    e. None of the above.

_____9. Adjustment d is a debit and credit to which accounts

    a. Debit, Salaries Payable; Credit, Salaries Expense.
    b. Debit, Insurance Expense; Credit, Prepaid Insurance.
    c. Debit, Salaries Expense; Credit, Interest Payable.
    d. Debit, Supplies Expense; Credit, Supplies.
    e. None of the above.

_____10. In order to connect data from the worksheet to the Income Statement, which of the following Excel features to you use?

    a. Copy/Paste.
    b. =Sum
    c. Paste alone.
    d. Paste Link.
    e. None of the above.

True/Make True: If the statement is true, write the word "True" in the space provided. If the statement is *not* true, write the correct answer in the space provided.

11. Prestored Excel files that are going to have additional information added to them are called documents.

_____

_____

12. Tabular analysis is a way to create an accounting worksheet that will show adjusting entries.

_____

_____

13. When you change the conditions of an existing spreadsheet, this is called what-if analysis.

_____

_____

14. On the Chapter 4-2 adjusted worksheet, adjustment a shows accrued wages.

_____

_____

15. On the Chapter 4-2 adjusted worksheet, adjustment b shows the amount of prepaid insurance that expired.

_____

_____

16. Adjustment c shows the inventory of supplies on hand at the beginning of the month.

_____

_____

17. Adjustment d shows accrued salaries of $900.

_____

_____

18. To prepare the Income Statement, you use data from the worksheet.

_____

_____

19. To prepare the Statement of Owner's Equity, you only need to use the worksheet.

————————————————————————————

————————————————————————————

20. The Statement of Owner's Equity shows beginning capital added to net income, less drawing to arrive at ending capital.

————————————————————————————

————————————————————————————

Exercise 4-1: Tabular Analysis and Transactions

1. Start Excel; then open the Exercise 4-1.xls file.

2. Complete the following transactions. Complete the Notes column for each revenue or expense transaction.

Date	Transactions
Jan. 2	Gave surfing lessons on account to Hilo Hotel guests on account for $700.
3	Purchased $500 of supplies on account.
10	Paid $550 for locker rent.
11	Paid amount due for supplies purchased on January 3.
15	Received cash for surf lessons, $900.
20	Received electric bill for $95 due at the end of the month.
25	After taking an inventory of supplies, there are $150 supplies on hand.

> 30 Gave lessons to Hilo Hotel guests for $250 on account.

3. Line one should be boldface and 18 point; line two should be boldface and 14 point.

4. Format the spreadsheet as follows:

    a. Change the setup so that the document prints in landscape.

    b. Change the margins so that the document is centered horizontally.

    c. Format the header so that your name is left aligned; the file name (Exercise 4-1_ answer) is centered; and today's date is right aligned.

5. Save your spreadsheet as **Exercise 4-1_answer**.

6. Print the spreadsheet.

Exercise 4-2: Tabular Analysis and Adjusting Entries

1. If necessary start Excel; open Exercise 4-2.xls.

2. Complete the following adjusting entries:

    Date   *Transactions*

    Jan. 31 Record the adjusting entry for $2,500 of depreciation. (Reference a.)

    31 $200 of prepaid insurance has expired. (Reference b.)

    31 You have $450 in supplies on hand. (Reference c.)

    31 Accrued salaries are $600. (Reference d.)

3. Enter the conditional formulas in the Balance Sheet and Income Statement columns to complete those columns.

4. Format your spreadsheet similar to Exercise 4-1. (See steps 4 a., b and c. above.) For the header, use your name; centered exercise number/name (Exercise 4-2 adjusted); and today's date.

5. Save your spreadsheet as **Exercise 4-2_adjusted**.

6. Print your spreadsheet.

Exercise 4-3: Tabular Analysis and Financial Statements.

1. If necessary, start Excel and open the Exercise 4-2_adjusted.xls spreadsheet.

2. Rename Sheet 1 Worksheet; rename Sheet 2 to Income Statement; rename Sheet 3 to Owner's Equity.

3. Insert another sheet. Rename the inserted sheet to Balance Sheet. Make the Balance Sheet the last tab.

4. Reposition the worksheet so that cell A5 is the top left cell showing on the spreadsheet. Make cell B7 the active cell. Freeze the panes of the worksheet so that column A and rows 5 and 6 are always displayed.

5. Make the Income Statement the active sheet and cell A1 the active cell. While holding down the Shift key, click on the Balance Sheet tab. This will highlight the Income statement, Owner's Equity and Balance Sheet tabs.

6. Type **Carol Surfing Stop** in cell A1. Format the font to be bold and 18 points.

7. Type **for the year ended 12/31/03** in Cell A3. Format the font to be bold and 12 points.

8. Hold down the Ctrl key and click on the Owner's Equity and Balance Sheet tabs to deselect them.

9. Make sure the Income Statement is the active sheet.

10.   Type **Income Statement** in cell A2. Format the font so that it is bold and 14 points.

11.   In cell A2 of Owner's Equity, and Balance Sheet type the correct financial statement name. The font should be bold and 14 points.

12.   Using the worksheet, create an Income Statement. Enter the appropriate formulas.

13.   Using the Worksheet and Income Statement, create a Statement of Owner's Equity. Enter the appropriate formulas.

14.   Using the Income Statement and Owner's Equity Statement, create a Balance Sheet. Enter the appropriate formulas.

15.   Format each financial statement similarly to the statements you created in Chapter 4. Include the file name in the header. (For example, use comma style with no decimal places; type the appropriate headers for each financial statement section; indent as needed.) Use dollar signs for lead numbers and add borders to the financial statements appropriately.

16.   Save your spreadsheet as **Exercise 4-3_answer**.

17.   Use the same header for the Worksheet that you used in Chapter 4.

18.   Print the Income Statement.

19. . Use the same header for the Statement of Owner's Equity that you used in Chapter 4. Print the Statement of Owner's Equity.

20.   Use the same header for the Balance Sheet that you used in Chapter 4. Print the Balance Sheet.

Exercise 4-4: What-if Analysis

1. Carol is considering buying new equipment for her business. The equipment would cost $5,000 and would be purchased on account. Change the data in the trial balance column to reflect this.

2. The purchase would affect depreciation and interest. Depreciation expense will increase by $1,000 and interest expense will be $250. Make these adjustments.

3. Update the Worksheet and the appropriate financial statements.

4. Save the workbook as **Exercise 4-4_whatif**.

5. Print the worksheet and financial statements.

6. Answer the questions that follow.

   a. What is the amount of depreciation expense after purchasing the new equipment? Does this increase or decrease depreciation? Indicate the amount of the increase or decrease.

   _____

   _____

   _____

   _____

b. What is the amount of net income? Did net income increase or decrease?

_____

_____

_____

c. What changes occurred on the Balance Sheet? Indicate the dollar amount of the increases or decreases.

_____

_____

_____

_____

CHAPTER 4 INDEX

Chapter 5 — Financial Accounting

SOFTWARE OBJECTIVES: In Chapter 5, you will use the software to:

1. Open template files from the CD that accompanies this book.

2. Make changes to an inventory valuation worksheet and determine how inventory methods affect net income.

3. Solve various what-if scenarios.

4. Prepare a cash receipts journal and prepare bank reconciliation.

5. Prepare an accounts receivable aging schedule.

6. Prepare a depreciation schedule using the declining balance method.

7. Complete a payroll register.

8. Make revenue decisions by doing a percentage of completion worksheet.

9. Complete bond amortization worksheets.

10. Complete financial statement analysis.

11. Complete the exercises and activities in Chapter 5.

WEB OBJECTIVES: In Chapter 5, you will do these Internet activities.

1. Use your Internet browser to go to the book's website.

2. Complete the Internet Activities.

In Chapter 5, you will work with preformatted templates again. The templates that you will use in Chapter 5 are included on the CD that accompanies this book. The file names of the templates that you will use with this chapter are:

- Chapter 5-1.xls
- Chapter 5-3.xls
- Chapter 5-5.xls
- Chapter 5-7.xls
- Chapter 5-9.xls

- Chapter 5-11.xls
- Chapter 5-13.xls
- Chapter 5-15.xls
- Chapter 5-17.xls
- Chapter 5-19.xls

GETTING STARTED

In Chapter 5, you will notice that the templates have light blue shaded areas. Whenever necessary, you will enter formulas in the light blue shaded cells. You will also enter data where indicated in the instructions. Follow these steps to start Excel and open the Chapter 5-1 template file.

1. Start Excel.

2. Open the Chapter 5-1 file from the CD that accompanies this textbook. *Or, if your instructor has saved the template files to a network or hard-drive location, open the Chapter 5-1 file from that location.*

3. Observe that numerous cells are shaded light blue.

ACCOUNTING FOR INVENTORY

Mike has come to you to do an analysis of his inventory to see which method would produce the highest net income.

1. Observe that cell B20 indicates an ending inventory of 50 units.

2. Enter the formula to calculate total inventory cost in the range D8:D15.

3. In the range E8:F15, enter a formula to calculate the cost of goods sold. (Hint: you should not include the cost of the remaining 50 items in the ending inventory.)

4. Use AutoSum in cells B17, D17, E18 and F18.

5. The cost of goods sold in cells D26 and E26 should be equal to the costs of goods sold calculated in cells E18 and F18. In cell F26, this amount must be calculated.

6. The ending inventory in cells D25 and E25 is calculated by subtracting the cost of goods sold from the cost of good purchased. You will have to calculate this amount in cell F25

7. Setup your page so that it prints on one page, is centered horizontally, does not print gridlines, and the header contains your name, the file name, and today's date.

8. Save the worksheet as Chapter 5-1 answer.xls.

9. Print the worksheet. Compare your worksheet to the one shown. (Hint: If done correctly, the ending inventory under the LIFO method should be $87.50.)

Student Name			Chapter 5-1 answer			Today's Date

Mike's Surf Shop
Inventory Valuation
For the month of January, 2003

				Cost of Goods Sold	
Month	Units Purchased	Unit Cost	Total Cost	FIFO	LIFO
Balance	75	$ 1.75	$ 131.25	$ 131.25	$ 43.75
5-Jan	25	$ 1.80	45.00	45.00	45.00
8-Jan	30	$ 1.82	54.60	54.60	54.60
10-Jan	25	$ 1.82	45.50	45.50	45.50
16-Jan	16	$ 1.85	29.60	29.60	29.60
23-Jan	18	$ 1.88	33.84	7.52	33.84
25-Jan	24	$ 1.90	45.60		45.60
29-Jan	12	$ 1.91	22.92		22.92
Net Purchases	225		$ 408.31		
Cost of goods sold				$ 313.47	$ 320.81
Ending inventory	50				

		FIFO	LIFO	Average Cost
Net Purchases		$ 408.31	$ 408.31	$ 408.31
Ending Inventory		94.84	87.50	90.74
Cost of goods sold		313.47	320.81	317.57

Based on your analysis, which inventory method will produce a higher net income?

Answer: FIFO will produce the highest net income because it produces the lowest cost of goods sold. As you know from your study of accounting, the amount of cost of goods sold is subtracted from net sales to arrive at gross profit. Then, the total operating expenses are subtracted from gross profit. As long as your gross profit is greater than your operating expenses, you will have a net income. Lower cost of good sold amounts will contribute to a greater gross profit, which can then result in a higher net income.

What–If Analysis

1. If necessary, open the file Chapter 5-1 answer.

2. Change the data as follows:

Units Purchased	Unit Cost
36	$ 1.91
23	$ 1.90
18	$ 1.88
27	$ 1.88
14	$ 1.85
27	$ 1.83
18	$ 1.83
9	$ 1.80

3. Change the ending inventory amount to 30.

4. Save the workbook as Chapter 5-2 answer.

5. Print the worksheet. Compare your worksheet to the one shown on the next page.

Mike's Surf Shop
Inventory Valuation
For the month of January, 2003

Month	Units Purchased	Unit Cost	Total Cost	Cost of Goods Sold FIFO	Cost of Goods Sold LIFO
Balance	36	$ 1.91	$ 68.76	$ 68.76	$ 11.46
5-Jan	23	$ 1.90	43.70	43.70	43.70
8-Jan	18	$ 1.88	33.84	33.84	33.84
10-Jan	27	$ 1.88	50.76	50.76	50.76
16-Jan	14	$ 1.85	25.90	25.90	25.90
23-Jan	27	$ 1.83	49.41	43.92	49.41
25-Jan	18	$ 1.83	32.94		32.94
29-Jan	9	$ 1.80	16.20		16.20
Net Purchases	172		$ 321.51		
Cost of goods sold				$ 266.88	$ 264.21
Ending inventory	30				

	FIFO	LIFO	Average Cost
Net Purchases	$ 321.51	$ 321.51	$ 321.51
Ending Inventory	54.63	57.30	56.08
Cost of goods sold	266.88	264.21	265.43

Based on this new data, which inventory method will produce the greatest net income?

> **Answer:** In this case LIFO produces the lowest cost of goods sold, so that would translate into the highest net income.

GROSS PROFIT METHOD

In your study of accounting, you learned that the ***gross profit method*** estimates the cost of ending inventory by applying the gross profit ratio to net sales (at retail). This method is often used when inventory is destroyed such as the example that follows.

Mike's Surf Shop has had a fire at their warehouse. Mike needs to determine how much inventory was destroyed in the fire. Because Mike uses the periodic inventory method, he does not know how much inventory was destroyed because he is unable to take a physical count.

The McGraw-Hill Companies, Inc., *Excel Accounting*

Mike has asked you to make an estimate of his ending inventory. From his accounting records, Mike gives you the information that follows.

Net sales	$ 250,000
Gross profit percent	30%
Beginning inventory	$ 50,000
Cost of goods purchased	$ 130,000

1. Open the file Chapter 5-3.

2. Input the information shown above in the appropriate cells.

3. Enter formulas where appropriate. (Hint: Formulas are entered into the shaded cells.)

4. Setup your page so that it prints on one page, is centered horizontally does not print gridlines, and the header contains your name, the file name, and today's date.

5. Save the worksheet as Chapter 5-3 answer.xls.

6. Print the worksheet. Observe that estimated cost of goods sold should be $175,000.

Student Name	Chapter 5-3 answer	Today's Date

Mike's Surf Shop
Gross Profit Method

Gross profit percent	30.00%
Net sales	250,000
Estimated gross profit	75,000
Estimated cost of goods sold	175,000
Beginning Inventory	50,000
Cost of goods purchased	130,000
Cost of goods available for sale	180,000
Estimated cost of goods sold	175,000
Estimated ending inventory	5,000

What-If Analysis

1.   Change the data as follows:

Net sales	$ 200,000
Gross profit percent	25%
Beginning inventory	$ 30,000
Cost of goods purchased	$ 120,000

2.   Save the workbook as Chapter 5-4 answer.xls.

3.   Print the worksheet.

<table>
<tr><td>Student Name</td><td align="center">Chapter 5-4 answer</td><td align="right">Today's Date</td></tr>
</table>

Mike's Surf Shop
Gross Profit Method

Gross profit percent	25.00%
Net sales	200,000
Estimated gross profit	50,000
Estimated cost of goods sold	150,000
Beginning Inventory	30,000
Cost of goods purchased	120,000
Cost of goods available for sale	150,000
Estimated cost of goods sold	150,000
Estimated ending inventory	-

ACCOUNTING FOR CASH

In this section, you will use Excel to prepare a cash receipts journal and a bank reconciliation.

Cash Receipts Journal

1.   Open the file Chapter 5-5.

2.   The entry for January 3 has already been completed for you. Copy the formulas in E8, F8, and J8 down to row 17. Notice that the

formula in E8 is set up to automatically calculate the debit to Cash when data is entered in columns G, H, and I.

3.   Make cell F8 the active cell and observe the formula. When Mike's Surf Shop sells merchandise on account, they use the terms 2/10, n/30. If a customer pays their account within the discount period, this formula [=IF(D8="y",G8*0.02,0)], will calculate the discount if there is a "y" for "yes" in column D.

4.   Make cell J8 the active cell and observe the formula. Mike's Surf Shop has a 20% gross profit rate. This formula will calculate the adjustment to the merchandise inventory account when you record a cash sale. Copy this cell down to the remaining cells in column J.

5.   Enter the following transactions.

Date	Transactions
Jan 5	Received payment from Hawaiian Hot Wax. Hawaiian Hot Wax's account balance was $5,600 and they paid within the discount period.
9	Mike made an additional investment of $3,000 cash. Credit MF, Capital.
10	Made cash sales of $8,000.
12	Received a payment from Zoe's Foam Shop less discount. Zoe owed $7,500.
15	Received payment for nine $100 surf lessons in advance. Credit Unearned Revenue.
18	Made cash sales of $3,000.
25	Gave six $100 surf lessons for cash. Credit Service Revenue.
29	Made cash sales of $250.

31   Received $700 payment from Beach Boy Surfing. Beach Boy Surfing did not pay within the discount period.

6.   Enter formulas in all cells with blue shading.

7.   Highlight the range A6:J19.

8.   From the menu bar, select Format, then Auto Format.

9.   Click on Options and be sure the Alignment and Width/Height checkboxes are unchecked.

10. Select List 1 and click [OK]. (Hint: scroll down the dialog box to List 1. The name appears below the sample.)

11. Format the page so that the worksheet prints on one page, is centered horizontally, and the header contains your name, the file name and today's date.

12. Save as Chapter 5-5 answer.xls.

13. Print your worksheet. If you entered all transactions and formulas correctly, Total Debits and Credits should be $49,350.

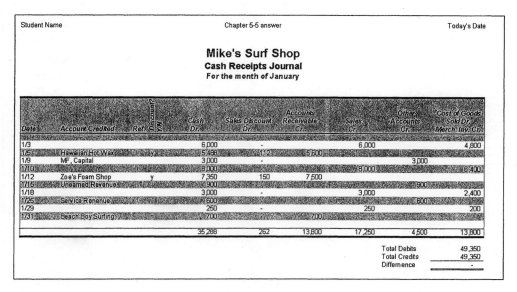

Date	Account Credited	Ref.	Discount? W/N	Cash Dr.	Sales Discount Dr.	Accounts Receivable Cr.	Sales Cr.	Other Accounts Cr.	Cost of Goods Sold Dr. Merch. Inv. Cr.
1/3				6,000	-		6,000		4,800
1/5	Hawaiian Hot Wax	y		5,488	112	5,600			
1/9	MF, Capital			3,000	-			3,000	
1/10				8,000				8,000	6,400
1/12	Zoe's Foam Shop	y		7,350	150	7,500			
1/15	Unearned Revenue			900				900	
1/18				3,000	-			3,000	2,400
1/25	Service Revenue			600				600	
1/29				250	-		250		200
1/31	Beach Boy Surfing	n		700		700			
				35,288	262	13,800	17,250	4,500	13,800

Student Name   Chapter 5-5 answer   Today's Date

Mike's Surf Shop
Cash Receipts Journal
For the month of January

Total Debits   49,350
Total Credits   49,350
Difference   -

What-If Analysis

Adjust the formulas on the worksheet to determine the total cash receipts if Mike's Surf Shop offered credit terms of 1/10,n/30 and the gross profit percent was 25%.

1. Change the formulas in columns F and J to account for these changes.

2. Change the AutoFormat option to List 3 but retain the current cell alignments and widths.

3. Change the alignment on cell D6 so that it appears at 90 degrees. (Hint: Right-click D6; left-click Format cells; choose the Alignment tab; type **90** in the Degrees field.)

4. Save the workbook as Chapter 5-6 answer.

5. Print the worksheet.

Student Name				Chapter 5-6 answer					Today's Date

Mike's Surf Shop
Cash Receipts Journal
For the month of January

Date	Account Credited	Ref.	Discount?	Cash Dr.	Sales Discount Dr.	Accounts Receivable Cr.	Sales Cr.	Other Accounts Cr.	Cost of Goods Sold Dr. Merch. Inv. Cr.
1/3				6,000	-		6,000		4,500
1/5	Hawaiian Hot Wax	y		5,544	56	5,600			
1/9	MF, Capital			3,000	-			3,000	
1/10				8,000	-		8,000		6,000
1/12	Zoe's Foam Shop	y		7,425	75	7,500			
1/15	Unearned Revenue			900	-			900	
1/18				3,000	-			3,000	2,250
1/25	Service Renenue			600	-			600	
1/29				250	-			250	188
1/31	Beach Boy Surfing	n		700	-	700			
				35,419	131	13,800	17,250	4,500	12,938

Total Debits	48,488
Total Credits	48,488
Differnence	-

Bank Reconciliation

In this section, you will use a worksheet to prepare bank reconciliation. *Bank reconciliation* is the process of bringing the balance of the bank statement and the balance of the cash account into agreement. Compare the following bank statement to the information from Mike's Surf Shop's checkbook on the next page.

North Shore Bank Sunset Beach, Hawaii						
Statement Date 12/31/2003					**Account Number** 12579	
Beginning Balance 13,543.82		**Deposits and Credits** 23,509.23		**Checks and Debits** 7,884.66	**Ending Balance** 29,168.39	
Checks and Debits			**Deposits and Credits**		**Daily Balance**	
Date	No.	Amount	Date	Amount	Date	Amount
12/3	135	500.60	12/4	3,500.00	12/1	13,579.82
12/5	136	125.36	12/10	8,659.23	12/3	13,079.22
12/6	138	865.23	12/17	2,800.00	12/4	16,579.22
12/12	137	1,563.00	CM 12/20	1,350.00	12/5	16,453.86
12/19	141	1,682.76	12/30	7,200.00	12/8	15,588.63
12/20	144	726.86			12/10	24,247,86
12/23	142	125.88			12/12	22,684.86
12/26	146	862.67			12/17	25,484.85
12/29	145	128.00			12/19	23,802.10
12/30	NSF	1,275.30			12/20	24,389.24
12/31	DM	29.00			12/23	24,263.36
					12/26	23,400.69
					12/29	23,272.69
					12/30	29,197.39
					12/31	29,168.39

- The NSF check was a payment from a customer on account.

- The Debit Memorandum indicates a bank service charge.

- The Credit Memorandum is a note that was collected by the bank. The principal amount was $1,200 with interest of $200. The bank charged Mike's Surf Shop $50 to collect the note.

- All of the checks and deposits on the bank statement are correct.

The following table is a schedule of checks from Mike's Surf Shop's checkbook.

Check No.	Amount	Check No.	Amount
134	1,256.40	144	762.86
135	500.60	145	128.00
136	125.36	146	862.67
137	1,563.00	147	189.98
138	865.23	148	1,276.57
139	265.00	149	1,928.60
140	123.58	150	125.36
141	1,682.76	151	1,295.30
142	125.88	152	865.30
143	166.00	153	291.80

Mike's Surf Shop made the following deposits during the month of December:

Date	Amount
12/4	3,500.00
12/10	8,659.23
12/17	2,800.00
12/30	7,200.00
12/31	3,500.00

Mike's Surf Shop's books show a cash balance of $24,874.80.

1. Open the file Chapter 5-7 from the student data files.

2. Input the necessary data in the yellow shaded areas. Use column A for descriptions such as check numbers. Use column B for the related amounts. Note that there may be extra rows that are shaded.

3. Input formulas in the blue shaded areas.

4. Setup the page so that the document prints on one page, is centered horizontally and the header includes your name, the file name and today's date.

5. Save as Chapter 5-7 answer.xls.

6. Print your worksheet. Observe that the balance per book should be $24,884.50.

Student Name	Chapter 5-7 answer	Today's Date

Mike's Surf Shop
Bank Reconciliation

Balance per bank		29,168.39
Deposits in transit		3,500.00
		32,668.39
Outstanding checks		
134	1,256.40	
139	265.00	
140	123.58	
143	166.00	
147	189.98	
148	1,276.57	
149	1,928.60	
150	125.36	
151	1,295.30	
152	865.30	
153	291.80	
		7,783.89
Adjusted balance per bank		24,884.50
Balance per books		24,874.80
Add:		
Collection by bank	1,350.00	
		1,350.00
Less:		
NSF check	1,275.30	
Bank service charge	29.00	
Check #144 error	36.00	
		1,340.30
Adjusted balance per book		24,884.50
Difference		-

What-If Analysis

Make the following changes to your worksheet.

1. Balance per bank is 28,224.00.

2. The error on check #144 is $75.00.

3. Change the formula in cell C40 so that it is equal to the Adjusted balance per bank.

4. Change the formula is cell C28 to calculate the balance per book.

5. Save your document as Chapter 5-8 answer.

6. Print the worksheet.

Student Name	Chapter 5-8 answer		Today's Date

Mike's Surf Shop
Bank Reconciliation

Balance per bank		28,224.00	
Deposits in transit		3,500.00	
		31,724.00	
Outstaning checks			
	134	1,256.40	
	139	265.00	
	140	123.58	
	143	166.00	
	147	189.98	
	148	1,276.57	
	149	1,928.60	
	150	125.36	
	151	1,295.30	
	152	865.30	
	153	291.80	
			7,783.89
Adjusted balance per bank			23,940.11
Balance per books			23,819.41
Add:			
Collection by bank		1,350.00	
Check #144 error		75.00	
			1,425.00
Less:			
NSF check		1,275.30	
Bank service charge		29.00	
			1,304.30
Adjusted balance per book			23,940.11
Difference			-

ACCOUNTS RECEIVABLE AGING SCHEDULE

In this exercise, you will use a worksheet to calculate the total uncollectible amount. An accounts receivable aging schedule is used to determine uncollectible amounts. Mike's Surf Shop estimates uncollectible accounts as follows:

Not yet due	1%
1-30 days	3%
31-60 days	5%
61-90 days	20%
Over 90 days	35%

Allowance for doubtful accounts has a debit balance of $150.00.

1. Open the file Chapter 5-9 from the student data files.

2. Enter the necessary data in the yellow shaded cells.

3. Enter the appropriate formulas in the blue shaded cells. Use AutoSum where possible.

4. Setup the page so that the worksheet prints on one page, is centered horizontally, and the header shows your name, the file name and today's date.

5. Save as Chapter 5-9 answer. Print the worksheet.

| Student Name | | Chapter 5-9 answer | | | | Today's Date |

Mike's Surf Shop
Aging Schedule

Customer	Total	Not Yet Due	Number of Days Past Due			
			1-30	31-60	61-90	Over 90
Zoe's Foam Shop	600.00	250.00	350.00			
Beach Boy Surfing	1,000.00		300.00	500.00	200.00	
Waikiki Hotel	2,500.00	350.00	1,700.00	450.00		
S&S Surfing	550.00		200.00	100.00		250.00
Shredding Surfers	275.00	175.00	100.00			
	4,925.00	775.00	2,650.00	1,050.00	200.00	250.00
Percent uncollectable		1%	3%	5%	20%	35%
Estimated Bad Debts	267.25	7.75	79.50	52.50	40.00	87.50
Current balance in Allowance for doubtful accounts				debit/(credit)		150.00
Bad Debt Expense						117.25

What-If Analysis

Mike's Surf Shop is considering changing their credit policies. The new credit policies would change the uncollectible amounts as follows:

Not yet due	2%
1-30 days	5%
31-60 days	20%
61-90 days	40%
Over 90 days	50%

What would the bad debt expense be if the allowance account had a credit balance of $200.00?

1. Make adjustments to the worksheet to reflect the changes in the credit policies.

2. Save the document as Chapter 5-10 answer. Print the worksheet.

Student Name   Chapter 5-10 answer   Today's Date

Mike's Surf Shop
Aging Schedule

Customer	Total	Not Yet Due	1-30	31-60	61-90	Over 90
Zoe's Foam Shop	600.00	250.00	350.00			
Beach Boy Surfing	1,000.00		300.00	500.00	200.00	
Waikiki Hotel	2,500.00	350.00	1,700.00	450.00		
S&S Surfing	550.00		200.00	100.00		250.00
Shredding Surfers	275.00	175.00	100.00			
	4,925.00	775.00	2,650.00	1,050.00	200.00	250.00
Percent uncollectable		2%	5%	20%	40%	50%
Estimated Bad Debts	563.00	15.50	132.50	210.00	80.00	125.00

Current balance in Allowance for doubtful accounts   debit/(credit)   (200.00)

Bad Debt Expense   763.00

DEPRECIATION

In this section, you will prepare a depreciation schedule using the declining balance method. **Depreciation** is the process of allocating the cost of a fixed asset (also called plant asset) to expense in the accounting periods benefiting from its use. Mike's Surf Shop has purchased a new vehicle for $20,000. It is estimated that the vehicle will have a salvage value of $5,000 and is expected to last five years. Use double declining balance (200%) to calculate depreciation over the asset's life.

1. Open the file Chapter 5-11.

2. Enter the appropriate data in the range D5:D8.

3. In cell B14, insert a function to calculate declining balance depreciation. If DDB is *not* listed in the Select a function dialog box, follow these steps. (Refer to 3b. for the Function Arguments dialog box.)

    a. From the menu bar, select Insert; Function. In the Search for a function field, type **depreciation**; then click [Go].

    b. In the Select a function area, select DDB; then [OK]. Complete the function arguments as shown below.

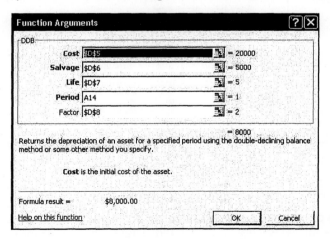

(Hint: When you reference any data in the range D5:D8, you should make the reference absolute. (Use the F4 function key.)

4. Calculate Accumulated depreciation by adding the current depreciation expense (B14) to the previous period's accumulated depreciation (C13). Make sure your formula in C14 will work correctly when copied down the column.

5. Copy the formulas in the range B14:D14 to the cell B15:D23.

6. Setup the page so that the worksheet prints on one page, is centered horizontally, and the header show your name, the file name and today's' date.

7. Save as Chapter 5-11 answer.

8. Print. Compare your worksheet to the one below.

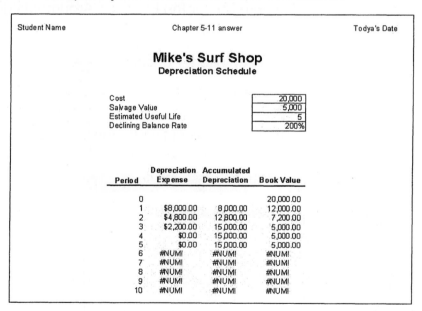

Student Name	Chapter 5-11 answer		Todya's Date

Mike's Surf Shop
Depreciation Schedule

Cost	20,000
Salvage Value	5,000
Estimated Useful Life	5
Declining Balance Rate	200%

Period	Depreciation Expense	Accumulated Depreciation	Book Value
0			20,000.00
1	$8,000.00	8,000.00	12,000.00
2	$4,800.00	12,800.00	7,200.00
3	$2,200.00	15,000.00	5,000.00
4	$0.00	15,000.00	5,000.00
5	$0.00	15,000.00	5,000.00
6	#NUM!	#NUM!	#NUM!
7	#NUM!	#NUM!	#NUM!
8	#NUM!	#NUM!	#NUM!
9	#NUM!	#NUM!	#NUM!
10	#NUM!	#NUM!	#NUM!

Comment

Excel calculates the depreciation until the book value reaches the salvage value. Anything after the useful life will not be calculated. That's why rows 6 through 10 show #NUM.

What-If Analysis

1. Change the data to show a $30,000 vehicle cost with a $6,000 salvage value, nine year life and 150% declining balance.

2. Save the file as Chapter 5-12 answer. Print the worksheet. Compare your worksheet to the one shown below.

Student Name	Chapter 5-12 answer	Todya's Date

Mike's Surf Shop
Depreciation Schedule

Cost	30,000
Salvage Value	6,000
Estimated Useful Life	9
Declining Balance Rate	150%

Period	Depreciation Expense	Accumulated Depreciation	Book Value
0			30,000.00
1	$5,000.00	5,000.00	25,000.00
2	$4,166.67	9,166.67	20,833.33
3	$3,472.22	12,638.89	17,361.11
4	$2,893.52	15,532.41	14,467.59
5	$2,411.27	17,943.67	12,056.33
6	$2,009.39	19,953.06	10,046.94
7	$1,674.49	21,627.55	8,372.45
8	$1,395.41	23,022.96	6,977.04
9	$977.04	24,000.00	6,000.00
10	#NUM!	#NUM!	#NUM!

PAYROLL REGISTER

In this exercise, you will complete a payroll register.

1. Open the file Chapter 5-13.xls.

2. Enter 10% as the State Income Tax rate.

3. Enter 87,000 at the FICA Limit.

4. Enter 6.2% as the FICA Rate.

5. In cell J14, enter the formula =IF(G14-F14>$B$5,0,IF(G14>$B$5,(G14-$B$5)*$B$6,F14*$B$6)). This formula will calculate the FICA tax with limits.

6. Enter appropriate formulas in cell I14. Remember that you will be copying this formula.

7. Enter formulas in the range K14:N14.

8. Copy the formulas down to row 18.

9. Enter appropriate formulas in the range D20:N20.

10. Highlight the range A12:N20.

11. Select List 1 from the AutoFormat dialog box.

12. Setup the page so that the worksheet prints in landscape and on one page, is centered horizontally, and shows you name, the file name and today's date.

13. Save as Chapter 13 answer.xls.

14. Print the worksheet. Compare it to the one shown below.

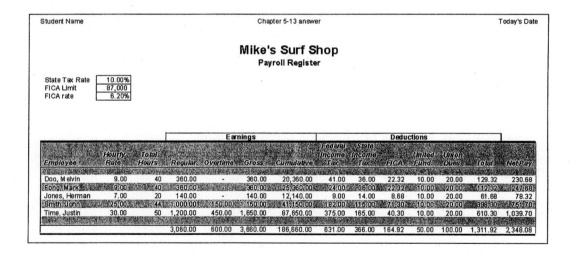

What-If Analysis

1. Change the FICA Limit to $41,000.

2. Change Melvin Doo's hours to 44.

3. Save the workbook as Chapter 5-14 answer.

4. Print the worksheet. Compare it to the one shown below.

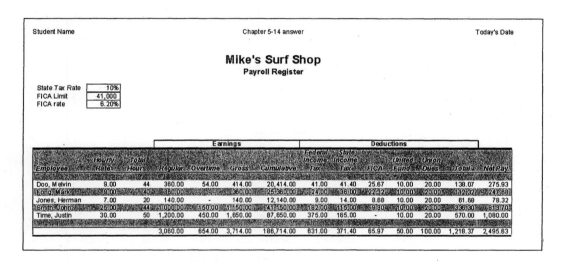

| Student Name | | | | | Chapter 5-14 answer | | | | | | | Today's Date | |

Mike's Surf Shop
Payroll Register

State Tax Rate   10%
FICA Limit   41,000
FICA rate   6.20%

			Earnings				Deductions						
Employee	Hourly Rate	Total Hours	Regular	Overtime	Gross	Cumulative	Federal Income Tax	State Income Tax	FICA	United Fund	Union Dues	Total	Net Pay
Doo, Melvin	9.00	44	360.00	54.00	414.00	20,414.00	41.00	41.40	25.67	10.00	20.00	138.07	275.93
Long, Mark	9.00	40	360.00	-	360.00	25,360.00	24.00	36.00	22.32	10.00	20.00	112.32	247.68
Jones, Herman	7.00	20	140.00	-	140.00	12,140.00	9.00	14.00	8.68	10.00	20.00	61.68	78.32
Smith, John	25.00	44	1,000.00	150.00	1,150.00	41,150.00	182.00	115.00	9.30	10.00	20.00	336.30	813.70
Time, Justin	30.00	50	1,200.00	450.00	1,650.00	87,650.00	375.00	165.00	-	10.00	20.00	570.00	1,080.00
			3,060.00	654.00	3,714.00	186,714.00	631.00	371.40	65.97	50.00	100.00	1,218.37	2,495.63

PERCENTAGE-OF-COMPLETION

Mike's Surf Shop has entered into a long term construction contract. Use the template to determine how much revenue the company will have to recognize each year. The contract will generate $3,000,000 in revenues and is expected to cost $2,300,000.

1. Open the file Chapter 5-15.

2. Enter the appropriate data in the range C5:C6.

3. Make cell C11 equal to the total estimated cost. This cell reference should be absolute.

4. Enter the appropriate formulas in the range D11:E11.

The McGraw-Hill Companies, Inc., *Excel Accounting*

5. Copy the formulas in the range C11:E11 down to row 14.

6. Use AutoSum in Row 16.

7. Format the page so that the worksheet prints on one page, is centered horizontally, and prints your name, the file name and today's date in the header.

8. Save as Chapter 5-15 answer. Print the worksheet. Compare it to the one shown below.

Student Name   Chapter 5-15 answer   Today's Date

Mike's Surf Shop
Percentage of Completion

Contract Price	3,000,000
Total Estimated Cost	2,300,000

Year	Cost Incurred (current period)	Total Estimated Cost	Percent Complete	Revenue Recognized Gross Profit
2002	600,000	2,300,000	26%	782,609
2003	750,000	2,300,000	33%	978,261
2004	750,000	2,300,000	33%	978,261
2005	200,000	2,300,000	9%	260,870
	2,300,000		100%	3,000,000

What-If Analysis

1. Change the contract price to $3,500,000.

2. Change the total estimated cost to $1,750,000.

3. Change the cost incurred in year 2002 to $50,000.

4. Enter a formula to calculate the cost incurred in year 2005 to the appropriate amount.

5. Print the worksheet.

6. Save the file as Chapter 5-16 answer.xls. Compare your worksheet to the one shown below.

Student Name   Chapter 5-16 answer   Today's Date

Mike's Surf Shop
Percentage of Completion

Contract Price   3,500,000
Total Estimated Cost   1,750,000

Year	Cost Incurred (current period)	Total Estimated Cost	Percent Complete	Revenue Recognized Gross Profit
2002	50,000	1,750,000	3%	100,000
2003	750,000	1,750,000	43%	1,500,000
2004	750,000	1,750,000	43%	1,500,000
2005	200,000	1,750,000	11%	400,000
	1,750,000		100%	3,500,000

BOND AMORTIZATION

In this section, you will prepare a bond amortization schedule. Mike's Surf Shop is selling bonds with a face value of $100,000 at 102. The bonds pay 5% interest semiannually for 15 years.

Comment:

The payment (column B) is equal to the face value (C6) of the bond times the contract rate (C7) divided by the payments per year (C9). The annual amortization (column D) is equal to the premium or discount in year 0 (E15) divided by the term of the bond (C8). Interest is the difference between the payment and the amortization. Carrying value (column F) is the Face value (C6) plus the unamortized premium or less the unamortized discount (column D).

1. Open the file Chapter 5-17.

2. Enter the appropriate data in the range C6:C10.

3. Enter formulas in row 16 to calculate Payment, Interest, Amortization, Unamortized Premium (Discount), and Carrying Value. Use absolute references when referencing data in the range C6:C10.

4.   Copy the formulas from the range B16:F16 to the range B17:F20. The remaining rows will be calculated for you.

5.   Format the worksheet so that it prints on one page, centers horizontally, and shows your name, the file name and today's date in the header.

6.   Save your file as Chapter 5-17 answer; then print.

If you have entered data and formulas properly, the carrying value should be equal to the face value at the end of the 15th year (period 30), as shown on the next page.

Mike's Surf Shop
Bond Amortization Schedule

Face Value	100,000	
Contract Rate	5.00%	
Term	15	Years
Payments/Year	2	
Bonds selling at	102%	

Period	Payment	Interest	Amortization	Premium (Discount)	Carrying Value
0				2,000.00	102,000.00
1	2,500.00	2,433.33	66.67	1,933.33	101,933.33
2	2,500.00	2,433.33	66.67	1,866.67	101,866.67
3	2,500.00	2,433.33	66.67	1,800.00	101,800.00
4	2,500.00	2,433.33	66.67	1,733.33	101,733.33
5	2,500.00	2,433.33	66.67	1,666.67	101,666.67
6	2,500.00	2,433.33	66.67	1,600.00	101,600.00
7	2,500.00	2,433.33	66.67	1,533.33	101,533.33
8	2,500.00	2,433.33	66.67	1,466.67	101,466.67
9	2,500.00	2,433.33	66.67	1,400.00	101,400.00
10	2,500.00	2,433.33	66.67	1,333.33	101,333.33
11	2,500.00	2,433.33	66.67	1,266.67	101,266.67
12	2,500.00	2,433.33	66.67	1,200.00	101,200.00
13	2,500.00	2,433.33	66.67	1,133.33	101,133.33
14	2,500.00	2,433.33	66.67	1,066.67	101,066.67
15	2,500.00	2,433.33	66.67	1,000.00	101,000.00
16	2,500.00	2,433.33	66.67	933.33	100,933.33
17	2,500.00	2,433.33	66.67	866.67	100,866.67
18	2,500.00	2,433.33	66.67	800.00	100,800.00
19	2,500.00	2,433.33	66.67	733.33	100,733.33
20	2,500.00	2,433.33	66.67	666.67	100,666.67
21	2,500.00	2,433.33	66.67	600.00	100,600.00
22	2,500.00	2,433.33	66.67	533.33	100,533.33
23	2,500.00	2,433.33	66.67	466.67	100,466.67
24	2,500.00	2,433.33	66.67	400.00	100,400.00
25	2,500.00	2,433.33	66.67	333.33	100,333.33
26	2,500.00	2,433.33	66.67	266.67	100,266.67
27	2,500.00	2,433.33	66.67	200.00	100,200.00
28	2,500.00	2,433.33	66.67	133.33	100,133.33
29	2,500.00	2,433.33	66.67	66.67	100,066.67
30	2,500.00	2,433.33	66.67	(0.00)	100,000.00

What-If Analysis

1. Change the data to reflect the sale of $200,000 face value bonds at 98. The bonds pay interest of 6% quarterly for five years.

2. Save your workbook as Chapter 5-18 answer; then print. Compare your results to those shown on the next page.

Mike's Surf Shop
Bond Amortization Schedule

Face Value	200,000	
Contract Rate	6.00%	
Term	5	Years
Payments/Year	4	
Bonds selling at	98%	

Period	Payment	Interest	Amortization	Premium (Discount)	Carrying Value
0				(4,000.00)	196,000.00
1	3,000.00	3,200.00	(200.00)	(3,800.00)	196,200.00
2	3,000.00	3,200.00	(200.00)	(3,600.00)	196,400.00
3	3,000.00	3,200.00	(200.00)	(3,400.00)	196,600.00
4	3,000.00	3,200.00	(200.00)	(3,200.00)	196,800.00
5	3,000.00	3,200.00	(200.00)	(3,000.00)	197,000.00
6	3,000.00	3,200.00	(200.00)	(2,800.00)	197,200.00
7	3,000.00	3,200.00	(200.00)	(2,600.00)	197,400.00
8	3,000.00	3,200.00	(200.00)	(2,400.00)	197,600.00
9	3,000.00	3,200.00	(200.00)	(2,200.00)	197,800.00
10	3,000.00	3,200.00	(200.00)	(2,000.00)	198,000.00
11	3,000.00	3,200.00	(200.00)	(1,800.00)	198,200.00
12	3,000.00	3,200.00	(200.00)	(1,600.00)	198,400.00
13	3,000.00	3,200.00	(200.00)	(1,400.00)	198,600.00
14	3,000.00	3,200.00	(200.00)	(1,200.00)	198,800.00
15	3,000.00	3,200.00	(200.00)	(1,000.00)	199,000.00
16	3,000.00	3,200.00	(200.00)	(800.00)	199,200.00
17	3,000.00	3,200.00	(200.00)	(600.00)	199,400.00
18	3,000.00	3,200.00	(200.00)	(400.00)	199,600.00
19	3,000.00	3,200.00	(200.00)	(200.00)	199,800.00
20	3,000.00	3,200.00	(200.00)	-	200,000.00

FINANCIAL STATEMENT ANALYSIS

1. Open the file Chapter 5-19.

2. Enter the appropriate formulas to calculate the vertical and horizontal ratios.

Comment:

The vertical ratio in the income statement is calculated by dividing the line item by Net Sales (Net Sales amount should be absolute). For example, the formula to calculate the ratio for Cost of goods sold in cell E10 would be =D10/$D$9. Once you compute and format the first ratio, copy it to the remaining cells. On the balance sheet, the ratio is calculated by dividing the amount by Total Assets.

The ratio for the horizontal analysis is calculated by dividing the change by the base year. For example, the formula in cell J9 would be =I9/D9.

3. Enter the appropriate formulas to calculate the ratios. Since 2002 was the first year of business, there is no data for 2001. For example, the formula in cell D53 should be =D41/((B32+D32)/2) (columns B and C are hidden).

4. Format the page so that it prints on two pages with only the Ratio Analysis on the second page (use page break preview). The pages should be centered horizontally and your name, the file name and today's date should print in the header.

  Read Me

To use Page Break Preview, click on Page Break Preview from the View menu. Drag the blue line to the point you want your page break located. Select Normal from the View menu to return to normal view.

5. Save your worksheet as Chapter 5-19 answer; then print your worksheet. Compare your worksheets to the ones shown on pages 170 and 171.

Mike's Surf Shop
Financial Statement Analysis

	2002	Vertical Analysis %	2003	%	Horizontal Analysis Change	%
Income Statement						
Net sales	8,201	100.00%	11,875	100.00%	3,674	44.80%
Cost of goods sold	3,996	48.73%	4,744	39.95%	748	18.72%
Gross profit	4,205	51.27%	7,131	60.05%	2,926	69.58%
Operating expenses	3,021	36.84%	4,653	39.18%	1,632	54.02%
Income from operations	1,184	14.44%	2,478	20.87%	1,294	109.29%
Other revenue and gains	100	1.22%	-	0.00%	(100)	-100.00%
Other expenses and losses	(201)	-2.45%	-	0.00%	201	-100.00%
Net income	1,385	16.89%	2,478	20.87%	1,093	78.92%
Balance Sheet						
Cash	431	2.73%	745	4.20%	314	72.85%
Accounts receivable	1,198	7.59%	2,204	12.44%	1,006	83.97%
Inventories	751	4.76%	1,233	6.96%	482	64.18%
Prepaid expenses and other assets	3,395	21.52%	3,933	22.20%	538	15.85%
Total current assets	5,775	36.60%	8,115	45.80%	2,340	40.52%
Property, plant and equipment	5,589	35.42%	5,447	30.74%	(142)	-2.54%
Investments	748	4.74%	961	5.42%	213	28.48%
Intangibles and other assets	3,667	23.24%	3,197	18.04%	(470)	-12.82%
Total Assets	15,779	100.00%	17,720	100.00%	1,941	12.30%
Current liabilities	1,580	10.01%	2,813	15.87%	1,233	78.04%
Long-term liabilities	2,320	14.70%	2,319	13.09%	(1)	-0.04%
Total liabilities	3,900	24.72%	5,132	28.96%	1,232	31.59%
Stockholders' equity	11,879	75.28%	12,588	71.04%	709	5.97%
Total liabilities and stockholders' equity	15,779	100.00%	17,720	100.00%	1,941	12.30%
Net cash provided by operating activities	1,819		2,185			
Weighted average number of shares	170		240			
Market price per share	16.02		24.00			

Mike's Surf Shop
Financial Statement Analysis

	Vertical Analysis				Horizontal Analysis
	2002	%	2003	%	
Ratio Analysis					
Current ratio	3.66 :1		2.88 :1		
Acid test (quick) ratio	1.03 :1		1.05 :1		
Current cash debt coverage ratio	2.30 :1		0.99 :1		
Receivables turnover	13.69 times		6.98 times		
Inventory turnover	10.64 times		4.78 times		
Profit margin	16.89%		20.87%		
Cash return on sales	22.18%		18.40%		
Asset turnover	1.04 times		0.71 times		
Return on assets	17.55%		14.79%		
Return on common stockholders' equity	23.32%		20.26%		
Earnings per share	8.15		10.33		
Price-earnings ratio	1.97		2.32		

INTERNET ACTIVITIES

1. From your Internet browser, go to the textbook's website at www.mhhe.com/yachtexcel. Go to the Student link. Link to Internet Activities, then WEB EXCERCISES, Part 2-Chapter 5.
2. Access this website. http://office.microsoft.com/excel/assistance. In the Search field, select Assistance. Type **What if Analysis**; click Go.
3. Explore two links on this site. Write up a summary of what you have seen. Your summary should have no more than 100 words or less than 75 words. Include the appropriate website addresses.
4. Go to Recent News Headlines for Accounting website. Write two brief essays (maximum length 75 words; minimum length 50 words.) Include the appropriate website address with each essay.
5. Go to this website www.thecycles.com/business/accounting. Explore three links on this site. Write up a summary of what you have seen. Your summary should have no more than 125 words or less than 75 words. Include the appropriate website addresses.

SUMMARY AND REVIEW

SOFWARE OBJECTIVES: In Chapter 5, you used to software to:

1. Open template files from the CD that accompanies this book.

2. Make changes to an inventory valuation worksheet and determine how inventory methods affect net income.

3. Solve various what-if scenarios.

4. Prepare a cash receipts journal and prepare a bank reconciliation.

5. Prepare an accounts receivable aging schedule.

6. Prepare a depreciation schedule using the declining balance method.

7. Complete a payroll register.

8. Make revenue decisions by doing a percentage of completion worksheet.

9. Complete bond amortization worksheets.

10. Complete financial statement analysis.

11. Complete the exercises and activities in Chapter 5.

WEB OBJECTIVES: In Chapter 3, you did these Internet activities:

1. Used your Internet browser to go the book's website.

2. Completed the Internet Activities.

Multiple-Choice Questions: In the space provided, write the letter that best answers each question.

_____1. On the templates, the cells that are shaded in light blue, indicate that you should enter:

    a. Analysis data.
    b. Test data..
    c. The appropriate depreciation method.
    d. Formulas.
    e. None of the above.

_____2. Using the Chapter 5-1 answer.xls worksheet, what inventory method produces the lowest net income?

    a. Average cost.
    b. LIFO.
    c. FIFO.
    d. Double-declining balance method.
    e. All of the above.

_____3. If the purchase price of inventory is rising, which method will result in the highest net income?

    a. LIFO.
    b. FIFO.
    c. Average cost.
    d. None of the above.
    e. All of the above.

_____4. Open your Chapter 5-3 answer worksheet. What is Mike's Surf Shop estimated cost of goods sold?

    a. $150,000.
    b. $200,000.
    c. $175,000.
    d. $0.00.
    e. None of the above.

_____5. Open the Chapter 5-6 answer worksheet. After completing
         what-if analysis on the Cash Receipts Journal, Mike's Surf
         Shop's Cost of Goods Sold debit and Merchandise Inventory
         credit is?

         a. $13,800.
         b. $48,488.
         c. $49,350.
         d. $12,938.
         e. None of the above.

_____6. The ending balance on Mike's bank statement (Chapter 5-7
         answer) is?

         a. $13,079.22
         b. $29,168.39
         c. $13,579.82
         d. $29,568.39
         e. None of the above.

_____7. The principal amount of the note that was collected by the bank
         is?

         a. $1,200.00
         b. $1,320.00
         c. $1,350.00
         d. $120.00
         e. None of the above.

_____8. What-if analysis on the bank statement shows that the error on
         the check was $75.00 instead of?

         a. $29.00.
         b. $29.50.
         c. $36.50.
         d. $36.00.
         e. None of the above.

_____9. On the accounts receivable aging schedule, the current
         balance in Allowance for doubtful accounts is?

         a. $200.00.
         b. $159.75.
         c. $150.00.
         d. $350.00.
         e. None of the above.

_____10. Excel calculates depreciation until the book value reaches?

         a. Book value..
         b. Salvage value.
         c. Double declining balance.
         d. Original cost.
         e. All of the above.

True/Make True: If the statement is true, write the word "True" in the
space provided. If the statement is *not* true, write the correct answer in
the space provided.

11. The FICA limit used in Chapter 5 is $87,000. (*Hint: Refer to the
     payroll register used in this chapter.*)

     _____

     _____

12. The FICA percentage stated in the text is 1.44 percent.

     _____

     _____

13. Before what-if analysis, the payroll register shows gross earnings of $3,060.

    _____

    _____

14. Based on the long-term construction contract, Mike will have to recognize $2,300,000 of revenue in 2002? (Hint: This amount was determined *before* what-if analysis.)

    _____

    _____

15. Using the same worksheet that you used in question 14, Mike is planning to complete 26% of the job in 2005 based on the contract price and total estimated cost.

    _____

    _____

16. Mike's new construction contract will generate $3,000,000 in revenue over the specified period of time.

    _____

    _____

17. Mike purchased a new vehicle for the surf shop at a cost of $20,000 with a salvage value of $4,000. (*Hint: This is before what-if analysis.*)

_____

_____

18. Mike may decide to purchase a vehicle that cost $30,000 and has a salvage value of $6,000.

_____

_____

19. In the Chapter 5-17 answer file, Mike's Surf Shop is selling bonds at $100,000 face value at 102.

_____

_____

20. If you have entered the data and formulas properly for bond amortization, the carrying value does *not* equal the face value at the end of the 15th year (period 30).

_____

_____

Exercise 5-1: Accounting for Inventory

1. Start Excel; then open the Exercise 5-1.xls file.

2. Enter the formula to calculate total inventory cost.

3. Enter the formulas to calculate cost of goods sold.

4. Enter all other appropriate formulas.

5. Setup your page so that is prints similarly to the chapter work.

6. Save the worksheet as Exercise 5-1_inventory.

7. Print the worksheet.

8. Based on your analysis, which inventory method will produce the highest net income? Indicate why.

_____

_____

_____

_____

Exercise 5-2: Gross Profit Method

1. Open the Exercise 5-2.xls file.

2. Input the following information.

Net sales	$ 150,000
Gross profit percent	20%
Beginning inventory	$ 30,000
Cost of goods purchased	$ 120,000

3. Enter formulas where appropriate.

4. Setup your page so that is prints similarly to the chapter work.

5. Save the worksheet as Exercise 5-2_gross profit.

6. Print the worksheet.

7. Change the data as follows:

Net sales	$ 250,000
Gross profit percent	30%
Beginning inventory	$55,000
Cost of goods purchased	$ 185,000

8. Based on your analysis, what is the estimated ending inventory based on this data?

_____

_____

9. Save this worksheet as Exercise 5-2_whatif; then print it.

Exercise 5-3: Cash Receipts Journal

1. Open the Exercise 5-3.xls file.

2. The entry for January 3 has already been completed. Copy appropriate formulas down to row 17.

3. When merchandise is sold on account, the terms are 2/10, n/30.

4. Assume a 20% gross profit rate.

5. Enter the following transactions:

    Date   *Transactions*

    Jan 5   Received payment from Jerry's Wax Products. The account balance was $4,600 and they paid within the discount period.

10   Carol made an additional investment of $4,000 cash.
Credit CY, Capital.

11   Made cash sales of $7,500.

12   Received a payment from K's Foam Shop less discount.
They owed $7,000.

15   Received payment for nine $100 surf lessons in advance.

18   Made cash sales of $2,000.

25   Gave six $100 surf lessons for cash. Credit Service
Revenue.

29   Made cash sales of $350.

31   Received $600 payment from The Surf Shoppe. They did
not pay within the discount period.

6.   Set up your page so that it is similar to your other worksheets.

7.   Save the worksheet as Exercise 5-3_cash receipts. Then, print it.

Exercise 5-4: Accounts Receivable Aging Schedule

1.   Open the Exercise 5-4.xls file.

2.   Enter the following data. Allowance for doubtful account has a debit
balance of $125.00.

Not yet due	1%
1-30 days	3%
31-60 days	5%
61-90 days	20%
Over 90 days	35%

3.   Enter the appropriate formulas. Use AutoSum where possible.

4.   Setup the page similarly to your other worksheets.

5. Save as Exercise 5-4_aging schedule.

6. Carol's Surfing Stop is considering changing credit policies. The new credit policies would change the uncollectible amounts as follows:

Not yet due	2%
1-30 days	5%
31-60 days	20%
61-90 days	40%
Over 90 days	50%

7. What would the bad debt expense be if the allowance account had a credit balance of $150?

_____

8. Save your worksheet as Exercise 5-4_whatif; then print it.

Exercise 5-5: Bond Amortization

1. Open the file Exercise 5-5.

2. Prepare a Bond Amortization Schedule for Carol's Surfing Stop based on the following information.

   Carol's Surfing Stop is selling bonds at $85,000 face value at 101. The bonds pay 3% interest semiannually for 20 years.

3. Setup the page similarly to the other worksheets.

4. Save as Exercise 5-5_bond amortization.

CHAPTER 5 INDEX

Chapter 6 — Managerial Accounting

SOFTWARE OBJECTIVES: In Chapter 6 you will use the software to:

1. Open template files from the CD that accompanies this book.

2. Prepare a schedule of the cost of goods manufactured.

3. Solve various what-if scenarios.

4. Determine the total cost and unit cost of a job.

5. Prepare a production cost report.

6. Complete break-even analysis.

7. Prepare a flexible budget.

8. Calculate the price, quantity and total variance for direct materials.

9. Determine make or buy decisions.

10. Complete the exercises and activities in Chapter 6.

WEB OBJECTIVES: In Chapter 6 you will do these Internet activities.

1. Use your Internet browser to go to the book's website.

2. Complete the Internet Activities.

This chapter is similar to Chapter 5. You will be presented with partially completed templates. You will be asked to enter formulas and data to complete the templates. After completing the template, you will be asked to test your work through What-If Analysis.

GETTING STARTED

Managerial accounting is the area of accounting aimed at serving the decision-making needs of owners, managers, and others working within a business. The reports used by managers are usually for internal use by the business. Internal reports try to answer questions such as these:

1. What are costs per product?
2. What service mix is most profitable?
3. Are sales sufficient to break even?
4. Which activities are most profitable?
5. What costs vary with sales?

The templates in this chapter exemplify some of the reports used by managers. The templates that you will use in Chapter 6 include the following:

> ➤ Chapter 6-1.xls: Schedule of Cost of Goods Manufactured
> ➤ Chapter 6-3.xls: Job Order Cost Sheet
> ➤ Chapter 6-5.xls: Production Cost Report
> ➤ Chapter 6-7.xls: Break Even Analysis
> ➤ Chapter 6-9.xls: Flexible Budget
> ➤ Chapter 6-11.xls: Variance Analysis
> ➤ Chapter 6-13.xls: Make or Buy

SCHEDULE OF COST OF GOODS MANUFACTURED

As you know from your study of accounting, the ***general ledger*** is a record containing all accounts used by a company. Often in business, you summarize selected general ledger accounts in a schedule. Accounts that relate to the cost of goods manufactured and sold are organized into a Schedule of Cost of Goods Manufactured. The result of the Cost of Goods Manufactured appears in the income statement.

In this exercise, you will complete the formulas in the schedule of cost of goods manufactured (COGM). This workbook contains two worksheets. The sheet labeled COGM contains the schedule of cost of good manufactured. After completing this schedule, link the cost of goods manufactured in cell D29 to the sheet labeled Income Statement (cell B11).

1. Open the file Chapter 6-1.

2. Make the COGM sheet the active sheet.

3. Enter the appropriate formulas in the blue shaded cells.

4. Make the Income Statement the active sheet.

5. Click in cell B11 to make it the active cell.

6. Enter the equal sign (=).

7. Click on the COGM sheet tab.

8. Click in cell D29. When you press <Enter>, this links cell B11 of the Income Statement to cell D29 of the COGM sheet.

9. Enter the appropriate formulas in the blue shaded cells.

10. On both sheets, setup the page so that the spreadsheet prints on one page, is centered horizontally, and the header contains your name, the file name and today's date.

11. Save the workbook as Chapter 6-1 answer.

12. Print both sheets.

Mike's Surf Shop
Cost of Goods Manufactured Schedule
For the year ended December 31, 2003

Beginning work in process		90,000
Direct materials		
Beginning raw materials inventory	25,000	
Raw materials purchased	300,000	
Raw materials available for use	325,000	
Less: Ending raw materials inventory	30,000	
Direct materials used		295,000
Direct Labor		425,000
Manufacturing overhead		
Indirect labor	75,000	
Indirect materials	15,000	
Utilities	5,000	
Depreciation	34,000	
Insurance	4,000	
Taxes	7,000	
Total manufacturing overhead		140,000
Total manufacturing costs		860,000
Total cost of work in process		950,000
Less Ending work in process		75,000
Cost of goods manufactured		875,000

Mike's Surf Shop
Income Statement
For the year ended December 31, 2003

Net Sales		$ 1,800,000
Cost of goods sold		
Beginning finished goods inventory	$ 90,000	
Cost of goods manufactured	875,000	
Cost of goods available for sale	965,000	
Less: Ending finished goods inventory	85,000	
Cost of goods sold		880,000
Gross Profit		920,000
Operating expenses		
Selling expenses	475,000	
Administrative expenses	320,000	
Total operating expenses		795,000
Net Income		125,000

What-If Analysis

Mike's Surf Shop would like to show net income of $150,000. Use the steps that follow to accomplish this.

1. Using Excel's Goal Seek tool, change the ending raw materials inventory in the COGM sheet to make net income equal to $150,000. (Hint: Review the use of Goal Seek in Chapter 4, page 113.)

2. Save the workbook as Chapter 6-2 answer.

3. Print both sheets.

Student Name	Chapter 6-2 answer	Today's Date

Mike's Surf Shop
Cost of Goods Manufactured Schedule
For the year ended December 31, 2003

Beginning work in process		90,000	
Direct materials			
Beginning raw materials inventory	25,000		
Raw materials purchased	300,000		
Raw materials available for use	325,000		
Less: Ending raw materials inventory	55,000		
Direct materials used		270,000	
Direct Labor		425,000	
Manufacturing overhead			
Indirect labor	75,000		
Indirect materials	15,000		
Utilities	5,000		
Depreciation	34,000		
Insurance	4,000		
Taxes	7,000		
Total manufacturing overhead		140,000	
Total manufacturing costs			835,000
Total cost of work in process			925,000
Less Ending work in process			75,000
Cost of goods manufactured			850,000

Student Name	Chapter 6-2 answer	Today's Date

Mike's Surf Shop
Income Statement
For the year ended December 31, 2003

Net Sales		$	1,800,000
Cost of goods sold			
Beginning finished goods inventory	$ 90,000		
Cost of goods manufactured	850,000		
Cost of goods available for sale	940,000		
Less: Ending finished goods inventory	85,000		
Cost of goods sold		855,000	
Gross Profit		945,000	
Operating expenses			
Selling expenses	475,000		
Administrative expenses	320,000		
Total operating expenses		795,000	
Net Income		150,000	

JOB ORDER COST SHEET

In this exercise, you will use the job order cost sheet to determine the total cost and unit cost of a job. Mike's Surf Shop has received an order (job number 479) from Joe Shredders to make 300 long boards. Mike applies manufacturing overhead at a rate of 80% of direct labor costs.

1.   Open the Chapter 6-3 file.

2.   Enter formulas in the range D14:D18 to calculate manufacturing overhead as 80% of direct labor costs.

3.   Enter the appropriate formulas in the remaining blue shaded cells.

4.   Setup the page so that the document prints on one page, is centered horizontally, and the header contains your name, the file name and today's date.

5.   Save the file as Chapter 6-3 answer.

6.   Print the spreadsheet.

Mike's Surf Shop
Job Order Cost Sheet

Job Number	479
Item	Long Board
For	Joe Shredders
Quantity	300
Date requested	01/02/03
Date completed	01/15/03

Date	Direct Materials	Direct Labor	Manufacturing Overhead
1/3/03	15,000		-
1/6/03		10,000	8,000
1/7/03	7,500		-
1/9/03	3,000		-
1/15/03		5,000	4,000
	25,500	15,000	12,000

Cost of completed job

Direct Materials	25,500
Direct Labor	15,000
Manufacturing Overhead	12,000
Total Cost	52,500
Unit Cost	175.00

What-If Analysis

How much would the unit cost be if the order was for 450 units instead of only 300?

1. Change the quantity to 450.

2. Save the workbook as Chapter 6-4 answer.

3. Print the spreadsheet.

Mike's Surf Shop
Job Order Cost Sheet

Job Number		479	
Item		Long Board	
For		Joe Shredders	
Quantity		450	
Date requested		01/02/03	
Date completed		01/15/03	

Date	Direct Materials	Direct Labor	Manufacturing Overhead
1/3/03	15,000		-
1/6/03		10,000	8,000
1/7/03	7,500		-
1/9/03	3,000		-
1/15/03		5,000	4,000
	25,500	15,000	12,000

Cost of completed job

Direct Materials	25,500
Direct Labor	15,000
Manufacturing Overhead	12,000
Total Cost	52,500
Unit Cost	116.67

PRODUCTION COST REPORT

In this exercise, a production cost report has been partially completed. Mike's Surf Shop has asked you to prepare a production cost report and has provided you with the information that follows.

On January 1, 500 units that were 60% complete were in process in the glassing department. During January, 1,200 units were transferred into the glassing department. On January 31, 600 units that were 55% complete are still in process. (*Hint: All materials are added at the beginning of the process.*)

The following cost information was also available:

Beginning work in process	$ 5,000	Labor	$ 45,000
Materials	$ 60,000	Overhead	$ 30,000

1. Open the file Chapter 6-5.

2. Enter the information above in the yellow shaded cells.

3. Enter the appropriate formulas in the blue shaded cells.

4. Setup the document so that it prints on one page, is centered horizontally and the header prints your name, the file name and today's date.

5. Save your document as Chapter 6-5 answer.

6. Print your document. Compare it to the one shown on the next page.

Mike's Surf Shop
Glassing Department
Production Cost Report
For the month ended January 31, 2003

QUANTITIES	Physical Units	Equivalent Units	
		Materials	Conversion Costs
Units charged to department			
Units in process, January 1	500		
Transferred in	1,200		
Total units charged	1,700		
Units accounted for			
Transferred out			
Units in process, January 1	500	-	200
Started and finished	1,800	1,800	1,800
	2,300	1,800	2,000
Units in process, January 31	600	600	330
Total units accounted for	1,700	1,200	1,670

COSTS	Materials	Conversion Costs	Total
Unit costs			
Costs in January	$ 60,000	$ 75,000	$ 135,000
Equivalent units	1,200	1,670	
Unit cost	$ 50.00	$ 44.91	$ 94.91
Costs charged to department			
In process, January 1			$ 5,000
Costs in January			135,000
Total costs charged to department			$ 140,000
Costs accounted for			
Transferred out			
In process, January 1	$ 5,000		
Conversion costs	8,982	$ 13,982	
Started and finished		170,838	$ 184,820
In process, January 31			
Materials		30,000	
Conversion costs		14,820	44,820
Total costs accounted for			$ 140,000

What-If Analysis

This exercise assumes that all of the materials are added at the beginning of the process and that the ending work in process is 55% complete.

1. Change the spreadsheet to show ending work in process as 80% complete.

2. Save your file as Chapter 6-6 answer. Print the document with the appropriate header information.

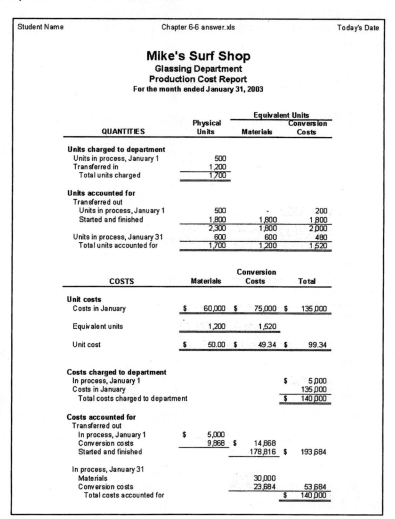

BREAK-EVEN ANALYSIS

The break-even point is where the contribution margin equals total fixed costs. A company neither earns a profit nor incurs a loss at the break-even point. Net income at break-even is zero. Follow the steps below to complete break-even analysis.

1. Open the file Chapter 6-7 from the student data files.

2. Enter the appropriate formulas in the blue shaded cells.

3. Setup the spreadsheet so that it prints on one page, is centered horizontally, and the header contains your name, the file name, and today's date.

4. Save the file as Chapter 6-7 answer.

5. Print the document with the appropriate header information.

Student Name		Chapter 6-7 answer			Today's Date

Mike's Surf Shop
Break Even Analysis

	Units	Cost	Total	Percent
Sales	500	$ 7.50	$3,750.00	100%
Variable costs		$ 2.00	$1,000.00	27%
Contribution margin		$ 5.50	$2,750.00	73%
Fixed costs			$ 750.00	20%
Net Income			$2,000.00	53%

What-If analysis

Use Excel's Goal Seek tool or change the data to determine the answers to each of the following situations separately. Print a copy of each answer.

1. Using the Chapter 6-7 answer file, determine how many units Mike's Surf Shop must sell in order to break even. Save the file as Chapter 6-8 answer. Print the document.

Student Name   Chapter 6-8 answer   Today's Date

Mike's Surf Shop
Break Even Analysis

	Units	Cost	Total	Percent
Sales	136	$ 7.50	$1,022.73	100%
Variable costs		$ 2.00	$ 272.73	27%
Contribution margin		$ 5.50	$ 750.00	73%
Fixed costs			$ 750.00	73%
Net Income			$ -	0%

2. Using the Chapter 6-8 answer file, determine how many units Mike's Surf Shop will have to sell in order to have net income of $3,000. Save the file as Chapter 6-8a answer. Print the document.

Student Name   Chapter 6-8a answer   Today's Date

Mike's Surf Shop
Break Even Analysis

	Units	Cost	Total	Percent
Sales	682	$ 7.50	$5,113.64	100%
Variable costs		$ 2.00	$1,363.64	27%
Contribution margin		$ 5.50	$3,750.00	73%
Fixed costs			$ 750.00	15%
Net Income			$3,000.00	59%

3. Mike's Surf Shop is considering raising prices to $8.00 each but this will decrease sales 10%. Using the Chapter 6-7 answer file, determine how much net income will be recognized? Save the file as Chapter 6-8b answer. Print the document.

Student Name   Chapter 6-8b answer   Today's Date

Mike's Surf Shop
Break Even Analysis

	Units	Cost	Total	Percent
Sales	450	$ 8.00	$3,600.00	100%
Variable costs		$ 2.00	$ 900.00	25%
Contribution margin		$ 6.00	$2,700.00	75%
Fixed costs			$ 750.00	21%
Net Income			$1,950.00	54%

4. Mike's Surf Shop would like to offer commissions of $ 1.00 per unit. They believe this will increase sales by 20%. Using the Chapter 6-7 answer file, make these changes and save the document as Chapter 6-8c answer. Print the document.

Student Name   Chapter 6-8c answer   Today's Date

Mike's Surf Shop
Break Even Analysis

	Units	Cost	Total	Percent
Sales	600	$ 7.50	$4,500.00	100%
Variable costs		$ 3.00	$1,800.00	40%
Contribution margin		$ 4.50	$2,700.00	60%
Fixed costs			$ 750.00	17%
Net Income			$1,950.00	43%

FLEXIBLE BUDGET

Mike's Surf Shop's production ranges between 8,000 and 10,000 units. In this exercise, you will produce a flexible budget for this range in increments of 1,000 units. The unit costs and fixed costs have already been entered for you.

1. Open the file Chapter 6-9.

2. In cell C8 enter the formula =$B8*C$5. Notice the dollar sign ($) before the column in the reference B8 and before the row number in the reference C5. This indicates that the first part of the formula will

always reference column B and the second part of the formula will always reference row 5. We do this so we can easily copy the formula to the remaining cells.

3.   Make cell C8 the active cell.

4.   Point to the fill handle and drag it to cell C10.

5.   With the range C8:C10 still highlighted, drag the fill handle to cell E10.

6.   Make the cell D14 equal to cell C14.

7.   Make cell D14 the active cell.

8.   Point to the fill handle and drag it down to cell E16.

9.   Enter appropriate formulas in rows 11, 17 and 19.

10.   Setup your document so that it prints on one page, is centered horizontally and the header prints your name, the file name and today's date.

Student Name			Chapter 6-9 answer			Today's Date	
			Mike's Surf Shop				
			Flexible Budget				
				Production Units			
		Budget per unit		**8,000**	**9,000**	**10,000**	
Variable costs							
Indirect materials	$	20.00	$	160,000	$ 180,000	$ 200,000	
Indirect labor	$	25.00		200,000	225,000	250,000	
Utilities	$	18.00		144,000	162,000	180,000	
Total variable costs				504,000	567,000	630,000	
Fixed costs							
Salaries				60,000	60,000	60,000	
Depreciation				5,000	5,000	5,000	
Insurance				3,000	3,000	3,000	
Total fixed costs				68,000	68,000	68,000	
Total costs			$	572,000	$ 635,000	$ 698,000	

What-If Analysis

Mike's Surf Shop would like to see the costs between the relevant range of 10,000 to 14,000 units in increments of 2,000 units.

1. Change the production units to the relevant range in increments of 2,000 units.

2. Save your file as Chapter 6-10 answer.

3. Print the file with the appropriate header information. Compare your spreadsheet to the one shown below.

Student Name			Chapter 6-10 answer			Today's Date

Mike's Surf Shop
Flexible Budget

	Budget per unit		Production Units		
			10,000	12,000	14,000
Variable costs					
Indirect materials	$	20.00 $	200,000 $	240,000 $	280,000
Indirect labor	$	25.00	250,000	300,000	350,000
Utilities	$	18.00	180,000	216,000	252,000
Total variable costs			630,000	756,000	882,000
Fixed costs					
Salaries			60,000	60,000	60,000
Depreciation			5,000	5,000	5,000
Insurance			3,000	3,000	3,000
Total fixed costs			68,000	68,000	68,000
Total costs		$	698,000 $	824,000 $	950,000

VARIANCE ANALYSIS

In this exercise, you will calculate the price, quantity and total variance for direct materials. The Chapter 6-11 file contains a partially completed direct materials matrix.

Mike's Surf Shop provides the following information:

Actual quantity	4,800 lbs
Actual price per pound	$3.80
Standard quantity	5,000 lbs
Standard price per pound	$3.75

1.   Open the file Chapter 6-11.

2.   Enter the data from the table above into the appropriate yellow shaded cells.

3.   Enter the appropriate formulas in the blue shaded cells.

4.   Setup the document so that it prints on one page in landscape, is centered horizontally, and the header prints your name, the file name and today's date.

5.   Save the document as Chapter 6-11 answer.

6.   Print the spreadsheet.

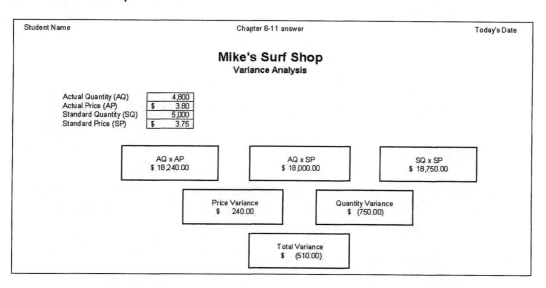

What-If Analysis

1. Change the data to the following:

Actual quantity	4,600 lbs
Actual price per pound	$3.95
Standard quantity	4,500 lbs
Standard price per pound	$4.00

2. Save your file as Chapter 6-12 answer.

3. Print the worksheet with the appropriate header information.

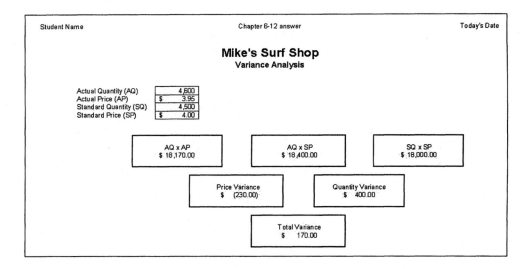

MAKE OR BUY

Mike's Surf Shop must decide if they want to have a glasser finish their surfboards or if they should continue to finish the boards themselves. Mike's Surf Shop provides the following information:

Purchase price	$150,000
Direct materials	$ 75,000
Direct labor	$50,000
Variable manufacturing costs	$12,000
Fixed manufacturing costs	$10,000

1. Open the file Chapter 6-13.

2. Enter the data in the yellow shaded cells.

3. Enter the appropriate blue shaded cells.

4. Setup the document so that it prints on one page, is centered horizontally, and the header prints your name, the file name and today's date.

5. Save the file as Chapter 6-13 answer. Print the document.

Student Name		Chapter 6-13 answer		Today's Date
		Mike's Surf Shop		
		Make or Buy		
				Net Income
	Make	Buy	Incr./(Decr.)	
Purchase price	-	150,000	(150,000)	
Direct materials	75,000	-	75,000	
Direct labor	50,000	-	50,000	
Variable manufacturing costs	12,000	-	12,000	
Fixed manufacturing costs	10,000	10,000	-	
Total Costs	147,000	160,000	(13,000)	

What-If Analysis

1. Using Goal Seek, determine the most Mike's Surf Shop should pay the glasser to finish their surfboards.

2. Save your file as Chapter 6-14 answer.

3. Print your document with the appropriate header information.

Student Name		Chapter 6-14 answer		Today's Date
		Mike's Surf Shop		
		Make or Buy		
				Net Income
	Make	Buy	Incr./(Decr.)	
Purchase price	-	137,000	(137,000)	
Direct materials	75,000	-	75,000	
Direct labor	50,000	-	50,000	
Variable manufacturing costs	12,000	-	12,000	
Fixed manufacturing costs	10,000	10,000	-	
Total Costs	147,000	147,000	-	

	INTERNET ACTIVITIES
1.	From your Internet browser, go to the textbook's website at http://www.mhhe.com/yachtexcel. Go to the Student link.
2.	Link to Internet Activities, then WEB EXERCISES, PART 2-Chapter 6.
3.	Link to http://office.microsoft.com/assistance/excel. In the Search field, select Assistance. Type **Budgets**, then click Go.
4.	If available, link to Manage Your Personal Budget with Excel. Follow the steps shown in this article. Print your budget. If this article is *not* available, go to another link.
5.	Go to this website www.webcpa.com. Explore two links on this site. Write up a summary of what you have seen. Your summary should have no more than 75 words or less than 50 words. Include the appropriate URLs.

SUMMARY AND REVIEW

SOFWARE OBJECTIVES: In Chapter 6, you used the software to:

1. Open template files from the CD that accompanies this book.

2. Prepare a schedule of the cost of goods manufactured.

3. Solve various what-if scenarios.

4. Determine the total cost and unit cost of a job.

5. Prepare a production cost report.

6. Complete break-even analysis.

7. Prepare a flexible budget.

8. Calculate the price, quantity and total variance for direct materials.

9. Determine make or buy decisions.

10. Complete the exercises and activities in Chapter 6.

WEB OBJECTIVES: In Chapter 6, you did these Internet activities:

1. Used your Internet browser to go the book's website.

2. Completed the Internet Activities.

Multiple-Choice Questions: In the space provided, write the letter that best answers each question.

_____1. The area of accounting aimed at serving the decision-making needs of owners, managers, and others working within a business is called:

   a. Payroll accounting.
   b. Cost accounting.
   c. Service accounting.
   d. Managerial accounting.
   e. None of the above.

_____2. Businesses summarize selected general ledger accounts in an internal report called a/an:

   a. Schedule.
   b. Accounts receivable journal.
   c. Accounts Payable journal.
   d. Income statement.
   e. None of the above.

_____3. If Mike's Surf Shop would like to show net income of $150,000, what amount did he change on his Chapter 6-1 answer.xls file?

   a. Ending raw materials inventory
   b. Beginning materials inventory
   c. Raw materials purchased
   d. Beginning work in process
   e. None of the above

_____4.   On the Chapter 6-2 answer.xls file, *after* what-if analysis, the net income is?

    a. $125,000
    b. $150,000
    c. $140,000
    d. None of the above

_____5.   On the Chapter 6-2 answer.xls file, what is the formula to calculate manufacturing overhead?

    a. =B14*0.8
    b. =C13*0.8.
    c. =SUM(B18:B23).
    d. =Sum(D14:D18)
    e. None of the above

_____6.   When completing what-if analysis on the Job Order Cost Sheet, you change the quantity from 300 units to?

    a. 479
    b. 450
    c. 350
    d. 379
    e. None of the above.

_____7.   On the Production Cost Report, what is the formula to determine the unit cost of materials?

    a. =B18*D31
    b. =B19-B20
    c. =C27/C290
    d. =B27/B29
    e. None of the above

Managerial Accounting 205

_____8. When you change the Production Cost Report to show ending work in process as 80% complete, which cell do you enter the formula in?

a. D21
b. C20
c. D20
d. C21
e. None of the above

_____9. The point where the contribution margin equals total fixed costs is called?

a. Flexible budget
b. Variance analysis
c. Production vs. cost analysis
d. Break-even point
e. None of the above

_____10. The difference between the two Flexible Budget spreadsheets has to do with which of the following?

a. Salaries
b. Depreciation
c. Production units
d. Budget per unit
e. Both b. and c.

True/Make True: If the statement is true, write the word "True" in the space provided. If the statement is *not* true, write the correct answer in the space provided.

11. Net income at break-even is zero.

_____

_____

12. Each spreadsheet that you print or display shows your name, exercise number, and the current date.

_____

_____

13. In the Chapter 6-1.xls file, you link two worksheets—the income statement and balance sheet.

_____

_____

14. The Chapter 6-1 answer.xls file shows $945,000 as the cost of goods sold amount.

_____

_____

15. Mike applies manufacturing overhead at a rate of 80% of direct labor costs.

_____

_____

16. On the Job Order Cost Sheet, the unit cost for 450 units is $175.

_____

_____

17. According to the Production Cost Report, on January 31, 600 units that were 55% complete are still in process.

_____

_____

18. The break-even point is where the contribution margin equals total fixed costs.

_____

_____

19. On the Flexible Budget, the unit costs and fixed costs have *not* been determined.

_____

_____

20. On the production cost report, to determine the total costs charged to the department, you subtract beginning work in process from all the costs in January.

_____

_____

Exercise 6-1: Cost of Goods Manufactured

1. Open the file Exercise 6-1.xls file. Verify that the COGM sheet is the active sheet.

2. Enter the appropriate formulas in the blue shaded cells.

3. Make the Income Statement the active sheet. Link the cost of goods manufactured from the COGM sheet to the income statement.

4. Enter the appropriate formulas in the blue shaded cells.

5. On both sheets, setup the page so that the spreadsheet prints on one page; is centered horizontally; and the header contains your name; the file name; and today's date.

6. Save the workbook as Exercise 6-1_answer.

7. Print both sheets.

8. Complete the following what-if analysis: Carol's Surfing Stop would like to show net income of $175,000 by changing the ending raw materials inventory. (*Hint:* Use Excel's Goal Seek tool to change the ending raw materials inventory in the COGM sheet.)

9. Save the workbooks as Exercise 6-1_whatif.

10. Print both sheets.

Exercise 6-2: Job Order Cost Sheet

Transaction: Carol's Surfing Stop has received an order (job number 378) from Susan King to make 500 long boards. Carol applies manufacturing overhead at a rate of 75% of direct labor costs.

1. Open the Exercise 6-2 file.

2. Enter the appropriate formulas in the remaining blue shaded cells.

3. Setup the page so that the document prints on one page, is centered horizontally, and the header contains your name, the file name and today's date.

4. Save the file as Exercise 6-2_answer.

5. Print the spreadsheet.

6. Complete the following what-if analysis: How much would the unit cost be if the order was for 650 long boards?

7. Save the workbook as Exercise 6-2_whatif.

8. Print the spreadsheet.

Exercise 6-3: Flexible Budget

Transaction: Carol's Surfing Stop's production ranges between 8,000 and 10,000 units. In this exercise, you will produce a flexible budget for this range in increments of 1,000 units. The unit costs and fixed costs have already been entered for you.

1. Open the Exercise 6-3.xls file.

2. In cell C8, enter the formula =$B8*C$5.

3. Make cell C8 the active cell. Point to the fill handle and drag it to cell E10.

4. Make the cell D14 equal to cell C14.

5. Make cell D14 the active cell.

6. Point to the fill handle and drag it down to cell E16.

7. Enter appropriate formulas in rows 11, 17 and 19.

8. Save the file as Exercise 6-3_answer.

9. Setup your document so that it prints on one page, is centered horizontally and the header prints your name, the file name and today's date.

Exercise 6-4: Variance Analysis

1. Open the Exercise 6-4.xls file.

2. Change the data to the following:

Actual quantity	4,850 lbs
Actual price per pound	$4.05
Standard quantity	4,450 lbs
Standard price per pound	$5.00

3. Save your file as Exercise 6-4_answer.

4. Print the worksheet with the appropriate header information.

CHAPTER 6 INDEX

Part

3   Model Building

In Part 3, you will build Excel spreadsheets from scratch. This is called model building. Since you are building your model from the data presented in the chapters, you will *not* use any partially completed templates from the student CD. It is your job to create the model template from scratch.

There are 10 chapters in Part 3.

In Chapter 7, Financial Statements, you will build models to solve various problems using Excel. Once you have completed your model, you will be asked to input a new set of data to test your model.

In Chapter 8, Inventory, model-building activities continue. You build a cost of goods sold schedule from scratch.

In Chapter 9, Payroll, you prepare spreadsheets to calculate an employee's earnings record and a payroll register. Similar to the other model building activities that you completed in Chapters 7 and 8, data will be provided so that you can complete the spreadsheets.

In Chapter 10, Depreciation, you prepare a declining-balance depreciation schedule. You will also prepare a schedule that will calculate depreciation using the units-of-activity (or production) method.

In Chapter 11, Amortization, you will prepare an amortization schedule for a note. You will use a formula to calculate the minimum payment required for a note. You will also calculate the amount of interest being paid with each payment and calculate the remaining principal balance after each payment is made.

In Chapter 12, Cost of Goods Manufactured, you prepare a cost of goods manufactured schedule. Your workbook will contain two linked sheets. One sheet is for input data and the other sheet is the actual cost of goods manufactured schedule which is linked to the input data.

In Chapter 13, Job Order Cost Accounting, you complete job order cost projections.

In Chapter 14, Process Costing, you complete worksheets that show equivalent units as well as production costs.

In Chapter 15, Cost-Volume-Profit, you will determine break-even points using the contribution margin.

In Chapter 16, Budgeting and Analysis, you will use Excel to prepare a master budget.

The table on this page and pages 215–217 shows the chapter, file name, and page numbers where you save Excel files.

Chapter	File Name	Page Nos.
7	Chapter 7.xls	222-223
	Chapter 7 test.xls	223-225
	Chapter 7 analysis.xls	226-228
	Exercise 7-1.xls	235
	Exercise 7-2 test.xls	236
	Exercise 7-3 analysis.xls	236

Chapter	File Name	Page Nos.
8	Chapter 8-1.xls	243
	Chapter 8-1 test.xls	243
	Chapter 8-1 analysis.xls	243-244
	Chapter 8-2.xls	245
	Chapter 8-2 test.xls	246
	Chapter 8-2 analysis.xls	246
	Chapter 8-3.xls	247
	Chapter 8-3 test.xls	248
	Chapter 8-3 analysis.xls	249
	Chapter 8-4.xls	250
	Chapter 8-4 test.xls	250
	Chapter 8-4 analysis.xls	250
	Exercise 8-1.xls	257
	Exercise 8-2 test.xls	258
	Exercise 8-2 analysis.xls	258
	Exercise 8-3.xls	259
	Exercise 8-4 test.xls	260
	Exercise 8-4 analysis.xls	260
9	Chapter 9-1.xls	266
	Chapter 9-1 test.xls	266
	Chapter 9-1 analysis.xls	267
	Chapter 9-2.xls	269
	Chapter 9-2 test.xls	270
	Chapter 9-2 analysis a.xls	270
	Chapter 9-2 analysis b.xls	271
	Chapter 9-3.xls	272
	Chapter 9-3 test.xls	272
	Chapter 9-3 analysis.xls	272
	Exercise 9-1.xls	279
	Exercise 9-2 test.xls	279
	Exercise 9-3.xls	281
	Exercise 9-4 test.xls	282
	Exercise 9-4 analysis.xls	282
10	Chapter 10-1.xls	288
	Chapter 10-1 test.xls	289
	Chapter 10-1 analysis.xls	290
	Chapter 10-2.xls	291
	Chapter 10-2 test.xls	292
	Chapter 10-2 analysis.xls	293-294
	Chapter 10-3.xls	295
	Chapter 10-3 test.xls	295
	Chapter 10-3 analysis.xls	295
	Chapter 10-4.xls	296
	Chapter 10-4 test.xls	297
	Chapter 10-4 analysis.xls	297
	Exercise 10-1.xls	304

Chapter	File Name	Page Nos.
10	Exercise 10-2.xls	304
	Exercise 10-2 analysis.xls	305
	Exercise 10-3.xls	305
	Exercise 10-3 test.xls	306
	Exercise 10-4 analysis.xls	306
11	Chapter 11-1.xls	311-313
	Chapter 11-1 test.xls	314
	Chapter 11-1 analysis a.xls	314
	Chapter 11-1 analysis b.xls	314
	Chapter 11-2.xls	316-317
	Chapter 11-2 test.xls	317
	Chapter 11-2 analysis.xls	317
	Exercise 11-1.xls	324
	Exercise 11-2 test.xls	325
	Exercise 11-2 analysis a.xls	325
	Exercise 11-2 analysis b.xls	325
	Exercise 11-3.xls	326
	Exercise 11-4 test.xls	326
	Exercise 11-4 analysis.xls	326
12	Chapter 12-1.xls	331
	Chapter 12-1 test.xls	332
	Chapter 12-1 analysis.xls	332
	Chapter 12-2.xls	333
	Chapter 12-2 test.xls	334
	Chapter 12-2 analysis.xls	334
	Exercise 12-1.xls	341
	Exercise 12-2 test.xls	341
	Exercise 12-2 analysis.xls	341
	Exercise 12-3.xls	342
	Exercise 12-4 test.xls	342
	Exercise 12-4 analysis.xls	343
13	Chapter 13-1.xls	347
	Chapter 13-1 test.xls	348
	Chapter 13-1 analysis.xls	348
	Chapter 13-2.xls	349-350
	Chapter 13-2 test.xls	350
	Chapter 13-2 analysis.xls	351
	Exercise 13-1.xls	357
	Exercise 13-2 test.xls	357
	Exercise 13-2 analysis.xls	358
	Exercise 13-3.xls	359
	Exercise 13-4 test.xls	359
	Exercise 13-4 analysis.xls	359

Chapter	File Name	Page Nos.
14	Chapter 14-1.xls	362-363
	Chapter 14-1 test.xls	364
	Chapter 14-1 analysis.xls	364
	Chapter 14-2.xls	364-365
	Chapter 14-2 test.xls	366
	Chapter 14-2 analysis.xls	366
	Exercise 14-1.xls	372
	Exercise 14-2 test.xls	373
	Exercise 14-2 analysis.xls	373
	Exercise 14-3.xls	374
	Exercise 14-4 test.xls	374
	Exercise 14-4 analysis.xls	374
15	Chapter 15-1.xls	378
	Chapter 15-1 test.xls	379
	Chapter 15-1 analysis.xls	379
	Chapter 15-2.xls	383
	Chapter 15-2 test.xls	384
	Chapter 15-2 analysis a.xls	384
	Chapter 15-2 analysis b.xls	384
	Exercise 15-1.xls	391
	Exercise 15-2 test.xls	391
	Exercise 15-2 analysis.xls	391
	Exercise 15-3.xls	392
	Exercise 15-4 test.xls	393
	Exercise 15-4 analysis a.xls	393
	Exercise 15-4 analysis b.xls	393
16	Chapter 16-1.xls	396-397
	Chapter 16-1 test.xls	397
	Chapter 16-1 analysis.xls	398
	Chapter 16-2.xls	399-400
	Chapter 16-2 test.xls	400
	Chapter 16-2 analysis.xls	401
	Exercise 16-1.xls	408
	Exercise 16-2 test.xls	408
	Exercise 16-2 analysis.xls	408
	Exercise 16-3.xls	409
	Exercise 16-4 test.xls	410
	Exercise 16-4 analysis.xls	410

Chapter 7   Financial Statements

SOFTWARE OBJECTIVES: In Chapter 7 you will use the software to:

1.   Complete model-building exercises.

2.   Refer to the model-building checklist when completing assignments.

3.   Compare your spreadsheet's results to the check figures shown.

4.   Complete test data.

5.   Complete what-if analysis.

6.   Complete the exercises and activities in Chapter 7.

WEB OBJECTIVES: In Chapter 7 you will do these Internet activities.

1.   Use your Internet browser to go the book's website.

2.   Complete the Internet Activities.

When you begin a new project from scratch in Excel, you are building a model. In this chapter, you will be asked to build models to solve various problems using Excel. Once you have completed your model, you will be asked to input a new set of data to test your model.

 Read Me

The objective of Part 3 (Chapters 7-16) is to teach you how to create models. In other words, you will be creating "templates" that can be used with various model-building activities. Templates with Excel data are *not* provided. It is your turn to learn how to do this.

When preparing your models, use this checklist:

❑ Each model should contain a heading stating the name of the company, what the spreadsheet is for and a date.

❑ Use formulas whenever applicable. The formulas should contain cell references where necessary.

❑ Use proper formatting for numbers, dollar signs, and text. Add borders and rules as needed.

❑ In most cases, format numbers with no decimals.

❑ Use Print Preview to view your document.

❑ Try to fit the spreadsheet on one page. If it cannot print on one page, page breaks should be in logical places. Use Page Break Preview to see the page breaks. (*Hint:* From Excel's menu bar, select File; Print Preview; then click Page Break Preview. Follow these steps to close, Page Break Preview:

1. When the dialog box pops up, click on OK to close it.
2. Click on File; Print Preview. Observe that there is a Normal View button.
3. Click Normal View to return to your worksheet.)

❑ Center your spreadsheet horizontally.

❑ The header should contain your name, the file name and today's date.

❑ Since you will be asked to test your data, you should have a data section on most models.

GETTING STARTED

Use the following trial balance to prepare a multi-step income statement, statement of owner's equity, and a classified balance sheet for Mike's Surf and Sea for the month ended 6/30/03.

In the accounting cycle, the account balances from the general ledger are entered into a balance sheet to prove that debits equal credits. The data from the trial balance is then used to create the financial statements. The income statement is prepared first. Net income from the income statement then flows into the statement of owners' equity. The ending capital balance from the statement of owners' equity then flows into the balance sheet. By completing this model-building activity you will see the interrelationship of the financial statements.

BUILDING A MODEL

Mike's Surf and Sea		
Trial Balance		
For the month ended 6/30/03		
Account	Debit	Credit
Cash	$ 15,000	
Accounts receivable	2,000	
Supplies	800	
Prepaid insurance	1,200	
Equipment	5,000	
Accumulated depreciation - equipment		$ 50
Accounts payable		1,700
Notes payable		8,000
Unearned revenue		900
Salaries payable		700
Capital		12,300
Drawing	200	
Sales		12,000
Cost of goods sold	4,000	
Advertising expense	1,200	
Depreciation expense	50	
Insurance expense	100	
Salaries expense	5,000	
Rent expense	1,100	
	$ 35,650	$ 35,650

1.   The workbook should contain four sheets: trial balance, income statement, statement of owner's equity and balance sheet. (*Hint: You may want to review Chapter 2's coverage of copying and linking worksheets, pages 53-59.*)

2. Use appropriate labels on the sheet tabs.

3. Each statement should be linked to the trial balance and to each other (net income to the statement of owners' equity, and ending capital balance to the balance sheet). When you enter your test data, all of the statements should update themselves.

4. Save your workbook as Chapter 7. Compare your results to the statements shown below and on the next page.

Student Name	Chapter 7	Today's Date

Mike's Surf and Sea
Income Statement
For the month ended 6/30/03

Sales		$ 12,000
Cost of goods sold		4,000
Gross Profit		8,000
Operating Expenses		
Advertising expense	$ 1,200	
Depreciation expense	50	
Insurance expense	100	
Salaries expense	5,000	
Rent expense	1,100	
Total operating expenses		7,450
Net Income		$ 550

Student Name	Chapter 7	Today's Date

Mike's Surf and Sea
Statement of Owners' Equity
For the month ended 6/30/03

Capital, June 1	$ 12,300
Net Income	550
	12,850
Drawing	200
Capital, June 30	$ 12,650

Student Name	Chapter 7	Today's Date

Mike's Surf and Sea
Balance Sheet
As of 6/30/03

Assets

Current Assets

Cash	$	15,000
Accounts receivable		2,000
Supplies		800
Prepaid insurance		1,200
Total current assets		19,000

Property, Plant & Equipment

Equipment	$	5,000	
Accumulated depreciation - equipment		50	
Total property, plant and equipment			4,950
Total Assets			$ 23,950

Liabilities

Accounts payable		1,700
Notes payable		8,000
Unearned revenue		900
Salaries payable		700
Total liabilities		$ 11,300

Owners' Equity

Capital		12,650
Total liabilities and owners' equity		$ 23,950

Check Figure. After preparing all statements, total assets should be $23,950.

Test Data

1. If necessary, open the file Chapter 7.

2. Input the data shown on the next page into the trial balance and save the file as Chapter 7 test.

Mike's Surf and Sea
Trial Balance
For the month ended 6/30/03

Account	Debit	Credit
Cash	$ 15,500	
Accounts receivable	2,500	
Supplies	900	
Prepaid insurance	1,300	
Equipment	5,500	
Accumulated depreciation - equipment		$ 100
Accounts payable		1,600
Notes payable		8,500
Unearned revenue		1,000
Salaries payable		600
Capital		14,300
Drawing	500	
Sales		12,500
Cost of goods sold	4,500	
Advertising expense	1,100	
Depreciation expense	100	
Insurance expense	200	
Salaries expense	5,500	
Rent expense	1,000	
	$ 38,600	$ 38,600

Student Name   Chapter 7 test   Today's Date

Mike's Surf and Sea
Income Statement
For the month ended 6/30/03

Sales		$ 12,500
Cost of goods sold		4,500
Gross Profit		8,000
Operating Expenses		
Advertising expense	$ 1,100	
Depreciation expense	100	
Insurance expense	200	
Salaries expense	5,500	
Rent expense	1,000	
Total operating expenses		7,900
Net Income		$ 100

Mike's Surf and Sea
Statement of Owners' Equity
For the month ended 6/30/03

Capital, June 1	$	14,300
Net Income		100
		14,400
Drawing		500
Capital, June 30	$	13,900

Mike's Surf and Sea
Balance Sheet
As of 6/30/03

Assets

Current Assets

Cash			$	15,500
Accounts receivable				2,500
Supplies				900
Prepaid insurance				1,300
Total current assets				20,200

Property, Plant & Equipment

Equipment	$	5,500		
Accumulated depreciation - equipment		100		
Total property, plant and equipment				5,400
Total Assets			$	25,600

Liabilities

Accounts payable		1,600
Notes payable		8,500
Unearned revenue		1,000
Salaries payable		600
Total liabilities	$	11,700

Owners' Equity

Capital		13,900
Total liabilities and owners' equity	$	25,600

Check Figure. After preparing all statements, total assets should be $25,600.

What-If Analysis

1. If necessary, open the file Chapter 7 test.

2. In the trial balance, enter a formula for the capital amount so that it will adjust the difference between the total amount of the debit column and the account balances in the credit column.

> Normally, the data in the trial balance sheet comes directly from the general ledger. However, for purposes of illustrating how Excel can help you analyze your data, the authors are asking you to enter a formula to compute the capital balance.

3. In the trial balance, change the cost of goods sold to be 40% of sales.

4. In the income statement, use Goal Seek to determine how much Sales (from the trial balance) there would have to be in order to have $1,000 of net income. (*Hint: Use the sales figure from the trial balance in the By changing cell field of Goal Seek; this is cell C20 on the trial balance.*)

5. Save the workbook as Chapter 7 analysis.

Student Name	Chapter 7 analysis		Today's Date

Mike's Surf and Sea
Trial Balance
For the month ended 6/30/03

Account	Debit	Credit
Cash	$ 15,500	
Accounts receivable	2,500	
Supplies	900	
Prepaid insurance	1,300	
Equipment	5,500	
Accumulated depreciation - equipment		$ 100
Accounts payable		1,600
Notes payable		8,500
Unearned revenue		1,000
Salaries payable		600
Capital		13,400
Drawing	500	
Sales		14,833
Cost of goods sold	5,933	
Advertising expense	1,100	
Depreciation expense	100	
Insurance expense	200	
Salaries expense	5,500	
Rent expense	1,000	
	$ 40,033	$ 40,033

Student Name   Chapter 7 analysis   Today's Date

Mike's Surf and Sea
Income Statement
For the month ended 6/30/03

Sales		$ 14,833
Cost of goods sold		5,933
Gross Profit		8,900
Operating Expenses		
Advertising expense	$ 1,100	
Depreciation expense	100	
Insurance expense	200	
Salaries expense	5,500	
Rent expense	1,000	
Total operating expenses		7,900
Net Income		$ 1,000

Student Name   Chapter 7 analysis   Today's Date

Mike's Surf and Sea
Statement of Owners' Equity
For the month ended 6/30/03

Capital, June 1	$ 13,400
Net Income	1,000
	14,400
Drawing	500
Capital, June 30	$ 13,900

 Read Me

Your spreadsheets should match the ones shown on pages 226-228. Remember, you need to use Goal Seek to change the net income amount and link some of the cell data. If your individual amounts do *not* match the ones shown, make sure you have appropriately linked account balances when it is necessary to do so.

Student Name	Chapter 7 analysis	Today's Date

Mike's Surf and Sea
Balance Sheet
As of 6/30/03

Assets

Current Assets

Cash	$	15,500
Accounts receivable		2,500
Supplies		900
Prepaid insurance		1,300
Total current assets		20,200

Property, Plant & Equipment

Equipment	$	5,500	
Accumulated depreciation - equipment		100	
Total property, plant and equipment			5,400

Total Assets	$	25,600

Liabilities

Accounts payable		1,600
Notes payable		8,500
Unearned revenue		1,000
Salaries payable		600
Total liabilities	$	11,700

Owners' Equity

Capital	13,900

Total liabilities and owners' equity	$	25,600

	INTERNET ACTIVITIES
1.	From your Internet browser, go to the textbook's website at http://www.mhhe.com/yachtexcel. Go to the Student link.
2.	Link to Internet Activities, then WEB EXERCISES, PART 3-Chapter 7.
3.	Access this website http://office.microsoft.com/assistance/2002/articles/xlCalculator.aspx.
4.	Read the article "Let Excel be your calculator." Go to two links from this website. Complete two templates. Print two spreadsheets.
5.	Go to this website http://www.electronicaccountant.com. Explore two more links on this site. (*Hint: You also looked at this site in Chapter 6. Make sure you explore different links. For example, you could explore a couple links listed under "Resources; Recommended Reading."*) Write up a summary of what you have seen. Your summary should have no more than 75 words or less than 50 words. Include the appropriate URLs.

SUMMARY AND REVIEW

SOFWARE OBJECTIVES: In Chapter 7, you used to software to:

1.   Complete model-building exercises.

2.   Refer to the model-building checklist when assignments are complete.

3.   Compare your spreadsheet's results to the check figures shown.

4.   Complete test data.

5.   Complete what-if analysis.

6.   Complete the exercises and activities in Chapter 7.

WEB OBJECTIVES: In Chapter 7, you did these Internet activities:

1. Used your Internet browser to go the book's website.

2. Completed the Internet Activities.

Multiple-Choice Questions: In the space provided, write the letter that best answers each question.

_____1.   In Excel, when you build a spreadsheet from scratch, this is called:

        a. Modeling
        b. Testing
        c. What-if analysis
        d. Financial Statements
        e. None of the above

_____2. You should use the following when preparing your spreadsheets from scratch:

   a. Header information.
   b. Appropriate formulas.
   c. Proper number formatting.
   d. All of the above.
   e. None of the above.

_____3. The account balances that appear on the trial balance originated in the:

   a. Chart of accounts.
   b. Income statement.
   c. General ledger.
   d. Balance sheet.
   e. None of the above.

_____4. The spreadsheets completed in Chapter 7 are as of what date?

   a. 12/31/03
   b. 6/30/03
   c. 4/30/03
   d. None of the above

_____5. The following model-building activity is *not* included in Chapter 7's work:

   a. Cost of goods manufactured.
   b. Statement of owner's equity.
   c. Trial balance.
   d. Income statement.
   e. None of the above.

_____6. The name of one of the financial statements completed in Chapter 7 is:

   a. Multi-step trial balance.
   b. Balance sheet.
   c. Statement of cash flow.
   d. Certified income statement.
   e. None of the above.

_____7. After preparing the Chapter 7.xls sheets, total assets are:

   a. $19,000.
   b. $23,950.
   c. $11,300.
   d. $15,000.
   e. None of the above.

_____8. After preparing the Chapter 7 test.xls sheets, total assets are:

   a. $23,950.
   b. $25,600.
   c. $20,200.
   d. $11,700.
   e. None of the above.

_____9. After preparing the Chapter 7 analysis.xls sheets, cost of goods sold is:

   a. $4,000.
   b. $4,500.
   c. $5,933.
   d. $6,900.
   e. None of the above.

_____10. What-if analysis on the Chapter 7 test.xls file, includes changing the cost of goods sold to be what percentage of sales?

   a. 10%
   b. 20%
   c. 30%
   d. 40%
   e. None of the above

True/Make True: If the statement is true, write the word "True" in the space provided. If the statement is *not* true, write the correct answer in the space provided.

11. You use trial balance data to build a multi-step income statement.

_____

_____

12. When there are multiple worksheets in a workbook, you should label each sheet tab.

_____

_____

13. In Chapter 7, you create five sheets from the trial balance data supplied.

_____

_____

14. When you begin a new project from scratch in Excel, you are building a test spreadsheet.

_____

_____

15. Financial statements should be linked to the trial balance and to each other.

_____

_____

16. In most cases, you should format numbers with no decimal places.

_____

_____

17. In order to reach certain net income objectives, use Excel's goal seek feature.

_____

_____

18. All spreadsheets completed in Chapter 7 include a multi-step income statement.

_____

_____

19. The starting point for data in Chapter 7 is a trial balance.

_____

_____

20. On the Chapter 7 analysis file, net income is $1,200.

Exercise 7-1: Building the model

1. Use the following trial balance to prepare a multi-step income statement, statement of owner's equity, and a classified balance sheet for Carol's Surf Shop as of 9/30/03.

	A	B	C
1	**Carol's Surf Shop**		
2	**Trial Balance**		
3	**For the month ended 9/30/03**		
4			
5			
6	**Account**	**Debit**	**Credit**
7			
8	Cash	$ 12,050	
9	Accounts receivable	2,200	
10	Supplies	700	
11	Prepaid insurance	2,400	
12	Equipment	3,500	
13	Accumulated depreciation - equipment		$ 50
14	Accounts payable		2,000
15	Notes payable		6,250
16	Unearned revenue		900
17	Salaries payable		700
18	Capital		12,300
19	Drawing	200	
20	Sales		11,000
21	Cost of goods sold	4,500	
22	Advertising expense	950	
23	Depreciation expense	50	
24	Insurance expense	200	
25	Salaries expense	5,500	
26	Rent expense	950	
27			
28		$ 33,200	$ 33,200

2.   Use the Chapter 7 checklist to prepare your models.

3.   Save your data as Exercise 7-1

4.   Print each sheet. Check Figure: total assets should be $20,800.

Exercise 7-2: Testing the model

1.   If necessary, open the Exercise 7-1.xls file.

2.   Input the data shown below into the trial balance.

	A	B	C
1	**Carol's Surf Shop**		
2	**Trial Balance**		
3	For the month ended 9/30/03		
4			
5			
6	**Account**	**Debit**	**Credit**
7			
8	Cash	$ 14,000	
9	Accounts receivable	1,200	
10	Supplies	900	
11	Prepaid insurance	1,300	
12	Equipment	4,000	
13	Accumulated depreciation - equipment		$ 100
14	Accounts payable		1,600
15	Notes payable		6,500
16	Unearned revenue		1,000
17	Salaries payable		600
18	Capital		11,200
19	Drawing	500	
20	Sales		10,050
21	Cost of goods sold	3,250	
22	Advertising expense	1,100	
23	Depreciation expense	100	
24	Insurance expense	200	
25	Salaries expense	4,000	
26	Rent expense	500	
27			
28		$ 31,050	$ 31,050

3.   Save as Exercise 7-2 test.

4.   Print each sheet. Check Figure: total assets should be $21,300.

Exercise 7-3: What-if analysis

1.   If necessary, open the Exercise 7-2 test file.

2.   In the trial balance, enter a formula for capital so that it will adjust the difference between the total account balances of the debit column and the account balances in the credit column.

3.   In the trial balance, change the cost of goods sold to be 30% of sales.

4.   In the income statement, use Goal Seek to determine how much Sales (from the trial balance) there would have to be in order to have $1,500 of net income.

5.   Save as Exercise 7-3 analysis.

6.   Print the sheets.

Exercise 7-4

Answer the following questions:

1.   What are the total liabilities and owner's equity on the Exercise 7-1 and 7-2 test spreadsheets?

_____

_____

2. a) What is the difference between total assets on the Exercise 7-1
    file, the Exercise 7-2 test file, and the Exercise 7-3 analysis file?
    b) What caused this difference? c) What financial statement shows
    total assets?

    _____

    _____

    _____

    _____

3. What steps did you use to find a new net income amount in Exercise
    7-3?

    _____

    _____

    _____

    _____

    _____

    _____

CHAPTER 7 INDEX

Chapter 8 Inventory

SOFTWARE OBJECTIVES: In Chapter 8 you will use the software to:

1. Complete a cost of goods sold schedule.

2. Complete a worksheet to determine lower of cost or market.

3. Test your models.

4. Solve what-if scenarios.

5. Save your worksheets.

6. Design and build your own model.

7. Complete the exercises and activities in Chapter 8.

WEB OBJECTIVES: In Chapter 8 you will do these Internet activities.

1. Use your Internet browser to go to the book's website.

2. Complete the Internet Activities.

Model-building activities continue in Chapter 8. In this chapter you will build a cost of goods sold schedule. Since you are building your model from the data presented in this chapter, you will *not* use partially completed templates. It is your job to create the model from scratch. Then, you will be asked to enter formulas and data to complete the model. Remember, when you begin a new project from scratch in Excel, you are building a model.

Use the data that is shown on the following pages to build your model. You will build a model, test your model, and then complete what-if analysis. This is similar to the work completed in Chapter 7, except in this chapter you are focusing on inventory rather than financial statements.

GETTING STARTED

Mike's Surf and Sea had a beginning inventory of 200 long boards at a cost of $218 each. During the year, the following purchases were made.

Date	Cost/Unit	Units
March 3	$220	175
May 5	$225	215
August 10	$227	160
December 3	$229	180

Mike's Surf and Sea uses a periodic inventory system and sold 867 long boards during the year.

The long boards are sold for $400 each and operating expenses for the year were $123,756.

MODEL BUILDING 1: Cost of Goods Sold Schedule

As you know from your study of accounting, *cost of goods sold* is the cost of merchandise sold to customers during the period. On a merchandising business' income statement an item called cost of goods sold is listed. On the merchandising business' balance sheet, a current asset called inventory is shown.

In the model-building activity that follows you are going to prepare a cost of goods sold schedule.

 Read Me

Your worksheets should match the ones shown on pages 242-244. In the Model Building 1 activity, you will be shown the result of your work. In the Model Building 2 and 4 activities, which start on page 244 and 249, you will *not* be shown the result of your work. You may want to check with your instructor to see if the Model Building 2 and 4 activities should be turned in for a grade.

Prepare a cost of goods sold schedule for Mike's Surf and Sea for the calendar year ending December 31, 2003. The steps shown below outline what you should do.

1. Determine the cost of goods available for sale. Refer to the cost of goods sold schedule you prepared in Chapter 5.

2. Determine ending inventory under each of the cost flow assumptions (*FIFO*, *LIFO*, and *Average Cost*). The ending inventory is the difference between the cost of goods available for sale and the cost of goods sold.

   In your study of accounting you learned that FIFO is an abbreviation for first in, first out. The FIFO method assumes that the items in the beginning inventory are sold first. The LIFO (last in, first out) method assumes that the goods received last are sold first. The Average Cost is determined by dividing the total cost by the number of units.

3. Determine the cost of goods sold under each of the cost flow assumptions.

4. Determine gross profit and net income under each of the cost flow assumptions.

5. Save the workbook as Chapter 8-1.

6. Be sure the worksheet adheres to the style checklist on page 220 (Chapter 7).

7. Print the cost of goods sold schedule.

8. Verify your results. Check Figure: LIFO net income should be $28,763. Compare your workbook to the one shown on the next page.

Student Name	Chapter 8-1	Today's Date

Mike's Surf Shop
Cost of Goods Sold Schedule
For the year ended 12/31/03

Date	Cost/Unit	Units	Total Cost	FIFO	LIFO	Avg. Cost
1-Jan $	218	200 $	43,600 $	43,600 $	29,866	
3-Mar $	220	175	38,500	38,500	38,500	
5-May $	225	215	48,375	48,375	48,375	
10-Aug $	227	160	36,320	36,320	36,320	
3-Dec $	229	180	41,220	26,793	41,220	
Goods Available for sale		930 $	208,015			
Sales	$ 400	867		193,588	194,281 $	193,924
Ending Inventory		63		$ 14,427 $	13,734 $	14,091

	FIFO	LIFO	Avg. Cost
Sales	$ 346,800 $	346,800 $	346,800
Cost of Goods Sold	193,588	194,281	193,924
Gross Profit	153,212	152,519	152,876
Operating expenses	123,756	123,756	123,756
Net Income	$ 29,456 $	28,763 $	29,120

The Chapter 8-1.xls file is shown on page 242 so that you can make sure your data is correct *before* you test your data. Note that the test data will only work properly if you have built the necessary formulas in columns E, F, and G and rows 14 to 25.

Test Data

Assume that Mike's beginning inventory is unchanged. During the year ending December 31, 2003, Mike's Surf and Sea had the following purchases.

Date	Cost/Unit	Units
March 3	$228	325
May 5	$226	200
August 10	$225	175
December 3	$223	190

Use the following criteria to test your model.

1. Mike's Surf and Sea sold 775 long boards during the year.

2. The long boards are sold for $425 each and operating expenses for the year were $133,500.

3. Input the above data to recalculate the cost of goods available for sale, cost of goods sold, ending inventory, and net income under each of the cost flow assumptions.

4. Save your file as Chapter 8-1 test.

5. Verify your results. Check Figure: LIFO net income is $21,050.

Mike's Surf Shop
Cost of Goods Sold Schedule
For the year ended 12/31/03

Date	Cost/Unit	Units	Total Cost	FIFO	LIFO	Avg. Cost
1-Jan	$ 218	200	$ 43,600	$ 43,600	$ -	
3-Mar	$ 228	325	74,100	74,100	47,880	
5-May	$ 226	200	45,200	45,200	45,200	
10-Aug	$ 225	175	39,375	11,250	39,375	
3-Dec	$ 223	190	42,370	-	42,370	
Goods Available for sale		1,090	$ 244,645			
Sales	$ 425	775		174,150	174,825	$ 173,945
Ending Inventory		315		$ 70,495	$ 69,820	$ 70,700

	FIFO	LIFO	Avg. Cost
Sales	$ 329,375	$ 329,375	$ 329,375
Cost of Goods Sold	174,150	174,825	173,945
Gross Profit	155,225	154,550	155,430
Operating expenses	133,500	133,500	133,500
Net Income	$ 21,725	$ 21,050	$ 21,930

What-If Analysis

1. Open the Chapter 8-1 test file.

2. Using Excel's Goal Seek tool, determine how many long boards Mike's Surf and Sea would have to sell to break even under the LIFO method. (*Hint: Make the LIFO net income equal to zero.*)

3. Save your file as Chapter 8-1 analysis.

4. Verify your results. Check Figure: FIFO net income should be $411.

Mike's Surf Shop
Cost of Goods Sold Schedule
For the year ended 12/31/03

Date		Cost/Unit	Units	Total Cost	FIFO	LIFO	Avg. Cost
1-Jan	$	218	200	$ 43,600	$ 43,600	$ -	
3-Mar	$	228	325	74,100	74,100	23,518	
5-May	$	226	200	45,200	32,351	45,200	
10-Aug	$	225	175	39,375	-	39,375	
3-Dec	$	223	190	42,370	-	42,370	
Goods Available for sale			1,090	$ 244,645			
Sales	$	425	668		150,051	150,463	$ 149,962
Ending Inventory			422		$ 94,594	$ 94,182	$ 94,683

	FIFO	LIFO	Avg. Cost
Sales	$ 283,963	$ 283,963	$ 283,963
Cost of Goods Sold	150,051	150,463	149,962
Gross Profit	133,911	133,500	134,000
Operating expenses	133,500	133,500	133,500
Net Income	$ 411	$ -	$ 500

MODEL BUILDING 2: Cost of Goods Sold Schedule

Mike's Surf and Sea had a beginning inventory on January 1, 2004 of 150 long boards at a cost of $200 each. During the year, the following purchases were made:

Date	Cost/Unit	Units
March 6	$205	120
May 10	$210	200
June 10	$215	180
December 8	$220	160

Mike's Surf and Sea uses a periodic inventory system and sold 680 long boards during the year.

The long boards are sold for $450 each and operating expenses for the year were $117,000.

Prepare a cost of goods sold schedule for Mike's Surf and Sea for the calendar year ending December 31, 2004.

The following steps outline what you should do.

1. Determine the cost of goods available for sale.

2. Determine ending inventory under each of the cost flow assumptions (FIFO, LIFO, and Average Cost).

3. Determine the cost of goods sold under each of the cost flow assumptions.

4. Determine gross profit and net income under each of the cost flow assumptions.

5. Save the workbook as Chapter 8-2.

6. Be sure the worksheet is adheres to the style checklist on page 220 (Chapter 7).

7. Print the worksheet.

8. Check Figure: LIFO net income should be $44,500.

Test Data

During the year ending December 31, 2004, Mike's Surf and Sea had the following purchases.

Date	Cost/Unit	Units
April 15	$195	135
June 10	$190	187
August 10	$190	122
December 3	$188	156

Use the following criteria to test your model.

1. Mike's Surf and Sea sold 625 long boards during the year.

2. The long boards are sold for $525 each and operating expenses for the year were $167,500.

3.   Input the above data to recalculate the cost of goods available for sale, cost of goods sold, ending inventory, and net income under each of the cost flow assumptions.

4.   Save your file as Chapter 8-2 test.

5.   Check Figure: LIFO net income should be $41,262.

What-If Analysis

1.   Open the file Chapter 8-2 test.

2.   Using Excel's Goal Seek tool, determine the price Mike's Surf and Sea can sell the long boards for in order to break even under the FIFO method.

3.   Save your file as Chapter 8-2 analysis.

4.   Check Figure: LIFO net income should be $1,500.

MODEL BUILDING 3: Lower of Cost or Market

In this model-building activity, you will determine the *lower of cost or market* **(LOCM)**. As you know from your study of accounting, market in the term lower of cost or market is defined as the current market value (cost) of replacing inventory.

LOCM is applied in one of three ways:

    (1)   To each individual item separately.
    (2)   To major categories of items.
    (3)   To the entire inventory.

The less similar the items that make up inventory, the more likely companies are to apply LOCM to individual items.

Mike's Surf and Sea sells various clothing and surfing accessories. The table that follows details the items with their cost and market values on December 31, 2003.

Items	Cost	Market
Clothing		
T-shirts	65,000	57,000
Walk shorts	55,000	72,000
Board shorts	75,000	83,000
Accessories		
Wax	15,000	32,000
Leashes	35,000	45,000
Sun screen	18,000	16,000

1. Prepare a worksheet to calculate the lower of cost or market for each item, category and total inventory. (*Hint: Use the =MIN function*).

2. Format the worksheet correctly and print it on one page.

3. Save your worksheet as Chapter 8-3.

Student Name   Chapter 8-3   Today's Date

Mike's Surf and Sea
Lower of Cost or Market
12/31/2003

	Cost	Market	LOCM
Clothing			
T-shirts	65,000	57,000	57,000
Walk shorts	55,000	72,000	55,000
Board shorts	75,000	83,000	75,000
Total	195,000	212,000	195,000
Accessories			
Wax	15,000	32,000	15,000
Leashes	35,000	45,000	35,000
Sun screen	18,000	16,000	16,000
Total	68,000	93,000	68,000
Total inventory	263,000	305,000	263,000

Test Data

Enter the following data into your model.

Items	Cost	Market
Clothing		
T-shirts	60,000	65,000
Walk shorts	46,000	35,000
Board shorts	68,000	76,000
Accessories		
Wax	18,000	12,000
Leashes	32,000	40,000
Sun screen	20,000	18,000

Print the worksheet and save the file as Chapter 8-3 test.

Student Name	Chapter 8-3 test		Today's Date

Mike's Surf and Sea
Lower of Cost or Market
12/31/2003

	Cost	Market	LOCM
Clothing			
T-shirts	60,000	65,000	60,000
Walk shorts	46,000	35,000	35,000
Board shorts	68,000	76,000	68,000
Total	174,000	176,000	174,000
Accessories			
Wax	18,000	12,000	12,000
Leashes	32,000	40,000	32,000
Sun screen	20,000	18,000	18,000
Total	70,000	70,000	70,000
Total inventory	244,000	246,000	244,000

What-If Analysis

Using the Chapter 8-3 test file, determine how much the inventory should be if the total market value of the leashes was $42,000 and explain the difference.

Print the worksheet and save the file as Chapter 8-3 analysis.

Student Name	Chapter 8-3 analysis		Today's Date

Mike's Surf and Sea
Lower of Cost or Market
12/31/2003

	Cost	Market	LOCM
Clothing			
T-shirts	60,000	65,000	60,000
Walk shorts	46,000	35,000	35,000
Board shorts	68,000	76,000	68,000
Total	174,000	176,000	174,000
Accessories			
Wax	18,000	12,000	12,000
Leashes	32,000	42,000	32,000
Sun screen	20,000	18,000	18,000
Total	70,000	72,000	70,000
Total inventory	244,000	248,000	244,000

MODEL BUILDING 4: Student-Designed Lower of cost or Market Model

Create a table that computes LOCM. Using a merchandising business of interest to you, create two different item categories with at least two subcategories. For example, if you are building a model for a sporting goods store, you could have a category for Camping Gear and items such as sleeping bags, and cookware. A second category could be Accessories with items such as backpacks, sun glasses, and totes.

Complete the table shown on the next page. Remember: Use two categories with at least two items in each category.

Items	Cost	Market

1. Prepare a worksheet to calculate the lower of cost or market for each item, category and total inventory.

2. Format the worksheet correctly and print it on one page.

3. Save your worksheet as Chapter 8-4.

4. Test your data by changing the cost and market amounts.

5. Save your worksheet as Chapter 8-4 test.

6. Using the Chapter 8-4 test file, change the market value of one of the items and determine the new LOCM value of the total inventory. Explain the difference in the value of the total inventory.

7. Save your worksheet as Chapter 8-4 analysis.

	INTERNET ACTIVITIES
1.	Start your Internet browser. Go to the textbook's website at http://www.mhhe.com/yachtexcel.com. Go to the Student link.
2.	Link to Internet Activities, then WEB EXERCISES, PART 3-Chapter 8.
3.	Access this website http://office.microsoft.com/assistance/2002/articles/GetDataFromTheWebInExcel.aspx.
4.	Read the article "Getting Data from the Web in Excel." Write an essay about what you have learned. Your essay should have no more than 125 words or less than 100 words. Include the appropriate URLs.
5.	Go to this website http://www.webcpa.com. Explore two additional links on this site. (*Hint: Make sure the links you look at are not the same ones you looked at in Chapters 6 and 7. For example, you might want to look at one of the publications and write your summary based on a recent journal article.*) Write up a summary of what you have seen. Your summary should have no more than 75 words or less than 50 words. Include the appropriate URLs.

SUMMARY AND REVIEW

SOFWARE OBJECTIVES: In Chapter 8, you used to software to:

1. Complete a cost of goods sold schedule.

2. Complete a worksheet to determine lower of cost or market.

3. Test your models.

4. Solve what-if scenarios.

5. Save your worksheets.

6. Design and build your own model.

7. Complete the exercises and activities in Chapter 8.

WEB OBJECTIVES: In Chapter 8, you did these Internet activities:

1. Used your Internet browser to go to the book's website.

2. Completed the Internet Activities.

Multiple-Choice Questions: In the space provided, write the letter that best answers each question.

_____1. On the Chapter 8-1.xls file, Mike's Surf and Sea had a beginning inventory of long boards on December 31, 2003 of:

    a. 200.
    b. 175.
    c. 215.
    d. 160.
    e. None of the above.

_____2. Mike's Surf and Sea uses the following inventory method.

    a. Perpetual.
    b. Periodic.
    c. Sum-of-the years' digits.
    d. Straight line.
    e. All of the above.

_____3. On the Chapter 8.xls file, operating expenses for the year are:

    a. $346,800.
    b. $193,588.
    c. $153,212.
    d. $123,756.
    e. None of the above.

_____4. The model templates are written to determine cost flow assumptions for each of the following *except:*

    a. FIFO.
    b. LIFO.
    c. Average cost.
    d. Budget cost.
    e. COGM.

_____5. The model templates determine which of the following?

    a. Beginning inventory costs per item.
    b. Total assets.
    c. Total liabilities.
    d. Cost of goods available for sale.
    e. All of the above.

_____6. On the Chapter 8.xls file, LIFO net income is:

    a. $29,456.
    b. $28,763.
    c. $29,120.
    d. $13,734.
    e. None of the above.

_____7. On the Chapter 8-1 test.xls file, Mike's Surf and Sea sold how many long boards during the year?

    a. 600
    b. 190
    c. 775
    d. 325
    e. None of the above

_____8. On the Chapter 8-1 test.xls file, long boards sold for:

    a. $223.
    b. $425.
    c. $450.
    d. $325.
    e. None of the above.

_____9.   On the Chapter 8-1 test.xls file, the LIFO net income is:

   a. $21,050.
   b. $21,725.
   c. $21,930.
   d. $28,763.
   e. None of the above.

_____10.   On the Chapter 8-1 test.xls file, ending inventory in units is:

   a. 305.
   b. 315.
   c. 415.
   d. 221.
   e. None of the above.

True/Make True: If the statement is true, write the word "True" in the space provided. If the statement is *not* true, write the correct answer in the space provided.

11.   In Excel when you build a new project from scratch, you are building a model.

   _____

   _____

12.   In Chapter 8, you prepare a cost of goods manufactured schedule.

   _____

   _____

13. In Chapter 8, the cost flow assumptions are FIFO, LIFO, and Average Cost.

_____

_____

14. In Chapter 8, you determine gross profit and net income under each of the cost flow assumptions.

_____

_____

15. In order to determine how much total sales Mike's Surf and Sea needs to reach net income goals, you use Excel's editing feature.

_____

_____

16. In the what-if analysis for Model 1, you are determining how many long boards Mike needs to sell in order to break even under the LIFO method.

_____

_____

17. After completing what-if analysis, Mike's ending inventory is 422. (Refer to the Chapter 8-1 analysis file.)

_____

_____

18. Market in the term lower of cost or market is defined as the current market value (cost) of replacing inventory.

_____

_____

19. The more similar the items that make up inventory, the more likely companies are to apply LOCM to individual items.

_____

_____

20. The Chapter 8-3.xls file shows the lower of cost or market (LOCM) for the total inventory as $305,000.

_____

_____

Exercise 8-1: Cost of Goods Sold Schedule

Carol's Surf Shop had a beginning inventory of 220 long boards at a cost of $215 each. During the year, the following purchases were made:

Date	Cost/Unit	Units
February 28	$218	170
June 1	$220	210
September 15	$222	175
December 12	$225	160

Carol's Surf Shop uses a periodic inventory system and sold 820 long boards during the year.

The long boards are sold for $410 each and operating expenses for the year were $125,705.

Instructions

Prepare a cost of goods sold schedule for Carol's Surf Shop for the calendar year ending December 31, 2003. The following steps outline what you should do.

1. Determine the cost of goods available for sale.

2. Determine ending inventory under each of the cost flow assumptions (FIFO, LIFO, and Average Cost).

3. Determine the cost of goods sold under each of the cost flow assumptions.

4. Determine gross profit and net income under each of the cost flow assumptions.

5. Save the workbook as Exercise 8-1.

6. Be sure the worksheet adheres to the style checklist on page 220 (Chapter 7).

7. Print the worksheet.

Exercise 8-2: Test and Analyze Data

During the year ending December 31, 2003, Carol's Surf Shop had the following purchases.

Date	Cost/Unit	Units
February 28	$226	300
June 1	$228	210
September 15	$229	170
December 12	$230	180

1. Carol's Surf Shop sold 845 long boards during the year.

2. The long boards are sold for $415 each and operating expenses for the year were $130,550.

3. Input the above data to recalculate the cost of goods available for sale, cost of goods sold, ending inventory, and net income under each of the cost flow assumptions.

4. Save your file as Exercise 8-2 test.

5. To complete what-if analysis, complete these steps.

    a. Using Excel's Goal Seek tool, determine how many long boards Carol's Surf Shop would have to sell to break even under the LIFO method.

    b. Save your file as Exercise 8-2 analysis.

Exercise 8-3: Lower of Cost or Market

1. Carol Surf's Shop sells various clothing and surfing accessories. The following table details the items with their cost and market values on December 31, 2003.

Items	Cost	Market
Clothing		
Tank tops	55,000	61,000
Bathing suits	45,000	57,000
Sarongs	73,000	79,000
Accessories		
Wax	14,000	25,000
Leashes	32,000	44,000
Sun glasses	19,000	15,000
Sun screen	17,000	14,000

2. Prepare a worksheet to calculate the lower of cost or market for each item, category and total inventory. (*Hint: use the =MIN function*).

3. Format the worksheet correctly and print it on one page.

4. Save your worksheet as Exercise 8-3.

Exercise 8-4: Test and Analyze Data

1. Enter the data shown to test your model.

Items	Cost	Market
Clothing		
Tank tops	52,000	62,000
Bathing suits	48,000	37,000
Sarongs	66,000	79,000
Accessories		
Wax	15,000	11,000
Leashes	30,000	42,000
Sun glasses	18,000	15,000
Sun screen	12,000	14,000

2. Print the worksheet and save the file as Exercise 8-4 test.

3. Complete what-if analysis.

    a. Using the Exercise 8-4 test file, determine how much the inventory should be if the market value of the tank tops was $45,000. Explain the difference.

    b. Print the worksheet and save the file as Exercise 8-4 analysis.

CHAPTER 8 INDEX

Chapter 9 — Payroll

SOFTWARE OBJECTIVES: In Chapter 9 you will use the software to:

1. Complete an employee earnings record.

2. Complete a payroll register.

3. Test your models.

4. Solve what-if scenarios.

5. Save your spreadsheets.

6. Design and build your own model.

7. Complete the exercises and activities in Chapter 9.

WEB OBJECTIVES: In Chapter 9 you will do these Internet activities.

1. Use your Internet browser to go to the book's website.

2. Complete the Internet Activities.

As you know from your study of accounting, employees and employers are required to pay local, state, and federal payroll taxes. Employers must withhold taxes from each employee's paycheck. The amount withheld for federal taxes is determined from tax tables published by the Internal Revenue Service (IRS). Circular E, Employer's Tax Guide, is available from the IRS. It shows the applicable tax tables and forms that are necessary for filing employee payroll information.

The amount withheld also depends on the employee's earnings and the number of ***withholding allowances*** claimed by the employee. The number of withholding allowances usually includes one for the employee, one for the employee's spouse, and one for each dependent.

Also deducted from employees' paychecks are **FICA taxes** or social security taxes. This deduction from wages provides qualified workers who retire at age 62 or older with monthly payments from the federal government. The retiree also receives medical benefits called **Medicare** after reaching age 65. In addition to these retirement benefits, social security also provides payments to the surviving family of a qualified deceased worker.

Congress adjusts the income limit for the FICA tax annually. There is no income limit on amounts subject to the Medicare tax. The FICA tax percentage for social security is 6.2%; the percentage for Medicare, 1.45%.

Employees may also voluntarily deduct other amounts from wages. These voluntary deductions include: charitable contributions, medical insurance premiums, U.S. savings bonds, or union dues.

In this chapter, you will prepare spreadsheets to calculate an employee's earnings record and a payroll register. Similar to the other model-building activities that you completed in Chapters 7 and 8, data will be provided so that you can complete the spreadsheets. In this chapter, those spreadsheets are related to payroll accounting. You will also complete a payroll model of your own design. You may want to refer to Chapter 5 to review the formulas used in the payroll register (pages 161-163). Remember, it is the purpose of this chapter for you to build spreadsheets from scratch. In other words, you are creating the Excel template.

GETTING STARTED

The material that follows includes data for an employee earnings record. Use this data to create payroll accounting models.

MODEL BUILDING 1: EMPLOYEE EARNINGS RECORD

To comply with employment laws, an employer must keep track of each employee's earnings and deductions. Mike's Surf and Sea prepares an employee earnings record to keep track of these earnings and deductions. An **employee earnings record** shows the pay period dates, hours worked, gross pay, deductions, and net pay of each employee for each pay period.

Use the information for the following employee as you build the model. Make sure your model adheres to the style checklist on page 220 (in Chapter 7).

Name	Joe Surfa	Address	1234 Beach Road
SSN	123-45-6789		Waikiki, HI 96813
Date of Birth	1/10/1975	Telephone	(808) 955-6122
Date Hired	2/1/1999	Terminated	
Sex	M		
Status	Single	Exemptions	1
Pay Rate	$11.00		

Instructions

1. Set up a model in Excel for an employee earnings record. Joe is paid on an hourly basis and is paid time and one half for all hours worked over 40 a week. (*Hint: Set up an Overtime column for hours in excess of 40 hours per week*.) The earnings data for Joe Surfa is as follows:

Period Ending	Total Hours	FIT Withholdings
1/5/03	25	29.00
1/12/03	43	44.00
1/19/03	20	23.00
1/26/03	22	26.00
2/2/03	20	23.00
2/9/03	20	23.00

2. Use the following tax information:

Tax	Rate	Limits
State Tax	10%	none
FICA	6.2%	$84,000
Medicare	1.45%	none

You may not apply the FICA tax if the employee's earnings are more than the limit. Therefore, you must enter a nested conditional formula to calculate the FICA tax. Refer to the payroll exercise in Chapter 5.

3. Setup the page so that the entire document prints on one page. Insert a column for Union Dues.

4. Save the file as Chapter 9-1.

5. Print the spreadsheet.

Mike's Surf and Sea
Employee Earnings Record
For the year ending 12/31/03

Name	Joe Surfa			Address	1234 Beach Road						
SSN	123-45-6789				Waikiki, HI 96813						
Date of Birth	1/10/1975			Telephone	(808) 955-6122						
Date Hired	2/1/1999			Terminated							
Sex	M										
Status	Single			Exemptions	1						
Pay Rate	$ 11.00										

Period Ending	Total Hours	Regular	Gross Earnings Overtime	Total	Cummulative	FIT	State	FICA	Medicare	Union Dues	Total	Net Pay
1/5/03	25	275.00	-	275.00	275.00	29.00	27.50	17.05	3.99	-	77.54	197.46
1/12/03	43	440.00	49.50	489.50	764.50	44.00	48.95	30.35	7.10	-	130.40	359.10
1/19/03	20	220.00	-	220.00	984.50	23.00	22.00	13.64	3.19	-	61.83	158.17
1/26/03	22	242.00	-	242.00	1,226.50	26.00	24.20	15.00	3.51	-	68.71	173.29
2/2/03	20	220.00	-	220.00	1,446.50	23.00	22.00	13.64	3.19	-	61.83	158.17
2/9/03	20	220.00	-	220.00	1,666.50	23.00	22.00	13.64	3.19	-	61.83	158.17

Test Data

1. Change the data in the employee earnings record to the following.

Period Ending	Total Hours	Withholdings FIT
1/5/03	45	52.00
1/12/03	43	50.00
1/19/03	40	46.00
1/26/03	42	48.00
2/2/03	40	46.00
2/9/03	40	46.00

2. Save your spreadsheet as Chapter 9-1 test.

Mike's Surf and Sea
Employee Earnings Record
For the year ending 12/31/03

Name	Joe Surfa	Address	1234 Beach Road	
SSN	123-45-6789		Waikiki, HI 96813	
Date of Birth	1/10/1975	Telephone	(808) 955-6122	
Date Hired	2/1/1999	Terminated		
Sex	M			
Status	Single	Exemptions	1	
Pay Rate	$ 11.00			

Period Ending	Total Hours	Regular	Gross Earnings Overtime	Total	Cummulative	FIT	State	FICA	Medicare	Union Dues	Total	Net Pay
1/5/03	45	440.00	82.50	522.50	522.50	52.00	52.25	32.40	7.58	-	144.22	378.28
1/12/03	43	440.00	49.50	489.50	1,012.00	50.00	48.95	30.35	7.10	-	136.40	353.10
1/19/03	40	440.00	-	440.00	1,452.00	46.00	44.00	27.28	6.38	-	123.66	316.34
1/26/03	42	440.00	33.00	473.00	1,925.00	48.00	47.30	29.33	6.86	-	131.48	341.52
2/2/03	40	440.00	-	440.00	2,365.00	46.00	44.00	27.28	6.38	-	123.66	316.34
2/9/03	40	440.00	-	440.00	2,805.00	46.00	44.00	27.28	6.38	-	123.66	316.34

What-If Analysis

1.   Using the Chapter 9-1 test file, determine how much Joe's hourly pay should be if he wants his net pay to be $400.00 during the week ended January 5. *(Hint: Use Goal Seek to find the solution.)*

2.   Save your spreadsheet as Chapter 9-1 analysis.

Mike's Surf and Sea
Employee Earnings Record
For the year ending 12/31/03

Name	Joe Surfa	Address	1234 Beach Road	
SSN	123-45-6789		Waikiki, HI 96813	
Date of Birth	1/10/1975	Telephone	(808) 955-6122	
Date Hired	2/1/1999	Terminated		
Sex	M			
Status	Single	Exemptions	1	
Pay Rate	$ 11.56			

Period Ending	Total Hours	Regular	Gross Earnings Overtime	Total	Cummulative	FIT	State	FICA	Medicare	Union Dues	Total	Net Pay
1/5/03	45	462.21	86.66	548.88	548.88	52.00	54.89	34.03	7.96	-	148.88	400.00
1/12/03	43	462.21	52.00	514.21	1,063.09	50.00	51.42	31.88	7.46	-	140.76	373.45
1/19/03	40	462.21	-	462.21	1,525.30	46.00	46.22	28.66	6.70	-	127.58	334.63
1/26/03	42	462.21	34.67	496.88	2,022.18	48.00	49.69	30.81	7.20	-	135.70	361.18
2/2/03	40	462.21	-	462.21	2,484.39	46.00	46.22	28.66	6.70	-	127.58	334.63
2/9/03	40	462.21	-	462.21	2,946.60	46.00	46.22	28.66	6.70	-	127.58	334.63

MODEL BUILDING 2: PAYROLL REGISTER

A *payroll register* lists employees with all paycheck information for a specified period of time. The payroll register shows the hours worked, gross pay, deductions, and net pay of each employee.

Mike's Surf and Sea has five employees who are paid on an hourly basis. All employees are paid time and one half for all hours worked over 40 per week. Payroll data for the week ending November 23, 2003 are included in the following table.

Employee	Cumulative Wages(11/15)	Hours Worked	Hourly Rate	Federal Withholding	Union Dues
Joe Surfa	$23,000	25	$11.00	$58.00	$0.00
Malia Kimi	$38,000	43	$13.00	$100.00	$5.00
Michele Ihilani	$43,000	40	$13.00	$100.00	$5.00
Irene Walker	$82,000	47	$30.00	$300.00	$5.00
Sharon Pocho	$85,000	50	$35.00	$450.00	$5.00

Tax rates are as follows:

Tax	Rate	Limits
State Tax	10%	none
FICA	6.2%	$84,000
Medicare	1.45%	none

Instructions

1. Use the above data to prepare a payroll register for Mike's Surf and Sea for the week ending November 23, 2003. Your spreadsheet should have an input section for the rates and limits.

2. The spreadsheet should calculate regular wages, overtime wages, total wages, federal and state withholdings, FICA withholdings, Medicare withholdings, union dues, and net pay for each employee as well as totals for all amount columns.

3. Save the file as Chapter 9-2.

4. Print the spreadsheet.

5. Check figure: Total net pay should be $3,055.27.

Student Name						Chapter 9-2.xls						Today's Date

Mike's Surf and Sea
Payroll Register
For the week ending 11/23/03

	Rate	Limit
State Withholdings	10.00%	
FICA	6.20%	$ 64,000.00
Medicare	1.45%	

Employee Name	Cumulative Earnings	Hours Worked	Hourly Rate	Regular	Wages Overtime	Total	FIT Withholding	State Withholding	FICA Withholding	Medicare Withholding	Union Dues	Net Pay
Joe Surfa	$ 23,000.00	25	$ 11.00	$ 275.00	$ -	$ 275.00	$ 58.00	$ 27.50	$ 17.05	$ 3.99	$ -	$ 168.46
Malia Kimi	$ 36,000.00	43	$ 13.00	$ 520.00	$ 58.50	$ 578.50	$ 100.00	$ 57.85	$ 35.87	$ 8.39	$ 5.00	$ 371.39
Michele Ihilani	$ 43,000.00	40	$ 13.00	$ 520.00	$ -	$ 520.00	$ 100.00	$ 52.00	$ 32.24	$ 7.54	$ 5.00	$ 323.22
Irene Walker	$ 82,000.00	47	$ 30.00	$ 1,200.00	$ 315.00	$ 1,515.00	$ 300.00	$ 151.50	$ 93.93	$ 21.97	$ 5.00	$ 942.60
Sharon Pocho	$ 85,000.00	50	$ 35.00	$ 1,400.00	$ 525.00	$ 1,925.00	$ 450.00	$ 192.50	$ -	$ 27.91	$ 5.00	$ 1,249.59
		102.00		$ 3,915.00	$ 898.50	$ 4,813.50	$ 1,008.00	$ 481.35	$ 179.09	$ 69.80	$ 20.00	$ 3,055.27

Test Data

1. Open the file Chapter 9-2 and change the data in the spreadsheet to the following:

Employee	Cumulative Wages(11/15)	Hourly Rate
Joe Surfa	$25,000	$12.00
Malia Kimi	$36,000	$13.00
Michele Ihilani	$63,000	$20.00
Irene Walker	$82,000	$30.00
Sharon Pocho	$85,000	$35.00

2. Change the FICA limit to $64,000.

3. Print the spreadsheet.

4. Save the file as Chapter 9-2 test.

5. Check figure: Net pay is $3,306.43.

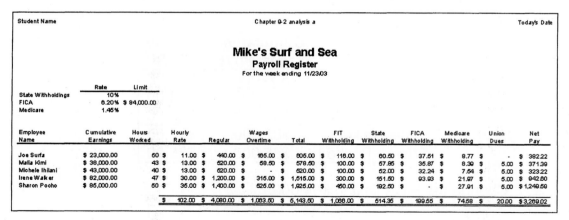

Student Name					Chapter 9-2 test									Today's Date

Mike's Surf and Sea
Payroll Register
For the week ending 11/23/03

	Rate	Limit
State Withholdings	10.00%	
FICA	6.20%	$ 84,000.00
Medicare	1.45%	

Employee Name	Cumulative Earnings	Hours Worked	Hourly Rate	Regular	Wages Overtime	Total	FIT Withholding	State Withholding	FICA Withholding	Medicare Withholding	Union Dues	Net Pay
Joe Surfa	$ 25,000.00	25 $	12.00 $	300.00 $	- $	300.00 $	58.00 $	30.00 $	18.60 $	4.35 $	- $	189.05
Malia Kimi	$ 36,000.00	43 $	13.00 $	520.00 $	58.50 $	578.50 $	100.00 $	57.85 $	35.87 $	8.39 $	5.00 $	371.39
Michele Ihilani	$ 63,000.00	40 $	20.00 $	800.00 $	- $	800.00 $	100.00 $	80.00 $	49.60 $	11.60 $	5.00 $	553.80
Irene Walker	$ 82,000.00	47 $	30.00 $	1,200.00 $	315.00 $	1,515.00 $	300.00 $	151.50 $	93.93 $	21.97 $	5.00 $	942.60
Sharon Pooho	$ 85,000.00	50 $	35.00 $	1,400.00 $	525.00 $	1,925.00 $	450.00 $	192.50 $	- $	27.91 $	5.00	$1,249.59
		$ 110.00	$ 4,220.00	$ 898.50	$ 5,118.50	$ 1,008.00	$ 511.85	$ 198.00	$ 74.22	$ 20.00	$3,306.43	

What-if Analysis

Mike's Surf and Sea is considering hiring another employee or doubling Joe Surfa's hours. The new employee, Abcde Sample, would be paid $11.00 per hour and work 30 hours.

1. Open the file Chapter 9-2 file and double the hours and FIT withholdings for Joe Surfa.

2. Print the worksheet and save the file as Chapter 9-2 analysis a.

Student Name					Chapter 9-2 analysis a									Today's Date

Mike's Surf and Sea
Payroll Register
For the week ending 11/23/03

	Rate	Limit
State Withholdings	10%	
FICA	6.20%	$ 84,000.00
Medicare	1.45%	

Employee Name	Cumulative Earnings	Hours Worked	Hourly Rate	Regular	Wages Overtime	Total	FIT Withholding	State Withholding	FICA Withholding	Medicare Withholding	Union Dues	Net Pay
Joe Surfa	$ 23,000.00	50 $	11.00 $	440.00 $	165.00 $	605.00 $	116.00 $	60.50 $	37.51 $	8.77 $	- $	382.22
Malia Kimi	$ 36,000.00	43 $	13.00 $	520.00 $	58.50 $	578.50 $	100.00 $	57.85 $	35.87 $	8.39 $	5.00 $	371.39
Michele Ihilani	$ 43,000.00	40 $	13.00 $	520.00 $	- $	520.00 $	100.00 $	52.00 $	32.24 $	7.54 $	5.00 $	323.22
Irene Walker	$ 82,000.00	47 $	30.00 $	1,200.00 $	315.00 $	1,515.00 $	300.00 $	151.50 $	93.93 $	21.97 $	5.00 $	942.60
Sharon Pooho	$ 85,000.00	50 $	35.00 $	1,400.00 $	525.00 $	1,925.00 $	450.00 $	192.50 $	- $	27.91 $	5.00	$1,249.59
		$ 102.00	$ 4,080.00	$ 1,063.50	$ 5,143.50	$ 1,066.00	$ 514.35	$ 199.55	$ 74.58	$ 20.00	$3,269.02	

3. Open the Chapter 9-2 file and add another employee, Abcde Sample (use your first and last name). The new employee will be paid $11.00 per hour for 30 hours. The FIT withholding is $60.00 and there are no union dues. (*Hint: Add a row above Joe Surfa.*) Print the worksheet and save the file as Chapter 9-2 analysis b.

| Student Name | | | | | Chapter 9-2 analysis b | | | | | | | Today's Date |

Mike's Surf and Sea
Payroll Register
For the week ending 11/23/03

	Rate	Limit
State Withholdings	10.00%	
FICA	6.20%	$84,000.00
Medicare	1.45%	

Employee Name	Cumulative Earnings	Hours Worked	Hourly Rate	Regular	Wages Overtime	Total	FIT Withholding	State Withholding	FICA Withholding	Medicare Withholding	Union Dues	Net Pay
Abcde Sample	$ -	30	$ 11.00	$ 330.00	$ -	$ 330.00	$ 60.00	$ 33.00	$ 20.46	$ 4.79	$ -	$ 211.75
Joe Surfa	$ 23,000.00	25	$ 11.00	$ 275.00	$ -	$ 275.00	$ 58.00	$ 27.50	$ 17.05	$ 3.99	$ -	$ 168.46
Malia Kimi	$ 38,000.00	43	$ 13.00	$ 520.00	$ 58.50	$ 578.50	$ 100.00	$ 57.85	$ 35.87	$ 8.39	$ 5.00	$ 371.39
Michele Ihilani	$ 43,000.00	40	$ 13.00	$ 520.00	$ -	$ 520.00	$ 100.00	$ 52.00	$ 32.24	$ 7.54	$ 5.00	$ 323.22
Irene Walker	$ 82,000.00	47	$ 30.00	$ 1,200.00	$ 315.00	$ 1,515.00	$ 300.00	$ 151.50	$ 93.93	$ 21.97	$ 5.00	$ 942.60
Sharon Pocho	$ 85,000.00	50	$ 35.00	$ 1,400.00	$ 525.00	$ 1,925.00	$ 450.00	$ 192.50	$ -	$ 27.91	$ 5.00	$1,249.59
		113.00		$ 4,245.00	$ 898.50	$ 5,143.50	$ 1,068.00	$ 514.35	$ 199.55	$ 74.59	$ 20.00	$3,267.02

Would Mike's Surf and Sea be better off doubling Joe Surfa's hours or hiring a new employee?

MODEL BUILDING 3: STUDENT-DESIGNED PAYROLL REGISTER

1. Create a table that lists four employees who are paid on an hourly basis. All employees are paid time and one half for all hours worked over 40 hours per week. Payroll data should be shown for one week. Use the blank table on the next page to complete your data.

2. Refer to earlier work to determine FIT (Federal) withholding.

Employee	Cumulative Wages	Hours Worked	Hourly Rate	Federal Withholding	Union Dues

3. Establish tax rates and limits. Note that state tax does not have a limit. (These rates should *not* be the same as the ones shown on page 265.)

Tax	Rate	Limits
State Tax		
FICA		
Medicare		

4. Use the above data to prepare a payroll register for a company that you name. Select an appropriate week-ending period. Your spreadsheet should have an input section for the rates and limits.

5. The spreadsheet should calculate regular wages, overtime wages, total wages, federal and state withholdings, FICA withholdings, Medicare withholdings, union dues, and net pay for each employee as well as totals for all amount columns.

6. Save the file as Chapter 9-3.

7. Print the spreadsheet. Use the style checklist on page 220 (Chapter 7) for appropriate formatting and printing criteria.

8. Test your data by increasing the cumulative wages, hourly rates, and the FICA limit. Print the spreadsheet. Save the file as Chapter 9-3 test.

9. Complete what-if analysis by adding another employee and doubling the hours of one of your employees. Save your spreadsheet as Chapter 9-3 analysis.

	INTERNET ACTIVITIES
1.	From your Internet browser, go to the textbook's website at www.mhhe.com/yachtexcel. Go to the Student link.
2.	Link to Internet Activities, then WEB EXERCISES, PART 3-Chapter 9.
3.	Go to this website www.ssa.gov/employer/. Link to General W-2 Filing Information, then answer these questions. 1. What are dates that employers must send W-2 information to the Social Security Administration? (Include the dates for both electronic and paper filing.) 2. By what date must employers give employees their W-2s? 3. What two forms do employers send to the Social Security Administration?
4.	Access this website http://www.microsoft.com/office/previous/xp/columns/column10.asp.
5.	Read the article "Count and Sum Your Data in Excel." Complete the spreadsheet shown in Figure 1. Then, complete the summing and counting activities shown, including conditional counting and summary. Print out your spreadsheet with an explanation of what you did.

SUMMARY AND REVIEW

SOFWARE OBJECTIVES: In Chapter 9, you used to software to:

1. Complete an employee earnings record.

2. Complete a payroll register.

3. Test your models.

4. Solve what-if scenarios.

5. Save your spreadsheets.

6. Design and build your own model.

7. Complete the exercises and activities in Chapter 9.

WEB OBJECTIVES: In Chapter 9, you did these Internet activities:

1. Used your Internet browser to go to the textbook's website.

2. Completed the Internet Activities.

Multiple-Choice Questions: In the space provided, write the letter that best answers each question.

_____1. According to Joe Surfa's employee earnings record, his hourly rate is

   a. $11.
   b. $12.
   c. $13.
   d. $14.
   e. None of the above.

_____2. Before testing your model, Joe Surfa's net pay was $355.12 on what date?

   a. 1/5/03
   b. 1/12/03
   c. 1/26/03
   d. 2/2/03
   e. All of the above

_____3. After testing your model, Joe Surfa's net pay was $320.46 on what date?

   a. 1/5/03
   b. 1/12/03
   c. 1/26/03
   d. 2/2/03
   e. None of the above

_____4. On Chapter 9-1 analysis, what is Joe Surfa's hourly rate when his take home pay on January 5 is $400?

    a. $11.00
    b. $11.50
    c. $11.56
    d. $11.75
    e. None of the above

_____5. The record that shows cumulative pay, hours worked, gross pay, deductions, and the net pay of all employees is called a/an

    a. Employee earnings schedule.
    b. Employee earnings record.
    c. Payroll register.
    d. Payroll journal.
    e. All of the above.

_____6. The income limit on the social security tax (FICA) is:

    a. The same each year.
    b. Determined by the number of exemptions.
    c. The FICA tax does not have an income limit.
    d. Adjusted yearly by Congress.
    e. None of the above.

_____7. Guidelines for employee and employer withholdings are found in the following IRS publication.

    a. Circular E, Employer's Tax Guide.
    b. Circular E, Employees Tax Guide.
    c. Circular F, Employee/Employer Tax Guide.
    d. Both a. and b.
    e. None of the above.

_____8. All of these payroll tax deductions are subtracted from an employee's gross pay EXCEPT:

   a. Federal income tax.
   b. Social security tax (FICA)
   c. Federal unemployment tax (FUTA).
   d. Medicare tax.
   e. None of the above.

_____9. The amount withheld from employees' paychecks depends on:

   a. How many employees a company has.
   b. The amount withheld changes on every paycheck.
   c. There are no withholdings.
   d. The number of withholding allowances.
   e. None of the above.

_____10. On the Chapter 9-2 analysis.xls file, what is the new employee paid per hour?

   a. $10.00.
   b. $11.00.
   c. $12.00.
   d. $13.50.
   e. None of the above.

True/Make True: If the statement is true, write the word "True" in the space provided. If the statement is *not* true, write the correct answer in the space provided.

11. To comply with employment laws, an employer must keep track of each employee's earnings and deductions.

_____

_____

12. Use a payroll register to keep track of an employee's earnings and deductions throughout the year.

_____

_____

13. For the week ended January 12, 2003, Joe Surfa worked 43 hours.

_____

_____

14. Joe Surfa was not owed any overtime pay for the period ended January 12, 2003.

_____

_____

15. In order for Joe Surfa to earn $400 net pay during the week of January 5, 2003, he needs to work 47 hours.

_____

_____

16. A payroll register lists employees with all paycheck information for a specified period of time.

_____

_____

17. Mike's Surf and Sea has five employees who are all salaried.

_____

_____

18. There is no income limit on either the Medicare tax or on the FICA tax.

_____

_____

19. The amount withheld from an employee's paycheck has to do with his total earnings.

_____

_____

20. The employee earnings record shows the pay period dates, hours worked, gross pay, deductions, and each employee's paycheck amount.

_____

_____

Exercise 9-1: Employee Earnings Record

1. Prepare an employee earnings record for Carol's Surf Shop for the
    employee shown below.

Name	Jackie Scruggs	Address	3211 North Ilikai Boulevard
SSN	433-55-8988		Honolulu, HI 96810
Date of Birth	1/10/1973	Telephone	(808) 555-6122
Date Hired	3/1/1998	Terminated	
Sex	F		
Status	Single	Exemptions	1
Pay Rate	$12.50		

2. The earnings data for Jackie Scruggs is:

Period Ending	Total Hours	FIT Withholdings
1/5/04	20	27.00
1/12/04	45	47.00
1/19/04	25	29.00
1/26/04	22	26.00
2/2/04	22	26.00
2/9/04	22	26.00

3. Use the following tax information to prepare the employee earning
    record:

Tax	Rate	Limits
State Tax	11.00%	none
FICA	6.20%	$87,000
Medicare	1.45%	none

4. Setup the page so that the entire document prints on one page.

5. Save the file as Exercise 9-1.

6. Print the spreadsheet. Verify these net pay amounts: Jackie
    Scruggs net pay on 1/26/04, 2/2/04 and 2/9/04 is $197.71.

Exercise 9-2: Test and Analyze Employee Earnings Record Data

1. To test your data, change the information in the employee earnings record as shown in the table below.

Period Ending	Total Hours	Withholdings FIT
1/5/04	40	46.00
1/12/04	42	48.00
1/19/04	45	52.00
1/26/04	43	50.00
2/2/04	40	46.00

2. The hours worked on 2/9/04 are the same as February 2, 2004.

3. Save your spreadsheet as Exercise 9-2 test.

4. Print the spreadsheet.

5. Using the Exercise 9-2 test file, determine how much Jackie's hourly pay would need to be if she wants to take home $500 during the week ended January 5.

6. Save your spreadsheet as Exercise 9-2 analysis.

7. Print the spreadsheet.

Exercise 9-3: Payroll Register

Carol's Surf Shop has five employees who are paid on an hourly basis. All employees are paid time and one half for all hours worked over 40 a week. Payroll data for the week ending November 21, 2004 are shown below.

Employee	Cumulative Wages (11/13)	Hours Worked	Hourly Rate	Federal Withholding	Union Dues
Jackie Scruggs	$25,000	27	$12.50	$60.00	$0.00
Mimi Peralto	$35,000	42	$13.50	$105.00	$7.00
Philip Marchon	$46,000	40	$13.00	$102.00	$7.00
Jean Ono	$89,000	43	$25.00	$200.00	$7.00
Kay Hara	$88,000	48	$30.00	$400.00	$7.00

Tax rates for the week are as follows:

Tax	Rate	Limits
State Tax	11.00%	none
FICA: Social Security	6.20%	$87,000
Medicare Tax	1.45%	none

Instructions

1. Use the above data to prepare a payroll register for Carol's Surf Shop for the week ending November 21, 2004. Your spreadsheet should have an input section for the rates and limits.

2. The spreadsheet should calculate regular wages, overtime wages, total wages, federal withholdings, state withholdings, FICA: Social Security withholdings, Medicare withholdings, union dues and net pay for each employee as well as totals for all amount columns.

3. Save the file as Exercise 9-3.

4. Print the spreadsheet.

Exercise 9-4: Test and Analyze Data the Payroll Register

1. Using the Exercise 9-3 file, change the data as shown below.

Employee	Cumulative Wages(11/13)	Hourly Rate
Jackie Scruggs	$28,000	$13.00
Mimi Peralto	$39,000	$14.50
Philip Marchan	$50,000	$14.00
Jean Ono	$90,000	$27.00
Kay Hara	$92,000	$32.50

2. Change the FICA: Social Security Tax limit to $75,000.

3. Save the file as Exercise 9-4 test.

4. Print the spreadsheet.

5. Complete what-if analysis by hiring another employee (use your name) and doubling Jackie Scruggs' hours and FIT withholding. The new employee should be paid $15 per hour; work 30 hours; and have $50 federal withholding. The new employee does not pay union dues. (*Hint: Make your changes to the Exercise 9-4 test file.*)

6. Save the file as Exercise 9-4 analysis.

7. Print the spreadsheet.

CHAPTER 9 INDEX

The McGraw-Hill Companies, Inc., *Excel Accounting*

Chapter 10 — Fixed Assets

SOFTWARE OBJECTIVES: In Chapter 10 you will use the software to:

1. Complete a depreciation schedule using the declining balance method.

2. Complete a depreciation schedule using units-of-activity method.

3. Test your models.

4. Solve what-if scenarios.

5. Save your spreadsheets.

6. Design and build your own models.

7. Complete the exercises and activities in Chapter 10.

WEB OBJECTIVES: In Chapter 10 you will do these Internet activities.

1. Use your Internet browser to go to the book's website.

2. Complete the Internet Activities.

In this chapter, you will be asked to prepare a depreciation schedule using the declining balance method. You will also be asked to prepare a schedule that will calculate depreciation using the units-of-activity method.

GETTING STARTED

As you know from your study of accounting, *fixed assets* (also called plant assets; plant and equipment; property, plant and equipment) are tangible assets used in a company's operations that have a useful life of

---

more than one accounting period. On the balance sheet, fixed assets are identified in a separate category called Plant and Equipment.

Fixed assets are set apart from other assets in two important ways.

1) Fixed assets are used in operations. This makes them different from inventory that is held for sale and not used in operations. The distinction is how the asset is used. For instance, a company that purchases a computer for purpose of reselling it reports that computer on the balance sheet as inventory. If the same company purchases the computer to use it in operations, then this computer is a fixed assets.

2) Fixed assets have useful lives extending over more than one accounting period. This makes fixed assets different from current assets, such as supplies that are consumed over a shorter period of time.

DEPRECIATION

Since fixed assets are used over more than one accounting period, companies allocate the cost of a plant asset over several periods. This process, called depreciation, allows a company to allocate fixed assets as an expense in the accounting periods benefiting from its use.

There are three factors relevant to determining depreciation:

1) Cost

2) Salvage value

3) Useful life

In the activities that follow, you will build spreadsheets to determine depreciation.

MODEL BUILDING 1: DECLINING BALANCE METHOD

In Chapter 5 you learned how to use Excel's financial function, DDB. When you use DDB, Excel calculates the depreciation of an asset for a specified period using the double-declining balance method, or other method that you specify.

The three factors relevant to determining depreciation (cost, salvage, useful life) are shown in the data that follow. To use the declining balance method, follow the steps below.

1) Compute the asset's straight-line deprecation rate. (1 divided by the asset's useful life.)

2) Multiply the asset's straight-line rate by the declining balance rate. (150%, 200%, etc.).

3) Compute depreciation expense by multiplying this rate by the asset's beginning-of-period book value.

Mike's Surf and Sea is considering purchasing some new equipment at the beginning of 2003. Compute depreciation based on the information in the following table. (*Hint: Refer to the tutorial in Chapter 5, pages 159-161.*)

Cost	$ 350,000
Salvage Value	$ 75,000
Useful Life	15 years
Declining Balance Rate	150%

1. Prepare a depreciation schedule that will calculate depreciation for a 20-year period. The schedule should show the current depreciation expense, accumulated depreciation and the asset's book value.

2. Create an input section for the cost, salvage value, life and declining balance rate.

3. Use the =DDB function to calculate the depreciation.

4. Setup the page so that it prints on one page. The header should include your name, the file name, and today's date.

5. Save the file as Chapter 10-1.

6. Print the document.

Mike's Surf and Sea
Depreciation Schedule
12/31/2003

Cost	350,000
Salvage Value	75,000
Estimated Useful Life	15
Declining Balance Rate	150%

Period	Depreciation Expense	Accumulated Depreciation	Book Value
0			350,000.00
1	$35,000.00	35,000.00	315,000.00
2	$31,500.00	66,500.00	283,500.00
3	$28,350.00	94,850.00	255,150.00
4	$25,515.00	120,365.00	229,635.00
5	$22,963.50	143,328.50	206,671.50
6	$20,667.15	163,995.65	186,004.35
7	$18,600.44	182,596.09	167,403.92
8	$16,740.39	199,336.48	150,663.52
9	$15,066.35	214,402.83	135,597.17
10	$13,559.72	227,962.55	122,037.45
11	$12,203.75	240,166.29	109,833.71
12	$10,983.37	251,149.66	98,850.34
13	$9,885.03	261,034.70	88,965.30
14	$8,896.53	269,931.23	80,068.77
15	$5,068.77	275,000.00	75,000.00
16	#NUM!	#NUM!	#NUM!
17	#NUM!	#NUM!	#NUM!
18	#NUM!	#NUM!	#NUM!
19	#NUM!	#NUM!	#NUM!
20	#NUM!	#NUM!	#NUM!

Test Data

1. Compute the depreciation for the following asset:

Cost	$ 750,000
Salvage value	$ 95,000
Useful life	20 years
Depreciation rate	200%

2. Save the file as Chapter 10-1 test.

3. Print the file.

Student Name	Chapter 10-1 test		Today's Date

Mike's Surf and Sea
Depreciation Schedule
12/31/2003

Cost	750,000
Salvage Value	95,000
Estimated Useful Life	20
Declining Balance Rate	200%

Period	Depreciation Expense	Accumulated Depreciation	Book Value
0			750,000.00
1	$75,000.00	75,000.00	675,000.00
2	$67,500.00	142,500.00	607,500.00
3	$60,750.00	203,250.00	546,750.00
4	$54,675.00	257,925.00	492,075.00
5	$49,207.50	307,132.50	442,867.50
6	$44,286.75	351,419.25	398,580.75
7	$39,858.08	391,277.33	358,722.68
8	$35,872.27	427,149.59	322,850.41
9	$32,285.04	459,434.63	290,565.37
10	$29,056.54	488,491.17	261,508.83
11	$26,150.88	514,642.05	235,357.95
12	$23,535.79	538,177.85	211,822.15
13	$21,182.22	559,360.06	190,639.94
14	$19,063.99	578,424.06	171,575.94
15	$17,157.59	595,581.65	154,418.35
16	$15,441.83	611,023.49	138,976.51
17	$13,897.65	624,921.14	125,078.86
18	$12,507.89	637,429.02	112,570.98
19	$11,257.10	648,686.12	101,313.88
20	$6,313.88	655,000.00	95,000.00

The McGraw-Hill Companies, Inc., *Excel Accounting*

What-If Analysis

1. Using the data from the Chapter 10-1 file, determine how much the salvage value should be in order to depreciate the asset no more than 10 years. (*Hint: Using the goal seek tool, make 10 years the goal for estimated useful life by changing the salvage value. Set cell B26 to 0.00 by changing cell D7.*)

3. Save it as Chapter 10-1 analysis.

4. Print the file.

Student Name	Chapter 10-1 analysis	Today's Date

Mike's Surf and Sea
Depreciation Schedule
12/31/2003

Cost		350,000
Salvage Value		123,000
Estimated Useful Life		15
Declining Balance Rate		150%

Period	Depreciation Expense	Accumulated Depreciation	Book Value
0			350,000.00
1	$35,000.00	35,000.00	315,000.00
2	$31,500.00	66,500.00	283,500.00
3	$28,350.00	94,850.00	255,150.00
4	$25,515.00	120,365.00	229,635.00
5	$22,963.50	143,328.50	206,671.50
6	$20,667.15	163,995.65	186,004.35
7	$18,600.44	182,596.09	167,403.92
8	$16,740.39	199,336.48	150,663.52
9	$15,066.35	214,402.83	135,597.17
10	$12,597.17	227,000.00	123,000.00
11	$0.00	227,000.00	123,000.00
12	$0.00	227,000.00	123,000.00
13	$0.00	227,000.00	123,000.00
14	$0.00	227,000.00	123,000.00
15	$0.00	227,000.00	123,000.00
16	#NUM!	#NUM!	#NUM!
17	#NUM!	#NUM!	#NUM!
18	#NUM!	#NUM!	#NUM!
19	#NUM!	#NUM!	#NUM!
20	#NUM!	#NUM!	#NUM!

MODEL BUILDING 2: UNITS-OF-ACTIVITY[1]

Units-of-activity depreciation charges a varying amount to expense for each period of an asset's useful life depending on its usage.

Mike's Surf and Sea needs to calculate depreciation for a delivery truck. The truck is expected to be used for 120,000 miles and has a useful life of five years. Actual miles driven for the first four years of the truck's life are as follows.

2000	25,000 miles
2001	34,000 miles
2002	32,000 miles
2003	29,000 miles

The truck's original cost was $90,000, and it is expected to be sold for $5,000 at the end of five years.

1. Using this data, prepare a schedule to calculate depreciation using the units-of-activity method. The schedule should show the units of activity for each year, the depreciable cost per unit (depreciable cost divided by estimated units of activity), annual depreciation (depreciable cost per unit times yearly activity), accumulated depreciation and book value.

2. Create an input section for the cost, salvage value, and total estimated units.

3. Be sure the schedule prints on one page. The header should include your name, the file name, and today's date.

4. Save the file as Chapter 10-2.

5. Print the file.

---

[1]The units-of-activity depreciation method is also called units-of-production. Since we are using mileage in the examples, units-of-activity is the term used.

| | | Student Name | | Chapter 10-2.xls | | | Today's Date |

Mike's Surf and Sea
Depreciation Schedule
12/31/2003

Cost	90,000
Salvage value	5,000
Total estimated units	120,000

Period	Units of Activity	Depreciable Cost/Unit	Annual Depreciation	Accumulated Depreciation	Book Value
					90,000.00
2000	25,000	$0.71	$17,708.33	17,708.33	72,291.67
2001	34,000	$0.71	$24,083.33	41,791.67	48,208.33
2002	32,000	$0.71	$22,666.67	64,458.33	25,541.67
2003	29,000	$0.71	$20,541.67	85,000.00	5,000.00

Test Data

Change the actual miles driven to the following:

2000	21,000 miles
2001	36,000 miles
2002	33,000 miles
2003	32,000 miles

1. Save the file as Chapter 10-2 test.

2. Print the file.

Mike's Surf and Sea
Depreciation Schedule
12/31/2003

Cost	90,000
Salvage value	5,000
Total estimated units	120,000

Period	Units of Activity	Depreciable Cost/Unit	Annual Depreciation	Accumulated Depreciation	Book Value
					90,000.00
2000	21,000	$0.71	$14,875.00	14,875.00	75,125.00
2001	36,000	$0.71	$25,500.00	40,375.00	49,625.00
2002	33,000	$0.71	$23,375.00	63,750.00	26,250.00
2003	32,000	$0.71	$22,666.67	86,416.67	3,583.33

What-If Analysis

Mike's Surf and Sea wants to reduce its depreciation expense. Mike believes that $0.55 per mile would be more reasonable.

1. Use the Goal Seek tool to determine how many total estimated units should be used in order to make the depreciable cost per unit equal to $.55. (*Hint: Use the Chapter 10-2 test file.*)

2. Save the file as Chapter 10-2 analysis.

3. Print the file.

Student Name	Chapter 10-2 analysis	Today's Date

Mike's Surf and Sea
Depreciation Schedule
12/31/2003

Cost		90,000
Salvage value		5,000
Total estimated units		154,526

Period	Units of Activity	Depreciable Cost/Unit	Annual Depreciation	Accumulated Depreciation	Book Value
					90,000.00
2000	21,000	$0.55	$11,551.42	11,551.42	78,448.58
2001	36,000	$0.55	$19,802.43	31,353.85	58,646.15
2002	33,000	$0.55	$18,152.23	49,506.07	40,493.93
2003	32,000	$0.55	$17,602.16	67,108.23	22,891.77

MODEL BUILDING 3: STUDENT-DESIGNED DEPRECIATION SCHEDULE USING DECLINING BALANCE

A company that you own is considering purchasing some new equipment. Decide on a type of business and then select equipment that your business will use in operations. Using the Internet or trade catalogs, determine a reasonable cost for this piece of equipment. List the cost, as well as other information needed to compute depreciation in the following table.

1. Prepare a depreciation schedule that will calculate depreciation for a 20-year period. The schedule should show the current depreciation expense, accumulated depreciation and the asset's book value.

2. Create an input section for the information in the table above.

3. Use the =DDB function to calculate the depreciation.

4. Setup the page so that it prints on one page.

5. Save the file as Chapter 10-3.

6. Print the document. Include appropriate header information.

Test Data

You have decided to purchase another piece of equipment for your business. Enter the information about that equipment in the table below. Refer to the chapter activity for the appropriate criteria needed to test your data.

1. Compute the depreciation for this asset.

2. Save the file as Chapter 10-3 test.

3. Print the file.

What-If Analysis

1. Using the data from the Chapter 10-3 file, determine how much the salvage value should be in order to depreciate the asset no more than 8 years. Hint: use the Goal Seek tool to set the depreciation in year 9 to zero.

2. Save it as Chapter 10-3 analysis.

3.   Print the file.

MODEL BUILDING 4: STUDENT DESIGNED DEPRECIATION SCHEDULE USING UNITS OF ACTIVITY

The company you own needs to calculate depreciation for a delivery van. The van is expected to be used for 120,000 miles and has a useful life of five years. Enter your estimates for the actual miles driven during the first four years of the van's life in the table below.

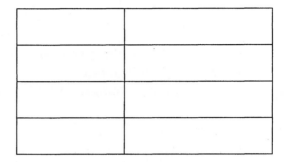

The van's original cost was $82,000 and is expected to be sold for $4,500 at the end of five years.

1.   Using this data, prepare a schedule to calculate depreciation using the units-of-activity method. The schedule should show the units of activity for each year, the depreciable cost per unit, annual depreciation, accumulated depreciation and book value.

2.   Create an input section for the cost, salvage value, and total estimated units.

3.   Set the schedule up to print on one page, inserting the appropriate header information.

4.   Save the file as Chapter 10-4.

5.   Print the file.

Test Data

Insert numbers in the table below for the actual number of miles driven during the first four years of the van's life.

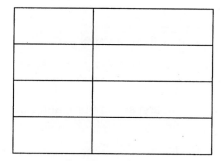

1. Insert the new numbers into the Chapter 10-4 file.

2. Save the file as Chapter 10-4 test.

3. Print the file.

What-If Analysis

Mike's Surf and Sea wants to reduce their depreciation expense. They believe $0.45 per mile would be more reasonable.

1. Use the Goal Seek tool to determine how much the total estimated units should be in order to make the depreciable cost per unit equal to $.45.

2. Save the file as Chapter 10-4 analysis.

3. Print the file.

	INTERNET ACTIVITIES
1.	From your Internet browser, go to the textbook's website at www.mhhe.com/yachtexcel. Go to the Student link.
2.	Link to Internet Activities, then WEB EXCERCISES, PART 3-Chapter 10.
3.	Go to this website http://office.microsoft.com/home/office.aspx?assetid=FX010380471033&CTT=98.
4.	Take the quiz. Are You a Whiz with Excel Formulas?
5.	Go to www.fixedassetinfo.com/calculator.htm. Read the directions and then use the depreciation calculator. Here's how you would use the online depreciation calculator for the Chapter 10-1 activity: 1. Property type: if necessary, select Furn. and Equipment 2. Placed in Service Date: type 1/1/2003. 3. Cost: type 350000; click [Next >]. 4. Depreciation Method: select Declining Balance 5. Deprecation Percent: select 150 6. Averaging Convention: select Full-Month 7. Depreciation Life (yrs): type 15; click [Depreciate]. Compare the depreciation calculator results to the Depreciation Schedule shown on page 288. 8. Click [Go Again] to use the depreciation calculator for another computation. Use similar steps to complete the Depreciation Schedules shown in Chapter 10. Compare the depreciation calculator's results to the Excel spreadsheets completed in Chapter 10. Explain any differences.

SUMMARY AND REVIEW

SOFWARE OBJECTIVES: In Chapter 10, you used to software to:

1. Complete a depreciation schedule using the declining balance method.

2. Complete a depreciation schedule using units-of-activity method.

3. Test your models.

4. Solve what-if scenarios.

5. Save your spreadsheets.

6. Design and build your own models.

7. Complete the exercises and activities in Chapter 10.

WEB OBJECTIVES: In Chapter 10, you did these Internet activities:

1. Used your Internet browser to go to the book's website.

2. Completed the Internet Activities.

Multiple-Choice Questions: In the space provided, write the letter that best answers each question.

_____1. Tangible assets used in a company's operations that have useful life of more than one accounting period are called

        a. Current assets.
        b. Long-term assets.
        c. Fixed assets.
        d. Liabilities.
        e. None of the above.

_____2. A company that purchases assets for resale reports those items on the balance sheet as

        a. Fixed assets.
        b. Current assets.
        c. Liabilities.
        d. Inventory.
        e. All of the above.

_____3. The process that allocates an asset's cost over several accounting periods is called:

        a. Declining balance.
        b. Unit-of-activity.
        c. Depreciation.
        d. Salvage value.
        e. None of the above.

_____4. All the following factors are relevant when determining depreciation *except*

    a. Resale value.
    b. Cost.
    c. Salvage value.
    d. Useful life.
    e. None of the above.

_____5. The declining balance method uses each one of the steps that follow *except*

    a. Compute the asset's straight-line depreciation rate.
    b. Determine units of activity.
    c. Double the straight-line rate.
    d. Compute depreciation expense by multiplying this rate by the asset's beginning-of-period value.
    e. All of the above.

_____6. On the Chapter 10-1.xls file, the declining balance rate is

    a. 200%.
    b. 100%.
    c. 150%.
    d. 250%.
    e. None of the above.

_____7. On the Chapter 10-1 test.xls file, the cost of equipment is

    a. $350,000.
    b. $750,000.
    c. $123,000.
    d. $95,000.
    e. None of the above.

_____8. This depreciation method charges a varying amount to expense for each period of an asset's useful life depending on its usage.

  a. Straight-line.
  b. Declining balance.
  c. Accelerated depreciation.
  d. Units-of-activity.
  e. None of the above.

_____9. Mike's Surf and Sea calculates this amount of cost per unit *before* what-if analysis.

  a. $.71.
  b. $.75.
  c. $.50.
  d. $.55.
  e. None of the above.

_____10. Mike's Surf and Sea completes what-if analysis because this amount of cost/unit seems more reasonable.

  a. $.71.
  b. $.75
  c. $.50.
  d. $.55.
  e. None of the above.

True/Make True: If the statement is true, write the word "True" in the space provided. If the statement is *not* true, write the correct answer in the space provided.

11. Fixed assets are also called plant assets.

_____

_____

12. Companies purchase fixed assets so they can resell them to their customers.

_____

_____

13. Assets that are purchased for resale show up on the balance sheet as inventory.

_____

_____

14. Supplies are consumed over a shorter period of time than fixed assets.

_____

_____

15. Fixed assets are different from inventory because fixed assets are used in business operations.

_____

_____

16. To depreciate a truck, van, or car, you may use the units-of-activity method.

_____

_____

17. In the Chapter 10-2.xls file, the total estimated units are 150,000 miles.

_____

_____

18. The original cost of Mike's truck was $95,000.

_____

_____

19. On the Chapter 10-2 depreciation schedule, annual depreciation is determined by multiplying depreciation cost per unit times yearly activity.

_____

_____

20. On the Chapter 10-2 analysis.xls file, the book value in 2003 is $40,493.93.

_____

_____

Exercise 10-1: Declining Balance

Carol's Surf Shop is considering purchasing some new equipment. Compute depreciation as of December 31, 2004 based on the information in the following table.

Cost	$ 500,000
Salvage value	$ 65,000
Useful life	20 years
Depreciation rate	200%

1. Prepare a depreciation schedule that will calculate depreciation for a 20-year period. The schedule should show the current depreciation expense, accumulated depreciation and the asset's book value.

2. Create an input section for the cost, salvage value, life and declining balance rate.

3. Use the =DDB function to calculate the depreciation.

4. Set up the page so that it prints on one page. Insert appropriate header information.

5. Save the file as Exercise 10-1.

6. Print the document.

Exercise 10-2: Test and Analyze Data

1. To test your data, compute the depreciation for the following asset.

Cost	$ 695,000
Salvage value	$ 150,000
Useful life	15 years
Depreciation rate	150%

2. Save the file as Exercise 10-2 test.

3. Print the file.

4. Using the data from the Exercise 10-1 file, determine how much the salvage value should be in order to depreciate the asset no more than 8 years.

5. Save your file as Exercise 10-2 analysis.

6. Print the file.

Exercise 10-3: Units-of-Activity

Carol's Surf Shop needs to calculate depreciation for a truck. The truck is expected to be used for 121,000 miles and has a useful life of five years. Actual miles driven for the first four years of the truck's life are as follows.

2001	26,000 miles
2002	28,000 miles
2003	32,000 miles
2004	35,000 miles

The truck's original cost is $82,000, and it is expected to be sold for $4,500 at the end of five years.

1. Using this data, prepare a schedule to calculate depreciation dated December 31, 2004, using the units-of-activity method. The schedule should show the units of activity for each year, the depreciable cost per unit, annual depreciation, accumulated depreciation and book value.

2. Create an input section for the cost, salvage value, and total estimated units.

3. Setup the page so that it prints on one page. Insert appropriate header information.

4. Save the file as Exercise 10-3.

5. Print the file.

Exercise 10-4: Test and Analyze Data

1. Change the actual miles driven to the following:

2001	20,000 miles
2002	30,000 miles
2003	40,000 miles
2004	27,000 miles

2. Save the file as Exercise 10-4 test.

3. Print the file.

4. Carol's Surf Shop wants to reduce its depreciation expense. Carol believes that $0.50 per mile would be more reasonable. Use the Goal Seek tool to determine how many total estimated units should used to make the depreciable cost per unit equal to $.50. (*Hint: Use the Exercise 10-4 test file.*)

5. Save the file as Exercise 10-4 analysis.

6. Print the file.

CHAPTER 10 INDEX

Chapter 11 — Amortization Schedule

SOFTWARE OBJECTIVES: In Chapter 11 you will use the software to:

1. Complete loan amortization schedules.

2. Complete bond amortization schedules.

3. Test your models.

4. Solve what-if scenarios.

5. Save your spreadsheets.

6. Complete the exercises and activities in Chapter 11.

WEB OBJECTIVES: In Chapter 11 you will do these Internet activities.

1. Use your Internet browser to go to the book's website.

2. Complete the Internet Activities.

GETTING STARTED

In this chapter, you will prepare amortization schedules for notes and bonds. You should use the appropriate formula to calculate the minimum payment required for a note. You will also calculate the amount of interest being paid with each payment and calculate the remaining principal balance after each payment is made.

For the bond amortization schedules, you will calculate the bond's selling price and premium or discount.

NOTES PAYABLE

As you know from your study of accounting, **notes payable** are issued to obtain assets such as cash. Usually notes are transacted with a single lender such as a bank.

Mike's Surf and Sea is considering replacing their old delivery van with a new one. The new vehicle will cost $37,000 plus $195 in license and documentation fees. Mike's Surf and Sea still owes $4,000 on the old delivery van, but they expect the dealer to give them a $6,500 trade-in allowance. The current sales tax rate on new vehicles in Hawaii is 4%.

Mike's Surf and Sea will finance the vehicle through the dealer for five years at a rate of 5% per year. Sixty monthly payments will be made.

Instructions:

1.   Prepare an input section with the following data:

Original cost of vehicle		$37,000.00
Trade-in value		6,500.00
Amount to pay off trade-in		4,000.00
License and documentation		195.00
Net cost of new vehicle		**Calculate**
Sales tax	4%	**Calculate**
Loan amount		**Calculate**
Interest rate		5.00%
Term in months		60
Payment		**Calculate**

2.   Use the Excel function =PMT to calculate the payment amount. (*Hint: You must convert the interest rate to a monthly rate since the terms are stated in months.*) Note that the payment appears as a negative number since it will reduce the amount of cash Mike has available.

3. Set up the amortization schedule with the following columns:

Month	Payment	Interest	Principal Reduction	Remaining Principal

4. Enter formulas to calculate the amounts for the first month and copy the formulas down to the sixtieth month. (*Hint: Use absolute references when referencing data from the input section.*)

5. Use Page Setup so that each page prints the row headings shown in step 3 above. (*Hint: Select Page Setup from the File menu then click on the Sheet Tab. In the Rows to Repeat at top field, enter the reference to the rows containing the heading information.*)

6. Be sure to format all numbers in the amortization schedule with two decimals.

7. Set up and print the worksheet. (*Hint: You should not print the whole document on one page.*) The header should include your name, the file name, and today's date.

8. Save the file as Chapter 11-1. Compare your amortization schedule with the one shown on the pages 312 (page 1) and page 313 (page 2).

Mike's Surf and Sea
Loan Amortization Schedule

Original cost of vehicle		37,000.00
Trade-in value		6,500.00
Amount to payoff trade-in		4,000.00
License and documentation		195.00
Net cost of new vehicle		34,695.00
Sales tax	4%	1,387.80
Loan amount		36,082.80
Interest rate		5.00%
Term in months		60
Payment		(680.93)

Month	Payment	Interest	Principal Reduction	Remaining Principal
0				36,082.80
1	680.93	150.35	530.58	35,552.22
2	680.93	148.13	532.79	35,019.43
3	680.93	145.91	535.01	34,484.41
4	680.93	143.69	537.24	33,947.17
5	680.93	141.45	539.48	33,407.69
6	680.93	139.20	541.73	32,865.96
7	680.93	136.94	543.99	32,321.98
8	680.93	134.67	546.25	31,775.72
9	680.93	132.40	548.53	31,227.20
10	680.93	130.11	550.81	30,676.38
11	680.93	127.82	553.11	30,123.27
12	680.93	125.51	555.41	29,567.86
13	680.93	123.20	557.73	29,010.13
14	680.93	120.88	560.05	28,450.08
15	680.93	118.54	562.38	27,887.70
16	680.93	116.20	564.73	27,322.97
17	680.93	113.85	567.08	26,755.89
18	680.93	111.48	569.44	26,186.44
19	680.93	109.11	571.82	25,614.63
20	680.93	106.73	574.20	25,040.43
21	680.93	104.34	576.59	24,463.84
22	680.93	101.93	578.99	23,884.84
23	680.93	99.52	581.41	23,303.43
24	680.93	97.10	583.83	22,719.61
25	680.93	94.67	586.26	22,133.34
26	680.93	92.22	588.70	21,544.64
27	680.93	89.77	591.16	20,953.48
28	680.93	87.31	593.62	20,359.86
29	680.93	84.83	596.09	19,763.77

Student Name		Chapter 11-1.xls		Today's Date

Month	Payment	Interest	Principal Reduction	Remaining Principal
30	680.93	82.35	598.58	19,165.19
31	680.93	79.85	601.07	18,564.12
32	680.93	77.35	603.58	17,960.54
33	680.93	74.84	606.09	17,354.45
34	680.93	72.31	608.62	16,745.83
35	680.93	69.77	611.15	16,134.68
36	680.93	67.23	613.70	15,520.98
37	680.93	64.67	616.26	14,904.72
38	680.93	62.10	618.82	14,285.90
39	680.93	59.52	621.40	13,664.50
40	680.93	56.94	623.99	13,040.51
41	680.93	54.34	626.59	12,413.91
42	680.93	51.72	629.20	11,784.71
43	680.93	49.10	631.82	11,152.89
44	680.93	46.47	634.46	10,518.43
45	680.93	43.83	637.10	9,881.33
46	680.93	41.17	639.75	9,241.58
47	680.93	38.51	642.42	8,599.16
48	680.93	35.83	645.10	7,954.06
49	680.93	33.14	647.79	7,306.27
50	680.93	30.44	650.48	6,655.79
51	680.93	27.73	653.19	6,002.60
52	680.93	25.01	655.92	5,346.68
53	680.93	22.28	658.65	4,688.03
54	680.93	19.53	661.39	4,026.64
55	680.93	16.78	664.15	3,362.49
56	680.93	14.01	666.92	2,695.57
57	680.93	11.23	669.70	2,025.88
58	680.93	8.44	672.49	1,353.39
59	680.93	5.64	675.29	678.10
60	680.93	2.83	678.10	0.00

 Read Me

The test data and what-if analysis spreadsheets will *not* be shown in the textbook. To make sure that your spreadsheets are done correctly, compare your work to the Check Figures shown.

Test Data

1. Change the input information to the following:

Original cost of vehicle	$43,000.00
Trade-in value	7,200.00
Amount to pay off trade-in	3,500.00
License and documentation	195.00
Interest Rate	4.85%

2. Save the file as Chapter 11-1 test. Check Figure: Verify that your Loan Amount shows $41,074.80. Your payment should be $772.31.

What-If Analysis

Mike's Surf and Sea does not want to pay more than $953.00 per month for the new vehicle. Use the Chapter 11-1 test file to complete the what-if analysis.

1. Using the Goal Seek tool, what is the most expensive vehicle Mike's Surf and Sea can purchase? Print and save the file as Chapter 11-1 analysis a. (*Hint: When using Goal Seek, change the payment To value -953, then point to the original cost of the vehicle.*)

   Check Figure: The loan amount is $50,684.51 with a payment of $953.00 per month.

2. Follow these steps to determine what the terms in months would be if the interest rate changed to 5.3%.

   a. Open the Chapter 11-1 test file.
   b. Type **5.3** as the Interest Rate.
   c. Make D16 the active cell.
   d. Use the Goal Seek tool to determine the terms. The To value field should be -953; then change the cell with the terms (By changing cell).
   e. Print and save the file as Chapter 11-1 analysis b.
   f. Check Figure: The term in months is 48.

BONDS PAYABLE

Bonds Payable is the liability account used to identify a company's bonds. A ***bond*** is its issuer's written promise to pay an amount identified as the face value (also known as par value) of the bond along with interest.

Mike's Surf and Sea is considering selling bonds to raise additional cash. Mike's Surf and Sea uses the straight line method to amortize the bond's premium or discount. Use Excel's functions to prepare an amortization schedule for the sale of bonds.

1. Set up an input section with the following information:

Face Value	$100,000.00
Stated Interest Rate	6.00%
Market Interest Rate	4.00%
Term (in years)	20
Bond Selling Price	**Calculate**
Premium/(Discount)	**Calculate**

2. Use Excel's =PV function to calculate the bond selling price. (*Hint: The rate should be the market interest rate. The PMT is the face value times the stated interest rate. The FV is the face value of the bond.*) If done correctly, the bond selling price should be $127,180.65. Make the bond selling price a positive number by putting a minus sign (-) in front of the formula.

3. Calculate the premium/(discount) by subtracting the face value from the bond selling price. A premium will be recorded if the bond's selling price is higher than the bond's face value. On the other hand, if the selling price is less than the face value, a discount will be recorded.

4. Prepare the amortization portion with the following column headers:

Period	Payment	Interest	Amortization	Unamortized Premium (Discount)	Carrying Value

5. Begin the schedule with period zero. This period should only have data in the Unamortized Premium (Discount) column and the Carrying Value column.

6. In period one, enter the formula to calculate the Payment. Use a conditional formula so that the payment will be zero if the carrying value in the pervious period is not equal to (<>) the face value. (*Hint: Use absolute references when referring to the data in the input section.*)

7. Enter a conditional formula to calculate the interest in period 1 if the payment is greater than zero (>0). (*Hint: Use absolute references when referring to the data in the input section.*)

8. Enter a conditional formula to calculate the amortization if the payment is greater than zero (>0).). In other words, if the payment is equal to zero, then enter a zero, else calculate the interest. (*Hint: Use absolute references when referring to the data in the input section.*)

9. The unamortized premium (discount) should be the previous unamortized premium (discount) minus the current amortization.

10. The carrying value is the face value plus the current unamortized premium (discount).

11. Copy the formulas from period one down to period 20. If the formulas are correct, the carrying value should be equal to the face value at maturity (period 20).

12. Set up the header to include your name, the file name, and today's date. Print the document.

13. Save your spreadsheet as Chapter 11-2.

Student Name   Chapter 11-2.xls   Today's Date

Mike's Surf and Sea
Bond Amortization Schedule

Face Value	$ 100,000.00
Stated Interest Rate	6.00%
Market Interest Rate	4.00%
Term	20
Bond Selling Price	$ 127,180.65
Premium/(Discount)	$ 27,180.65

Period	Payment	Interest	Amortization	Unamortized Premium (Discount)	Carrying Value
0				27,180.65	127,180.65
1	6,000.00	4,640.97	1,359.03	25,821.62	125,821.62
2	6,000.00	4,640.97	1,359.03	24,462.59	124,462.59
3	6,000.00	4,640.97	1,359.03	23,103.55	123,103.55
4	6,000.00	4,640.97	1,359.03	21,744.52	121,744.52
5	6,000.00	4,640.97	1,359.03	20,385.49	120,385.49
6	6,000.00	4,640.97	1,359.03	19,026.46	119,026.46
7	6,000.00	4,640.97	1,359.03	17,667.42	117,667.42
8	6,000.00	4,640.97	1,359.03	16,308.39	116,308.39
9	6,000.00	4,640.97	1,359.03	14,949.36	114,949.36
10	6,000.00	4,640.97	1,359.03	13,590.33	113,590.33
11	6,000.00	4,640.97	1,359.03	12,231.29	112,231.29
12	6,000.00	4,640.97	1,359.03	10,872.26	110,872.26
13	6,000.00	4,640.97	1,359.03	9,513.23	109,513.23
14	6,000.00	4,640.97	1,359.03	8,154.20	108,154.20
15	6,000.00	4,640.97	1,359.03	6,795.16	106,795.16
16	6,000.00	4,640.97	1,359.03	5,436.13	105,436.13
17	6,000.00	4,640.97	1,359.03	4,077.10	104,077.10
18	6,000.00	4,640.97	1,359.03	2,718.07	102,718.07
19	6,000.00	4,640.97	1,359.03	1,359.03	101,359.03
20	6,000.00	4,640.97	1,359.03	-	100,000.00

Test Data

1.   Test your spreadsheet by changing the input data to the following:

Face Value	$175,000.00
Stated Interest Rate	4.00%
Market Interest Rate	5.80%
Terms	15
Bond Selling Price	$144,002.62
Premium/(Discount)	$(30,997.38)

2.   Compare your bond selling price and premium/(discount) to the one shown above. If all of your formulas are correct, the carrying value should be equal to the face value in period 15.

3.   Print your document.

4.   Save the file as Chapter 11-2 test.

What-If Analysis

1.   Using the data from the Chapter 11-2 test file, determine what the stated interest rate should be if the bonds sell for $190,000.

     Check Figure: The stated interest rate will be 6.67% if the bonds sell for $190,000.

2.   Print the document.

3.   Save the file as Chapter 11-2 analysis.

INTERNET ACTIVITIES
1. From the textbook's website at www.mhhe.com/yachtexcel, go to the Student link. Then, link to Internet Activities, WEB EXERCISES, PART 3-Chapter 11.
2. Access this website http://officeupdate.microsoft.com/templategallery/.
3. From the template gallery, download a template of interest to you. (Hint: Try the Finance and Accounting; Personal Finance links. There is a bond amortization template and loan calculators.)
4. Go to this website http://1000bestlenders.com/bestlenders.html. Link to Auto Loan, Refinance or Lease; then link to the calculator for How much will your monthly payments be? Complete a two loan payment scenarios of your design. Print both reports.

SUMMARY AND REVIEW

SOFWARE OBJECTIVES: In Chapter 11, you used to software to:

1.   Complete loan amortization schedules.

2.   Complete bond amortization schedules.

3.   Test your models.

4. Solve what-if scenarios.

5. Save your spreadsheets.

6. Complete the exercises and activities in Chapter 11.

WEB OBJECTIVES: In Chapter 11, you did these Internet activities:

1. Used your Internet browser to go to the book's website.

2. Completed the Internet Activities.

Multiple-Choice Questions: In the space provided, write the letter that best answers each question.

_____1. In order to obtain assets such as cash without giving up voting rights, a corporation will issue the following:

    a. Bonds payable.
    b. Common Stock.
    c. Accounts payable.
    d. Warranty payable.
    e. None of the above.

_____2. On the Chapter 11-1.xls file, the payment on the delivery van is:

    a. $680.93.
    b. $953.00.
    c. $1,053.90.
    d. $891.35.
    e. None of the above.

_____3. On the loan amortization schedules, the sales tax in Hawaii is:

    a. 8%.
    b. 7%.
    c. 5%.
    d. 4%.
    e. None of the above.

_____4. On the Chapter 11-1 test.xls file, the amount to pay off trade in is:

    a. $4,000.
    b. $3,500.
    c. $7,200.
    d. $2,155.80.
    e. None of the above.

_____5. On the Chapter 11-1 test.xls file, the original cost of the vehicle is:

    a. $37,000.
    b. $40,000.
    c. $43,000.
    d. $45,000.
    e. None of the above.

_____6. On the Chapter 11-1.analysis b file, the interest rate is:

    a. 4.00%.
    b. 5.00%.
    c. 5.30%
    d. 5.75%
    e. None of the above.

_____7. On the Chapter 11-2.xls file, the stated interest rate is:

    a. 4%
    b. 5%.
    c. 6%.
    d. 7%
    e. None of the above.

_____8. On the Chapter 11-2.xls file, the premium/discount is:

    a. ($30,997.38).
    b. $27,180.65.
    c. $15,000.00.
    d. $26,170.65.
    e. None of the above.

_____9. On the Chapter 11-2 test.xls file, the face value of the bonds is:

    a. $175,000.00.
    b. $144,002.62.
    c. $100,000.00.
    d. $190,000.00.
    e. None of the above.

_____10. On the Chapter 11-2 analysis.xls file, the stated interest rate is:

    a. $6.00%.
    b. $4.00%
    c. $5.80%.
    d. $6.67%.
    e. None of the above.

True/Make True: If the statement is true, write the word "True" in the space provided. If the statement is *not* true, write the correct answer in the space provided.

11. In Chapter 11 you prepare amortization schedules for notes and bonds.

_____

_____

12. For the bond amortization schedule, you calculate the bond's selling price and premium or discount.

_____

_____

13. A company's notes may be transacted with a single lender such as a bank.

_____

_____

14. The terms of the car loan are 6 years or 72 months. (Refer to Chapter 11 loan amortization schedules.)

_____

_____

15. On the Chapter 11-1 test file, the terms are 4.85%.

_____

_____

16. The face value of a bond is also known as the par value.

_____

_____

17. A company considers selling bonds to raise additional cash.

_____

_____

18. Use Excel =PMT function to calculate the bond selling price.

_____

_____

19. To calculate the premium/(discount), subtract the face value from the bond selling price.

_____

_____

20. On the bond amortization schedules, the carrying value is the face value plus the current unamortized premium/(discount).

_____

_____

Exercise 11-1: Loan Amortization Schedule

Carol's Surf Shop is considering replacing its delivery van. The new vehicle will cost $42,500 plus $215 in license and documentation fees. Carol's Surf Shop still owes $5,000 on the old delivery van, but it expects the dealer to give it a $4,000 trade-in allowance. The current sales tax rate on new vehicles is 4%.

Carol's Surf Shop plans to finance the vehicle through the dealer for six years at a rate of 6% per year.

Instructions:

1. Prepare an input section with the following data:

Original cost of vehicle		$42,500.00
Trade-in value		5,000.00
Amount to pay off trade-in		4,000.00
License and documentation		215.00
Net cost of new vehicle		**Calculate**
Sales tax	4%	**Calculate**
Loan amount		**Calculate**
Interest rate		6.00%
Term in months		72
Payment		**Calculate**

2. Set up the loan amortization schedule similarly to the one completed in the chapter.

3. Enter formulas to calculate the amounts for the first month and copy the formulas down to the seventy-second month.

4. Set up each page so that the row heading prints on each page.

5. Insert appropriate header information. Format and print the two-page worksheet.

6. Save the file as Exercise 11-1.

Exercise 11-2: Test and Analyze Data

1. Using the Exercise 11-1 file, change the input information to the following:

Original cost of vehicle	$40,000.00
Trade-in value	5,000.00
Amount to pay off trade-in	4,500.00
License and documentation	215.00
Interest rate	5.75%

2.   Save the file as Exercise 11-2 test.

Analysis

Carol's Surf Shop does not want to pay more than $725 per month for the new vehicle. Use the Exercise 11-2 test file for *both* analysis a. and b.

1.   Using the Goal Seek tool, what is the most expensive vehicle Carol's Surf Shop can purchase? (*Hint: Change the payment to -725.*)

2.   Save the file as Exercise 11-2 analysis a, then print it.

3.   Using the information from the Exercise 11-2 test file, change the interest rate to 4.25%, then determine what the term in months should be to keep the payment at $725 per month.

4.   Save the file as Exercise 11-2 analysis b, then print it.

Exercise 11-3: Bond Amortization Schedule

Carol's Surf Shop is considering selling bonds to raise additional cash. Use Excel's functions to prepare an amortization schedule for the sale of bonds.

1.   Set up an input section with the following information:

Face Value	$100,000.00
Stated Interest Rate	7.00%
Market Interest Rate	5.00%
Term (in years)	20
Bond Selling Price	**Calculate**
Premium/(Discount)	**Calculate**

2.   Prepare the amortization schedule with the same column headings as the chapter activity.

3.   Refer to the steps on pages 315-317 for setting up your bond amortization schedule.

4. Insert appropriate header information. Save your spreadsheet as Exercise 11-3.

5. Print the document.

Exercise 11-4: Test and Analyze Data

1. Test your spreadsheet by changing the input data to the following:

Face Value	$195,000.00
Stated Interest Rate	5.50%
Market Interest Rate	7.25%
Term (in years)	15

2. Save the file as Exercise 11-4 test.

3. Print your document.

4. Using the data from the Exercise 11-4 test file, determine what the stated interest rate would be if the bonds sold for $205,000.

5. Save the file as Exercise 11-4 analysis.

6. Print the document.

CHAPTER 11 INDEX

Chapter 12

Cost of Goods Manufactured

SOFTWARE OBJECTIVES: In Chapter 12 you will use the software to:

1. Complete a cost of goods manufactured schedule.

2. Complete a multi-step income statement from the input data and cost of goods manufactured schedule worksheets.

3. Test your models.

4. Solve what-if scenarios.

5. Save your spreadsheets.

6. Complete the exercises and activities in Chapter 12.

WEB OBJECTIVES: In Chapter 12 you will do these Internet activities.

1. Use your Internet browser to go to the book's website.

2. Complete the Internet Activities.

GETTING STARTED

In this chapter, you will prepare a cost of goods manufactured schedule. The cost of goods manufactured schedule will contain two sheets linked together. You will also use the cost of goods manufactured schedule to prepare a multi-step income statement.

COST OF GOODS MANUFACTURED SCHEDULE

In this section, you will prepare a cost of goods manufactured schedule. Your workbook should contain two sheets. One sheet will be for your input data and the other will be the actual cost of goods manufactured schedule linked to the input data.

1. Rename Sheet1 of the spreadsheet to "Input."

2. Enter the data from the following table into the "Input" sheet.

Raw materials, 1/1/03	15,000
Raw materials, 12/31/03	22,000
Raw materials purchased	175,000
Indirect materials	16,000
Work in process, 1/1/03	19,000
Work in process, 12/31/03	18,000
Direct labor	180,000
Indirect labor	25,000
Factory repairs	10,000
Factory utilities	12,000
Factory maintenance	16,000
Factory depreciation	6,000
Factory insurance	11,000

3. Rename Sheet2 as "COGM."

4. Create a cost of goods manufactured schedule, referencing the cells on the input sheet as needed. Refer to the worksheet on page 331 for setting up the schedule. Use formatting techniques such as indents, borders, and font formatting to make your schedule easy to read.

5. Link the data from the input sheet to the COGM sheet to create a cost of goods manufactured schedule. (*Hint: Once you have linked all of your data to Sheet 2, you can easily move data by holding down the Shift key while dragging the border of the selected range. Another option is to cut the data, place the active cell where you want the data inserted, and then select "Insert Cut Cells" from the shortcut menu.*)

6. Set up a header on the COGM sheet that includes your name, the file name, and today's date. Save the file as Chapter 12-1.

7. Print the COGM Sheet.

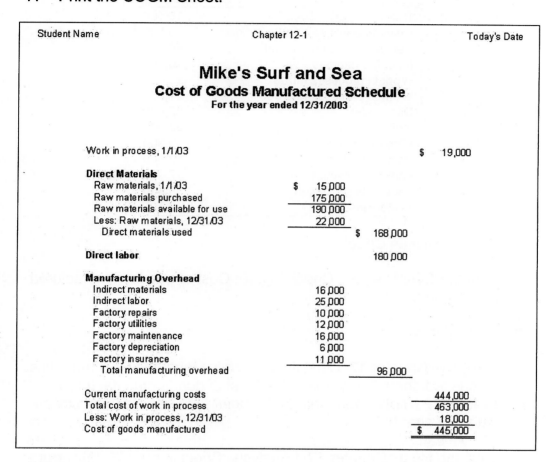

Mike's Surf and Sea
Cost of Goods Manufactured Schedule
For the year ended 12/31/2003

Work in process, 1/1/03			$ 19,000
Direct Materials			
Raw materials, 1/1/03	$ 15,000		
Raw materials purchased	175,000		
Raw materials available for use	190,000		
Less: Raw materials, 12/31/03	22,000		
Direct materials used		$ 168,000	
Direct labor		180,000	
Manufacturing Overhead			
Indirect materials	16,000		
Indirect labor	25,000		
Factory repairs	10,000		
Factory utilities	12,000		
Factory maintenance	16,000		
Factory depreciation	6,000		
Factory insurance	11,000		
Total manufacturing overhead		96,000	
Current manufacturing costs			444,000
Total cost of work in process			463,000
Less: Work in process, 12/31/03			18,000
Cost of goods manufactured			$ 445,000

Read Me

The test data and what-if analysis worksheets will *not* be shown in the textbook. Verify your worksheets by making sure your amounts agree with the Check Figures.

Test Data

1. Enter data from the following table into the Input sheet.

Raw materials, 1/1/03	16,500
Raw materials,12/31/03	20,500
Raw materials purchased	180,000
Indirect materials	15,000
Work in process, 1/1/03	23,000
Work in process, 12/31/03	21,500
Direct labor	165,000
Indirect labor	30,000
Factory repairs	9,000
Factory utilities	13,500
Factory maintenance	17,000
Factory depreciation	8,000
Factory insurance	9,500

2. Save the file as Chapter 12-1 test.

3. Print the COGM sheet. Check Figure: Cost of goods manufactured is $444,500.

What-if Analysis

1. Using the Chapter 12-1 test file, determine what the Raw materials purchased should be to make the Cost of goods manufactured $445,000. (*Hint: Using Goal Seek, point to the appropriate cell on the Input sheet.*)

2. Save the file as Chapter 12-1 analysis. Check Figure: Total current manufacturing costs are $443,500.

3. Print the COGM sheet.

INCOME STATEMENT

In this section, you will use the Chapter 12-1 test file to prepare a multi-step income statement for the year.

1. Open the Chapter 12-1 test file.

2. Enter the data from the following table into the Input sheet.

Sales	950,000
Finished goods, 1/1/03	115,000
Finished goods,12/31/03	130,000
Selling expenses	150,000
Administrative expenses	250,000

3. Rename Sheet3 to "Income Stmt."

4. Prepare a multi-step income statement in the Income Stmt sheet by linking the data from the Input sheet and the COGM sheet.

5. Set up a header on the Income Stmt sheet that includes your name, the file name, and today's date. Save the file as Chapter 12-2.

6. Print the Income Stmt sheet.

Student Name	Chapter 12-2	Today's Date

Mike's Surf and Sea
Income Statement
For the year ended 12/31/2003

Sales		950,000
Cost of Goods Sold		
Finished goods, 1/1/03	115,000	
Cost of goods manufactured	444,500	
Cost of goods available for sale	559,500	
Less: Finished goods, 12/31/03	130,000	
Cost of goods sold		429,500
Gross Profit		520,500
Operating expenses		
Selling expenses	150,000	
Administrative expenses	250,000	
Total operating expenses		400,000
Net income		120,500

Test Data

1. Change the data in the input section to the following:

Raw materials, 1/1/03	17,000
Raw materials,12/31/03	21,000
Sales	800,000
Finished goods, 1/1/03	120,000
Finished goods,12/31/03	110,000
Selling expenses	130,000
Administrative expenses	90,000

2. Save the file as Chapter 12-2 test.

3. Print the Income Stmt sheet. Check Figure: Net income is $125,500.

What-If Analysis

1. Open the Chapter 12-2 test file.

2. Using the Goal Seek tool, determine what the sales should be in order to break even. (*Hint: Using Goal Seek, point to the appropriate cell on the Input sheet.*)

3. Save the file as Chapter 12-2 analysis.

4. Print the Input and Income Stmt sheets. Check Figure: Both the Gross profit and Total operating expenses are $220,000, which means the Net income is $0.00.

	INTERNET ACTIVITIES
1.	From the book's website at www.mhhe.com/yachtexcel, go the Student link. Then, link to Internet Activities, WEB EXERCISES, PART 3-Chapter 12.
2.	Access this website http://officeupdate.microsoft.com/templategallery/.
3.	From the template gallery, download a template of interest to you.
4.	Go to this website http://pacioli.loyola.edu/aecm/. Define the acronym, AECM, and describe the list. How do you subscribe to AECM? Explore this site. Write a brief summary of what you find. Include the URL(s).

SUMMARY AND REVIEW

SOFWARE OBJECTIVES: In Chapter 12, you used to software to:

1. Complete a cost of goods manufactured schedule.

2. Complete a multi-step income statement from the input data and cost of goods manufactured schedule worksheets.

3. Test your models.

4. Solve what-if scenarios.

5. Save your spreadsheets.

6. Complete the exercises and activities in Chapter 12.

WEB OBJECTIVES: In Chapter 12, you did these Internet activities:

1. Used your Internet browser to go the book's website.

2. Completed the Internet Activities.

Multiple Choice Questions: In the space provided, write the letter that best answers each question.

_____1. On the Chapter 12-1 worksheet, the raw materials purchased for the year ended 12/31/2003 are:

   a. $190,000.
   b. $175,000.
   c. $180,000.
   d. $180,500.
   e. None of the above.

_____2. On the Chapter 12-1 worksheet, the total manufacturing overhead is:

    a. $22,000.
    b. $15,000.
    c. $168,000.
    d. $96,000.
    e.   None of the above.

_____3. The Chapter 12-1 test worksheet includes raw materials as of 1/1/03 of:

    a. $9,500.
    b. $20,500.
    c. $16,500.
    d. $175,000.
    e.   None of the above.

_____4. The Chapter 12-1 test worksheet includes current manufacturing costs of:

    a. $444,500.
    b. $443,000.
    c. $102,000.
    d. $21,500.
    e. None of the above

_____5. The Chapter 12-1 analysis worksheet includes total cost of work in process of:

    a. $466,500.
    b. $445,000.
    c. $102,000.
    d. $165,000.
    e.   None of the above.

_____6. On the Chapter 12-2 Income Stmt worksheet, the net income is:

    a. $120,500.
    b. $0.
    c. $125,500.
    d. $90,000.
    e. None of the above

_____7. On the Chapter 12-2 test Income Stmt worksheet, the sales are:

    a. $674,500.
    b. $800,000.
    c. $454,500.
    d. $220,000.
    e. None of the above.

_____8. On the Chapter 12-2 analysis.xls worksheet, the gross profit is:

    a. $345,500.
    b. $125,500.
    c. $220,000.
    d. $454,500.
    e. None of the above.

_____9. The Income Stmt worksheet indicates the break even point, when gross profit and total operating expenses are:

    a. Within $10,000 of each other.
    b. The same amount.
    c. $220,000 and $345,500, respectively.
    d. All of the above.
    e. None of the above.

_____10. The acronym AECM is an abbreviation for:

    a. Accounting Education using Computers & Multimedia.
    b. Accountants in education who use the Internet to teach introductory accounting.
    c. Listserv@listserve.loyola.edu.
    d. Loyola College in Maryland.
    e. None of the above.

True/Make True: If the statement is true, write the word "True" in the space provided. If the statement is *not* true, write the correct answer in the space provided.

11. You link input data to the COGM sheet to produce a cost of goods manufactured schedule.

12. When you compare the Chapter 12-1 test and Chapter 12-1 analysis worksheets to the Chapter 12-1 worksheet, there is a $500 difference in the cost of goods manufactured.

13. The raw materials purchased on the Chapter 12-1 analysis worksheet is $180,000.

14. The raw materials available for use on Chapter 12-1 worksheet is $196,500.

_____

_____

15. On the Chapter 12-1 test and analysis worksheets, the total cost of work in process is $463,000.

_____

_____

16. The sales amount is the same on the two additional spreadsheets that are done based on the Chapter 12-2 worksheet.

_____

_____

17. There is a $5,000 difference in net income between the Chapter 12-2 worksheet and the Chapter 12-2 test worksheet.

_____

_____

18. Net income is $0.00 on the Chapter 12-2 analysis worksheet.

_____

_____

19. Use the Goal Seek tool to determine what the sales should be in order to break even.

_____

_____

20. The net income on the Chapter 12-2 test worksheet is $220,000.

_____

_____

Exercise 12-1: Cost of Goods Manufactured Schedule

1. Prepare a cost of goods manufactured schedule for Carol's Surf Shop for the year ended 12/31/2004. Your workbook should contain two sheets linked together.

2. Type **Input** for the Sheet1 name.

3. Use the following information for the input data.

Raw materials, 1/1/04	15,000
Raw materials,12/31/04	22,000
Raw materials purchased	175,000
Indirect materials	16,000
Work in process, 1/1/04	19,000
Work in process, 12/31/04	18,000
Direct labor	180,000
Indirect labor	25,000
Factory repairs	10,000
Factory utilities	12,000
Factory maintenance	16,000
Factory depreciation	6,000
Factory insurance	11,000

4. Type **COGM** for the Sheet2 name.

5. Create a cost of goods manufactured schedule, linking the data from the Input sheet to the COGM sheet.

6. Format the sheets similarly to the ones completed in the chapter.

7. Save the file as Exercise 12-1.

8. Print the COGM Sheet. Check Figure: The Cost of goods manufactured for the year ended 12/31/2004 is $445,000.

Exercise 12-2: Test and Analyze Data

1. Enter data from the following table into the Input sheet.

Raw materials, 1/1/04	15,300
Raw materials,12/31/04	19,500
Raw materials purchased	195,000
Indirect materials	14,400
Work in process, 1/1/04	20,000
Work in process, 12/31/04	22,000
Direct labor	175,000
Indirect labor	28,000
Factory repairs	9,500
Factory utilities	14,000
Factory maintenance	15,500
Factory depreciation	7,500
Factory insurance	13,000

2. Save the file as Exercise 12-2 test.

3. Print the COGM sheet.

4. Using the Exercise 12-2 test file, determine what the Raw materials purchased should be to make the Cost of goods manufactured $457,500. (*Hint: You must change the data on the Input sheet.*)

5. Save the file as Exercise 12-2 analysis.

6. Print the COGM sheet.

Exercise 12-3: Income Statement

In this section, you will use the Chapter 12-2 test file to prepare a multi-step income statement for the year.

1. Use the Exercise 12-2 test file to prepare a multi-step income statement for the year ended 2004.

2. Enter the data from the following table into the Input sheet.

Sales	880,000
Finished goods, 1/1/04	105,000
Finished goods, 12/31/04	120,000
Selling expenses	160,000
Administrative expenses	225,000

3. Type **Income Stmt** for the Sheet3 name.

4. Prepare a multi-step income statement on the Income Stmt sheet by linking the data from the Input sheet and the COGM sheet.

5. Save the file as Exercise 12-3. Check Figure: Cost of goods manufactured is $465,700.

6. Print the Income Stmt sheet.

Exercise 12-4: Test and Analyze Data

1. Change the data in the input section to the following:

Raw materials, 1/1/04	16,600
Raw materials, 12/31/04	20,300
Sales	725,000
Finished goods, 1/1/04	102,000
Finished goods, 12/31/04	98,000
Selling expenses	120,000
Administrative expenses	95,000

2. Save the file as Exercise 12-4 test.

3. Print the Income Stmt sheet. Check Figure: Net income is $39,800.

4. Open the Exercise 12-4 test file.

5. Using the Goal Seek tool, determine what the sales should be in order to break even.

6. Save the file as Exercise 12-4 analysis.

7. Print the Input and Income Stmt sheets. Check Figure: Both the Gross profit and Total operating expenses are $215,000, which means the Net income is $0.00.

CHAPTER 12 INDEX

Chapter 13
Job Order Cost Accounting

SOFTWARE OBJECTIVES: In Chapter 13 you will use the software to:

1.   Complete a job cost sheet.

2.   Complete a projected manufacturing cost worksheet.

3.   Test your models.

4.   Solve what-if scenarios.

5.   Save your spreadsheets.

6.   Complete the exercises and activities in Chapter 13.

WEB OBJECTIVES: In Chapter 13 you will do these Internet activities.

1.   Use your Internet browser, to go to the book's website.

2.   Complete the Internet Activities.

GETTING STARTED

In this chapter, you will prepare a job cost sheet and complete job order cost projections.

As you know from your study of accounting, a cost accounting system designed to accumulate costs by jobs is *a job-order cost system*. Mike's Surf and Sea manufactures surfboards. In this chapter, you will track the costs to manufacture this product.

JOB COST SHEET

In a job order cost system, product costs are accumulated on a **job cost sheet**. This is also known as a job order cost sheet or a job record. A separate job cost sheet is prepared for each job. As the job moves through the various stages of production, detailed information regarding the cost of materials, labor, and overhead is added to the job cost sheet.

In this section, you will prepare a spreadsheet to track the cost of surfboards for each customer. Mike's Surf and Sea has just completed job number 613 for Hot Hawaiian Stix. The order for 10 modern long boards (MLB) was received on May 21, 2003 and completed on May 29, 2003. Manufacturing overhead is applied at a rate of 80% of direct labor costs.

1. Prepare a job cost sheet using the data in the following table.

Date	Direct Materials	Direct Labor
5/21/03	$75 each	$25 each
5/23/03	$50 each	$7 each
5/27/03	$10 each	
5/29/03		$40 each

Note: Labor is normally accumulated by the hour. However, in the surfboard industry, shapers, sanders and glassers are paid on a piece-rate (per surfboard) basis.

2. Set up an input section with cells for the following items:
    - Job number
    - Customer's name
    - Quantity
    - Item description
    - Date requested
    - Date completed

3. Track job costs by using separate columns for the Date, Direct Materials, Direct Labor, and Manufacturing Overhead.

4. Make sure the spreadsheet includes totals for Direct Materials, Direct Labor, and Manufacturing Overhead. You should also have a running total for the Total Cost as well as Unit Costs.

5. Set up a header that includes your name, the file name, and today's date. Save your file as Chapter 13-1.

6. Print the worksheet.

Student Name	Chapter 13-1	Today's Date

Mike's Surf and Sea
Job Order Cost Sheet

Job Number	613
Customer name	Hot Hawaiian Stix
Item description	MLB
Quantity	10
Date requested	05/21/03
Date completed	05/29/03

Date	Direct Materials	Direct Labor	Manufacturing Overhead
5/21/03	750	250	200
5/23/03	500	70	56
5/27/03	100		-
5/29/03		400	320
	1,350	720	576

Cost of completed job

Direct Materials	1,350
Direct Labor	720
Manufacturing Overhead	576
Total Cost	2,646
Unit Cost	264.60

 Read Me

The test data and what-if analysis spreadsheets will *not* be shown in the textbook. Verify your worksheets by making sure your amounts agree with the Check Figures.

Test Data

On June 2, 2003, Mike's Surf and Sea received job order number 617 for 20 short boards from Ocean Motion. The job is not yet complete.

1. Using the Chapter 13-1 file, input the above data into the appropriate cells.

2. Enter the data from the following table.

Date	Direct Materials	Direct Labor
5/21/03	$50 each	$20 each
5/23/03	$25 each	$5 each
5/29/03		$15 each

3. Save the file as Chapter 13-1 test.

4. Print the worksheet. Check Figure: Total Cost should be $2,940.

What-If Analysis

When analyzing the job cost sheet, the accountant for Mike's Surf and Sea believes that too much overhead is being assigned because the adjusting journal entry for the over applied manufacturing overhead has been much too large. The predetermined overhead rate needs to be adjusted to assign less overhead to short boards.

1. Open the Chapter 13-1 test file.

2. Add a row for the overhead rate in the input section.

3. Adjust the formulas in the Manufacturing Overhead column to reference the overhead percentage.

4. Using Excel's Goal Seek tool, determine what the overhead rate should be to make the unit costs $143.

5. Save the file as Chapter 13-1 analysis.

6.   Print the worksheet. Check Figure: Total Cost should be $2,860.

JOB ORDER COST PROJECTIONS

In this section, you will prepare a schedule to calculate the manufacturing costs of Mike's Surf and Sea's surfboard factory. The factory consists of three departments: Shaping, Glassing and Sanding.

The shapers use a foam blank that costs about $100 each, are paid $25 an hour and spend about an hour on each surfboard. The glassing department spends $10 in fiberglass and resin on each surfboard. The glassers are paid $15 an hour and spend about half an hour on each surfboard. Sanders use several sheets of sandpaper and polish (indirect materials) to finish the surfboards and are paid $10 an hour and spend about fifteen minutes on each surfboard. During the month of May, Mike's Surf and Sea is expected to produce 1,500 surfboards. Manufacturing overhead is applied at a rate of 70% of direct labor costs.

1.   Using the data above, prepare a schedule to calculate the projected manufacturing costs for Mike's Surf and Sea's factory.

2.   Set up an input section for the estimated production and the overhead rate.

3.   Gather the costs in columns for Direct Materials (multiply expected production times 100 for shaping; multiply expected production times 10 for glassing), Direct Labor (Rate, Hours, and Total) and Overhead (multiply overhead rate by the total direct labor costs).

4.   Calculate Total Costs as well as Unit Costs.

5.   Set up a header that includes your name, the file name, and today's date. Save the file as Chapter 13-2.

6.   Print the worksheet.

Student Name   Chapter 13-2   Today's Date

Mike's Surf and Sea
Projected Manufacturing Cost
For the month ended 5/31/03

Expected production   1,500
Overhead rate   70%

Department	Direct Materials	Rate	Direct Labor Hours	Total	Overhead
Shaping	150,000	25.00	1,500	37,500	26,250
Glassing	15,000	15.00	750	11,250	7,875
Sanding		10.00	375	3,750	2,625
	165,000			52,500	36,750

Direct Materials   165,000
Direct Labor   52,500
Manfacturing Overhead   36,750
Total Costs   254,250

Unit Costs $ 169.50

Test Data

1. Open the file Chapter 13-2.

2. Change the estimated production to 1,300.

3. Change the overhead rate to 68%.

4. Save the file as Chapter 13-2 test.

5. Print the worksheet. Check Figure: Total Costs $ 219,440.

What-if Analysis

Mike's Surf and Sea wants the unit costs to be no greater than $165.00.

1. Use the Chapter 13-2 test file.

2. Use the Goal Seek tool to determine how much the Shapers should be paid to make the unit costs equal to $165.00.

3. Save the file as Chapter 13-2 analysis.

4. Print the worksheet. Check Figure: Total Costs $214,500.

INTERNET ACTIVITIES	
1.	From the book's website www.mhhe.com/yachtexcel, link to Internet Activities, then WEB EXERCISES, PART 3-Chapter 13.
2.	Access this website http://office.microsoft.com/home/office.aspx?assetid=FX010380471033&CTT=98
3.	In the Excel section, take the quiz: Are you an Excel whiz?
4.	Go to the Salary Calculator website at http://www.homefair.com/homefair/cmr/salcalc.html. Read the directions on "The Salary Calculator" page. Compare salaries in two states and two cities. Write up your results, identifying the salary comparisons. Include the appropriate website addresses in your answer.
5.	Go back to "The Salary Calculator" website. Explore three other links. Write a summary of what you have found (minimum length 50 words; maximum length 75 words). Include the appropriate website addresses.

SUMMARY AND REVIEW

SOFWARE OBJECTIVES: In Chapter 13, you used to software to:

1. Complete a job cost sheet.

2. Complete a projected manufacturing cost worksheet.

3. Test your models.

4. Solve what-if scenarios.

5. Save your spreadsheets.

6. Complete the exercises and activities in Chapter 13.

WEB OBJECTIVES: In Chapter 13, you did these Internet activities:

1.   Used your Internet browser to go to the book's website.

2.   Completed the Internet Activities.

Multiple-Choice Questions: In the space provided, write the letter that best answers each question.

_____1.   A cost accounting system designed to accumulate costs by individual products is called a/an:

    a. Production cost system.
    b. Accumulated job ledger.
    c. Inventory record.
    d. Job order cost system.
    e. None of the above.

_____2.   Production costs are accumulated on the following worksheet:

    a. Job cost sheet.
    b. Job record.
    c. Job order cost sheet.
    d. All of the above.
    e. None of the above.

_____3.   On the Chapter 13-1 worksheet, the total costs are:

    a. $264.60.
    b. $2,646.00.
    c. $576.00.
    d. $1,350.00.
    e. None of the above.

_____4. On the Chapter 13-1 worksheet, the total manufacturing overhead is:

    a. $576.
    b. $1,350.
    c. $720.
    d. $250.
    e. None of the above.

_____5. The Chapter 13-1 test worksheet includes total direct materials of:

    a. $650.
    b. $800.
    c. $2,940.
    d. $1,500.
    e. None of the above.

_____6. The Chapter 13-1 test worksheet includes total direct labor of:

    a. $300.
    b. $800.
    c. $2,940.
    d. $400.
    e. None of the above.

_____7. The Chapter 13-1 analysis worksheet includes an overhead rate of?

    a. 40%.
    b. 50%.
    c. 60%.
    d. 70%.
    e. None of the above.

_____8. The Chapter 13-1 analysis worksheet includes a unit cost of:

    a. $147.00.
    b. $143.00.
    c. $1,500.00.
    d. $264.60.
    e. None of the above.

_____9. On the Chapter 13-2 worksheet, the expected production is:

    a. 1,500.
    b. 1,300.
    c. 70%.
    d. 68%.
    e. None of the above.

_____10. On the Chapter 13-2 test worksheet, the unit costs are:

    a. $165.00.
    b. $168.80.
    c. $325.00.
    d. $650.00.
    e. None of the above.

True/Make True: If the statement is true, write the word "True" in the space provided. If the statement is *not* true, write the correct answer in the space provided.

11. In Chapter 13, you track the costs to manufacture surfboards.

_____

_____

12. A separate job cost sheet is prepared for each job.

_____

_____

13. As each job moves through the various stages of production, detailed information regarding the cost of materials, labor, and overhead is added to the job cost sheet.

_____

_____

14. Job number 613 is for 15 modern long boards.

_____

_____

15. Job number 613 was received on 5/21/03 and completed on 5/31/03.

_____

_____

16. Job number 617 is for 20 short boards.

_____

_____

17. The unit cost for Job Number 617 is $147.

_____

_____

18. The projected manufacturing overhead costs of 1,500 surfboards with an overhead rate of 70% is $36,750 (Refer to the Chapter 13-2 worksheet.)

_____

_____

19. Mike's Surf and Sea consists of two departments, Shaping and Sanding.

_____

_____

20. Mike's Surf and Sea factory pays glassers $15/hour.

_____

_____

Exercise 13-1: Job Order Cost Accounting Schedule

1. Prepare a spreadsheet to track the cost of surfboards for each customer. Carol's Surf Shop has just completed job number 510 for Aloha Boards. The order for 15 modern long boards (MLB) was received on August 9, 2004 and completed on August 16, 2004. Manufacturing overhead is applied at a rate of 80% of direct labor costs.

2.   Prepare a job cost sheet using the data in the following table.

Date	Direct Materials	Direct Labor
8/9/04	$70 each	$20 each
8/11/04	$60 each	$6.50 each
8/13/04	$8 each	
8/16/04		$35 each

3.   Set up an input section with rows for the Job number, Customer's name, Quantity, Item description, Date requested and Date completed.

4.   Track job costs by using separate columns for the Date, Direct Materials, Direct Labor, and Manufacturing Overhead.

5.   Make sure the sheet includes totals for Direct Materials, Direct Labor, and Manufacturing Overhead. You should also have a running total for the Total Cost as well as Unit Costs.

6.   Set up a header that includes your name, the file name, and today's date. Save your file as Exercise 13-1.

7.   Print the document.

Exercise 13-2: Test and Analyze Data

1.   On August 30, Carol's Surf Shop received job order number 514 for 18 short boards (SB) from Sea Pines.

2.   Using the Exercise 13-1 file, enter the data from the following table.

Date	Direct Materials	Direct Labor
8/9/04	$40 each	$22 each
8/12/04	$50 each	$7 each
8/16/04		$20 each

3.   Save the file as Exercise 13-2 test.

4. Print the worksheet.

5. When analyzing the job cost sheet, the accountant believes that too much overhead is being assigned to the short boards. Lowering the predetermined overhead rate will reduce the cost of the short boards. Open the Exercise 13-2 test file.

6. Add a row for the overhead rate in the input section.

7. Adjust the formulas in the Manufacturing Overhead column.

8. Using Excel's Goal Seek tool, determine what the overhead rate should be to make the unit costs $170.

9. Save the file as Exercise 13-2 analysis.

10. Print the worksheet.

Exercise 13-3: Projected Manufacturing Cost

In this section, you will prepare a schedule to calculate the manufacturing costs of Carol's Surf Shop's surfboard factory. The factory consists of three departments: Shaping, Glassing and Sanding.

The shapers use a foam blank that costs about $100 each, are paid $20 an hour and spend about an hour on each surfboard. The glassing department spends $10 in fiberglass and resin on each surfboard. The glassers are paid $16 an hour and spend about half an hour on each surfboard. Sanders are paid $12.50 an hour and spend about fifteen minutes on each surfboard. Sanders use several sheets of sandpaper and polish (indirect materials) to finish the surfboards. During the month of August, Carol's Surf Shop expects to produce 1,000 surfboards. Manufacturing overhead is applied at a rate of 65% of direct labor costs.

1. Using the data above, prepare a schedule to calculate the projected manufacturing costs for Carol's Surf Shop's factory.

2. Set up an input section for the estimated production and the overhead rate.

3.   Gather the costs in columns for Direct Materials (multiply expected production times 100 for shaping; multiply expected production times 10 for glassing), Direct Labor (Rate, Hours, and Total) and Overhead (multiply overhead rate by the total direct labor costs).

4.   Calculate Total Costs as well as Unit Costs.

5.   Set up a header that includes your name, the file name, and today's date. Save the file as Exercise 13-3.

6.   Print the worksheet.

Exercise 13-4: Test and Analyze Data

1.   Open the file Exercise 13-3.

2.   Change the estimated production to 1,250.

3.   Change the overhead rate to 72%.

4.   Save the file as Chapter 13-4 test.

5.   Print the worksheet.

6.   Carol's Surf Shop wants the unit costs to be $155. Use the Goal Seek tool to determine how much the Shapers should be paid to make the unit costs no greater than to $155.

7.   Save the file as Exercise 13-4 analysis.

8.   Print the worksheet.

CHAPTER 13 INDEX

SOFTWARE OBJECTIVES: In Chapter 14 you will use the software to:

1.   Complete a worksheet that shows equivalent units.

2.   Complete production cost reports.

3.   Test your models.

4.   Solve what-if scenarios.

5.   Save your spreadsheets.

6.   Complete the exercises and activities in Chapter 14.

WEB OBJECTIVES: In Chapter 14 you will do these Internet activities.

1.   Use your Internet browser to go to the book's website.

2.   Complete the Internet Activities.

GETTING STARTED

In Chapter 13, you created worksheets that showed the job order cost system. In this chapter, you create worksheets that show the process cost system. A *process cost system* accumulates costs by departments for a specific period of time. The primary difference between a job order cost system and the process cost system is that costs are accumulated by department *not* by the specific job. In this chapter you will create worksheets that show equivalent units as well as production costs. Mike's Surf and Sea makes their own wax, formulated specifically for the Hawaiian weather. The wax factory consists of three departments: mixing, molding and packaging. All materials for each department are added at the beginning of the process and conversion costs are incurred uniformly throughout the process.

EQUIVALENT UNITS

Mike's Surf and Sea uses the weighted-average method to compute equivalent units (*Hint: The equivalent units under the weighted-average method are calculated by adding the equivalents of the ending work in process to the total units completed and transferred out.*)

During the month of May, the following transactions occurred:

- The mixing department began with 100,000 units in work in process that were 80% complete as to conversion costs.

- 600,000 more units were started into production during the month.

- 500,000 units were finished and transferred to the molding department.

- Work in process at the end of the month is 75% complete as to conversion costs.

Instructions

1. Using the data shown above, complete the schedule to calculate the mixing department's physical units.

2. Use the data from the physical units to calculate the mixing department's equivalent units.

3. Set up a header for the sheet that includes your name, the file name, and today's date. Save your file as Chapter 14-1.

4. Print the worksheet.

Mike's Surf and Sea
Equivalent Units
For the month ended 5/31/03

Mixing Department

	Physical Units	Percentage Complete Materials	Percentage Complete Conversion Costs
Work in process, 5/1/03	100,000	100%	80%
Started into production	600,000		
Total units	700,000		
Units transferred out	500,000		
Work in process, 5/31/03	200,000	100%	75%
Total units	700,000		

Equivalent Units

	Materials	Conversion Costs
Units transferred out	500,000	500,000
Work in process, 5/31/03	200,000	150,000
Total equivalent units	700,000	650,000

Test Data

During the month of May, the following transactions occurred in the molding department:

- On May 1, 80,000 units were in process that were 70% complete as to conversion costs.

- 500,000 more units were started into production during the month.

- 250,000 units were finished and transferred to the packaging department.

- Work in process at the end of the month is 80% complete as to conversion costs.

1. Open the Chapter 14-1 file.

2. Use the data above to calculate the physical and equivalent units for the molding department.

3. Save the file as Chapter 14-1 test.

4. Print the worksheet. Check Figure: The ending work in process for conversion costs is 264,000.

What-If Analysis

Mike's Surf and Sea believes the molding department's ending work in process is much too high.

1. Open the Chapter 14-1 test file.

2. Using the Goal Seek tool, determine how many units should be transferred to the packaging department to make the equivalent units as to conversion costs equal to 560,000.

3. Save the file as Chapter 14-1 analysis.

4. Print the worksheet. Check Figure: The ending work in process for materials is 100,000.

PRODUCTION COST REPORT

During the month of May, total material costs for the mixing department were $250,000. Conversion costs were $200,000. The costs assigned to the beginning work in process were $65,000.

Instructions

1. Use the data from the mixing department (Chapter 14-1) and the information above to prepare a production cost report for the mixing department. Be sure to use proper formatting.

2. Set up a header for the sheet that includes your name, the file name, and today's date. Save the file as Chapter 14-2.

3. Print the worksheet on one page.

| Student Name | Chapter 14-2 | | | Today's Date |

Mike's Surf and Sea
Production Cost Report
For the month ended 5/31/03

Mixing Department

QUANTITIES	Physical Units	Equivalent Units	
		Materials	Conversion Costs
Work in process, 5/1/03	100,000		
Started into production	600,000		
Total units	700,000		
Units transferred out	500,000	500,000	500,000
Work in process, 5/31/03	200,000	200,000	150,000
Total units	700,000	700,000	650,000

COSTS	Materials	Conversion Costs	Total
Unit costs			
Costs in May	$ 250,000	$ 200,000	$ 450,000
Equivalent units	700,000	650,000	
Unit costs	$ 0.36	$ 0.31	$ 0.66
Costs to be accounted for			
Work in process, 5/1/03			$ 65,000
Started into production			385,000
Total costs			$ 450,000

COST RECONCILIATION SCHEDULE

Costs to be accounted for		
Transferred out		$ 332,418
Work in process, 5/31/2003		
Materials	$ 71,429	
Conversion	46,154	117,582
Total costs		$ 450,000

Test Data

During the month of May, total material costs for the molding department were $75,000. Conversion costs were $50,000. The costs assigned to the beginning work in process were $18,000.

1. Open the file Chapter 14-2.

2. Change the data so the cost report represents the data from the molding department. Use information from the Chapter 14-1 test file.

3. Save the file as Chapter 14-2 test. Check Figure: The ending work in process amount (materials and conversion costs) is $68,353.

4. Print the worksheet.

What-If Analysis

The total unit cost in the molding department is too high. Mike's Surf and Sea believes they can bring the cost down by $.01 per unit by transferring more units to the packaging department.

1. Using the Goal Seek tool, determine how many units must be transferred to the packaging department in order to reduce the total unit costs by $.01.

2. Save the file as Chapter 14-2 analysis.

3. Print the worksheet. Check Figure: The ending work in process amount (materials and conversion costs) is $30,821.

	INTERNET ACTIVITIES
1.	From your Internet browser, go to the book's website at www.mhhe.com/yachtexcel. Link to Internet Activities, then WEB EXERCISES, PART 3-Chapter 14.
2.	Link to this website http://office.microsoft.com/home/office.aspx?assetid=FX010380471033&CTT=98. Complete the quiz, Are you a small business Excel whiz? Then, check your answers.
3.	Go to the FINANCIALjobs.com website at http://www.financialjobs.com.
4.	Explore two links from this website
5.	Write up a summary of what you have seen. Your summary should have no more than 75 words or less than 50 words. Include the appropriate URLs.

SUMMARY AND REVIEW

SOFWARE OBJECTIVES: In Chapter 14, you used to software to:

1. Complete a worksheet that shows equivalent units.

2. Complete production cost reports.

3. Test your models.
4. Solve what-if scenarios.
5. Save your spreadsheets.

6. Complete the exercises and activities in Chapter 14.

WEB OBJECTIVES: In Chapter 14, you did these Internet activities:

1. Used your Internet browser to go the book's website.

2. Completed the Internet Activities.

Multiple-Choice Questions: In the space provided, write the letter that best answers each question.

_____1. A system that accumulates costs by departments for a specific period of time is called a/an:

    a. Job order cost system.
    b. Process cost system.
    c. Inventory system.
    d. Equivalent unit system.
    e. None of the above.

_____2. Mike's Surf and Sea's wax factory consists of these departments:

    a. Mixing, molding and packaging.
    b. Conversion, materials and transfer.
    c. Work in process, equivalent units and waxing.
    d. All of the above.
    e. None of the above.

_____3. Mike's Surf and Sea uses the following method to compute equivalent units:

a. Straight-line.
b. Double-declining balance.
c. MACRS.
d. Weighted-average.
e. None of the above.

_____4. On the Chapter 14-1 worksheet, the percentage of work in process complete as to conversion costs on 5/31/03 is:

a. 100%.
b. 75%.
c. 80%.
d. 25%.
e. None of the above.

_____5. The Chapter 14-1 worksheet shows total equivalent units for materials of:

a.   500,000.
b.   150,000.
c.   700,000.
d.   200,000.
e. None of the above.

_____6. The Chapter 14-1 test worksheet includes total equivalent units for conversion costs of:

a.   250,000.
b.   264,000.
c.   580,000.
d.   514,000.
e. None of the above.

_____7. The Chapter 14-1 analysis worksheet shows the beginning
        work in process percentage for conversion costs of:

   a. 70%.
   b. 100%.
   c. 80%.
   d. 75%.
   e. None of the above.

_____8. The Chapter 14-2 test worksheet, the costs to be accounted
        for, work in process, on 5/1/03 are:

   a. $18,000.
   b. $65,000.
   c. $107,000.
   d. $125,000.
   e. None of the above.

_____9. On the Chapter 14-2 test worksheet, the unit costs for
        materials are:

   a. $0.36.
   b. $0.23.
   c. $0.10.
   d. $0.13.
   e. None of the above.

_____10. On the Chapter 14-2 analysis worksheet, the transferred out
        total is:

   a. $56,647.
   b. $94,179.
   c. $68,353.
   d. $30,821.
   e. None of the above.

True/Make True: If the statement is true, write the word "True" in the space provided. If the statement is *not* true, write the correct answer in the space provided.

11.   In Chapter 14, you track departmental costs.

_____

_____

12.   Mike's Surf and Sea makes their own wax, formulated specifically for the Hawaiian climate.

_____

_____

13.   The Chapter 14-1 worksheet shows equivalent units that calculate the molding department's physical units.

_____

_____

14.   The Chapter 14-1 test worksheet shows that 600,000 units were started into production during the month.

_____

_____

15. On the Chapter 14-1 test worksheet, conversion costs for work in process at the end of the month were 70% complete.

_____

16. In the Chapter 14-1 worksheet you are trying to keep conversion costs down.

_____

_____

17. On the Chapter 14-2 worksheet, the production cost report shows material costs for the mixing department of $250,000.

_____

_____

18. On the Chapter 14-2 test file, conversion costs per unit are $.22.

_____

_____

19. On the Chapter 14-2 analysis worksheet, costs in the ending work in process inventory for materials are $19,720.

_____

_____

20. On the Chapter 14-2 analysis worksheet, conversion costs are
    $11,101.

_____

_____

Exercise 14-1: Equivalent Units

Carol's Surf Shop makes its own special wax for Hawaii's climate
conditions. The wax factory consists of three departments: mixing,
molding and packaging. All materials for each department are added at
the beginning of the process and conversion costs are incurred uniformly
throughout the process.

Carol uses the weighted-average method to compute equivalent units.
During the month of July 2004, the following transactions occurred:

- The mixing department began with 110,000 units in work in process
  that were 70% complete as to conversion costs.

- 450,000 more units were started into production during the month.

- 525,000 units were transferred to the molding department.

- Work in process at the end of the month is 68% complete as to
  conversion costs.

Instructions:

1. Using the data shown above, complete the schedule to calculate
   the mixing department's physical units.

2. Use the data from the physical units to calculate the mixing
   department's equivalent units.

3. Set up a header for the sheet that includes your name, the file
   name, and today's date. Save your file as Chapter 14-1.

4.   Print the worksheet.

Exercise 14-2: Test and Analyze Data

During the month of July, the following transactions occurred in the molding department:

- On July 1, 50,000 units were in process that were 65% complete as to conversion costs.

- 500,000 more units were started into production during the month.

- 400,000 units were transferred to the packaging department.

- Work in process at the end of the month is 55% complete as to conversion costs.

Instructions:

1.   Open the Exercise 14-1 file.

2.   Use the data above to calculate the physical and equivalent units for the molding department.

3.   Save the file as Exercise 14-2 test.

4.   Print the worksheet.

5.   Carol's Surf Shop thinks that the molding department's ending work in process is too high. Open the Exercise 14-2 test file.

6.   Using the Goal Seek tool, determine how many units should be transferred to the packaging department to make the equivalent units as to conversion costs equal to 450,000.

7.   Save the file as Exercise 14-2 analysis.

8.   Print the worksheet.

Exercise 14-3: Production Cost Report

During the month of July, material costs for the mixing department were $200,000. Conversion costs were $150,000. The costs assigned to the beginning work in process were $50,000.

Instructions:

1. Use the data from the mixing department (Exercise 14-1) and the information above to prepare a production cost report for the mixing department. Be sure to use proper formatting.

2. Set up a header for the sheet that includes your name, the file name, and today's date. Save the file as Exercise 14-3.

3. Print the worksheet on one page.

Exercise 14-4: Test and Analyze Data

1. During the month of July, material costs for the molding department were $90,000. Conversion costs were $70,000. The costs assigned to the beginning work in process were $22,000.

2. Open the Exercise 14-3 file.

3. Change the data so the cost report represents the data from the molding department. Use your printout of the Exercise 14-2 test file for the necessary data.

4. Save the file as Exercise 14-4 test.

5. Print the worksheet.

6. The total unit cost in the molding department is too high. Carol's Surf Shop believes they can bring the cost down by $.015 per unit by transferring more units to the packaging department. Using the Goal Seek tool, determine how many units must be transferred to the packaging department in order to reduce the total unit costs to $.26.

7. Save the file as Exercise 14-4 analysis.

8. Print the worksheet.

CHAPTER 14 INDEX

Chapter

15 Cost-Volume-Profit

SOFTWARE OBJECTIVES: In Chapter 15 you will use the software to:

1. Complete a break-even analysis worksheet using the contribution margin.

2. Insert a column chart and bar chart.

3. Complete a contribution margin income statement.

4. Test your models.

5. Solve what-if scenarios.

6. Save your spreadsheets.

7. Complete the exercises and activities in Chapter 15.

WEB OBJECTIVES: In Chapter 15 you will do these Internet activities.

1. Use your Internet browser to go to the book's website.

2. Complete the Internet Activities.

GETTING STARTED

Changes in prices, costs and volume affect profitability. The accounting term used to identify this is known as *cost-volume-profit analysis* **(CVP)**. In this chapter, you will determine the break-even point by using the contribution margin. The *contribution margin* is the difference between sales revenue and variable costs. It is a measure of the amount available to cover fixed costs. It also provides a way to analyze a company's profitability.

The contribution margin approach will be used to construct an income statement. This approach is useful for analyzing the relationship between CVP variables.

BREAK-EVEN ANALYSIS

In this section, you will determine break even using the contribution margin. The surfboard sales division of Mike's Surf and Sea has a contribution margin ratio of 60%. The average selling price of surfboards is $450. The division's fixed costs per month are $150,000. During the month of May, Mike's Surf and Sea sold 700 units.

Instructions

1. Prepare a spreadsheet to calculate the net income for Mike's Surf and Sea. The spreadsheet should show the number of units sold, unit selling price, total sales, variable cost per unit, total variable cost, variable cost ratio, contribution margin per unit, total contribution margin, contribution margin ratio, total fixed cost and net income.

2. Enter the data from above and calculate the remaining amounts.

3. Set up a header for the sheet that includes your name, the file name, and today's date. Save the file as Chapter 15-1.

4. Print the worksheet.

Student Name			Chapter 15-1		Today's Date

Mike's Surf Shop
Break Even Analysis
For the month ended 5/31/03

	Units	Unit Price	Total	Percent
Sales	700	450	315,000	100%
Variable costs		180	126,000	40%
Contribution margin		270	189,000	60%
Fixed costs			150,000	
Net income			39,000	

Test Data

1. Change the unit sold to 900 units.

2. Change the contribution margin ratio to 55%.

3. Change the fixed cost to $145,000.

4. Save the file as Chapter 15-1 test.

5. Print the worksheet.

What-if Analysis

Mike's Surf and Sea would like to show a net income of $100,000. They believe they can sell more surfboards by paying commissions to their sales associates. The commission is a variable cost, and it will reduce the contribution margin ratio to 50%. Fixed cost will remain the same.

1. Open the Chapter 15-1 test file.

2. Adjust the contribution margin ratio to reflect the increased variable cost ratio.

3. Using the Goal Seek tool, determine how many surfboards Mike's Surf and Sea will have to sell to recognize $100,000 in net income.

4. Save the file as Chapter 15-1 analysis.

5. Print the worksheet.

INSERT A CHART

Many of the worksheets that you have created can be made into a chart or graph. Excel's chart feature includes numerous choices. In the steps that follow you use the Chapter 15-1.xls file to create a chart. You should also experiment with the chart feature using other worksheets.

1. Open the Chapter 15-1.xls file.

2. Click on Sheet2. Rename the sheet Chart 1.

3. Chart 1 should be the active sheet (formerly Sheet2). From the menu bar, select Insert; Chart (or, from the icon bar click 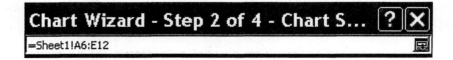). The Chart Wizard – Step 1 of 4 screen appears.

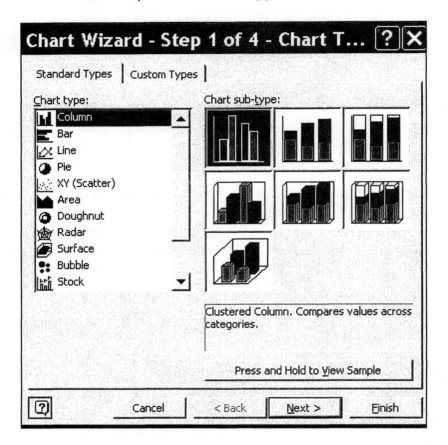

4. Accept the default for Column Chart type by clicking Next >.

5. The Chart Wizard – Step 2 of 4 screen appears. In the Data range field click. Click on Sheet1; type **A6:E12** (or highlight those cells on Sheet1).

Chart Wizard - Step 2 of 4 - Chart S...

=Sheet1!A6:E12

6. Press <Enter> or click 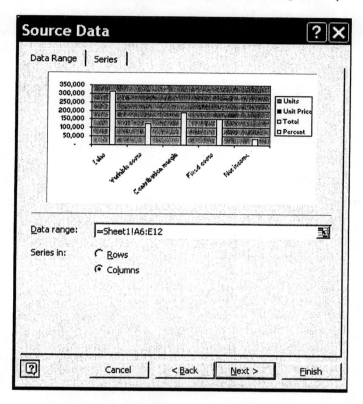 to close the Chart Wizard – Step 2 of 4 screen. The Source Data screen appears. Compare your screen to the one shown below. (If necessary, select Columns.)

7. Click [Next >]. Type **Break Even Analysis** in the Chart title field. Click [Next >].

8. At the Chart Wizard – Step 4 of 4 screen, click [Finish]. Your chart appears. Compare your screen with the one shown on the next page.

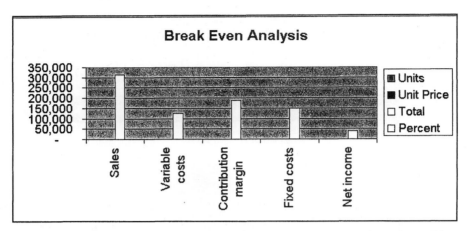

9. Right-click on the chart. From the drop-down menu, select Chart Type. Experiment with chart types. Select one or more to see your chart as different graph; for example, select Bar, then OK. This chart appears. Try some others, too.

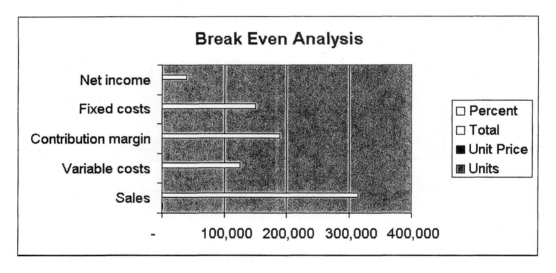

10. Save your worksheet.

CONTRIBUTION MARGIN FORMAT INCOME STATEMENT

In this section, you will prepare an income statement using the contribution margin format. The following table shows the allocation of costs between variable and fixed.

	Variable	Fixed
Cost of goods sold	$ 400,000	$ 125,000
Selling expenses	$ 80,000	$ 20,000
Administrative expenses	$ 25,000	$ 60,000

During the month of May, Mike's Surf and Sea recognized sales of $800,000.

Instructions:

1. Prepare an income statement using the contribution margin format.
2. Show all numbers as whole numbers. Use proper formatting on all numbers.

3. Use indents to show the difference between detail and category titles.

4. Set up a header for the sheet that includes your name, the file name, and today's date. Save the file as Chapter 15-2.

5. Print the worksheet.

Student Name　　　　　　　Chapter 15-2　　　　　　　Today's Date

Mike's Surf and Sea
Income Statement
For the Month Ended 5/31/03

Sales		$ 800,000
Variable expenses		
Cost of goods sold	$ 400,000	
Selling expenses	80,000	
Administrative expenses	25,000	
Total variable expenses		505,000
Contribution margin		295,000
Fixed expenses		
Cost of goods sold	125,000	
Selling expenses	20,000	
Administrative expenses	60,000	
Total fixed expenses		205,000
Net income		$ 90,000

Test Data

1. Open the Chapter 15-2 file.

2. Adjust the sales amount to $900,000.

3. Adjust the variable expenses to the following percent of sales (use formulas):

Cost of goods sold	55%
Selling expenses	14%
Administrative expenses	10%

4. Save the file as Chapter 15-2 test.

5. Print the worksheet.

What-If Analysis

1. Open the Chapter 15-2 test file.

2. Determine how much sales should be in order to break even.

3. Save the file as Chapter 15-2 analysis a.

4. Print the worksheet.

5. Determine how much sales should be to make $75,000 in net income.

6. Save the file as Chapter 15-2 analysis b.

7. Print the worksheet.

	INTERNET ACTIVITIES
1.	From your Internet browser, go to the book's website at www.mhhe.com/yachtexcel. Link to Internet Activities, then WEB EXERCISES, PART 3-Chapter 15.
2.	Link to http://office.microsoft.com/home/office.aspx?assetid=FX010380471033&CTT=98. Complete the quiz; Are You an Excel fiscal year whiz? Then, check your answers.
3.	From your Internet browser, go to the book's website. Link to Internet Activities, then WEB EXERCISES, PART 3-Chapter 15.
4.	Go to The Moving Calculator website at http://www.homefair.com/homefair/calc/movecalcin.html.
5.	Read the directions on "The Moving Calculator" page. Use the calculator to estimate interstate or local moving costs. Follow the steps on the screen.
6.	Print your report.
7.	Go to the StartHereGoPlaces.com website http://startheregoplaces.com/. This website is sponsored by the American Institute of Certified Public Accountants.
8.	Link to an area of interest. Write a short report (minimum length 75 words; maximum length 100 words.) Print your report.

SUMMARY AND REVIEW

SOFWARE OBJECTIVES: In Chapter 15, you used to software to:

1. Complete a break-even analysis worksheet using the contribution margin.

2. Insert a column chart and bar chart.

3. Complete a contribution margin income statement.

4. Test your models.

5. Solve what-if scenarios.

6. Save your spreadsheets.

7. Complete the exercises and activities in Chapter 15.

WEB OBJECTIVES: In Chapter 15, you did these Internet activities:

1.   Used your Internet browser to go the book's website.

2.   Completed the Internet Activities.

Multiple-Choice Questions: In the space provided, write the letter that best answers each question.

_____1.   The difference between sales revenue and variable costs is known as:

   a.   Cost-volume-profit margin.
   b.   Break-even analysis.
   c.   Contribution margin.
   d.   Ratio analysis.
   e.   None of the above.

_____2.   On the Chapter 15-1 worksheet, Mike's Surf and Sea's contribution margin ratio is:

   a.   100%.
   b.   60%.
   c.   40%.
   d.   25%.
   e.   None of the above

_____3.   On the Chapter 15-1 worksheet, units sold are at a cost of:

   a. $450.
   b. $180.
   c. $270.
   d. $700.
   e.   None of the above.

_____4.   On the Chapter 15-1 test worksheet, the net income is:

     a. $39,000.
     b. $77,750.
     c. $90,000.
     d. $100,000.
     e. None of the above.

_____5.   The Chapter 15-1 analysis worksheet shows the total
     contribution margin as:

     a. $245,000.
     b. $490,000.
     c. $222,750.
     d. $405,000.
     e. None of the above.

_____6.   The Chapter 15-1 analysis worksheet shows total sales of:

     a. $315,000.
     b. $222,750.
     c. $405,000.
     d. $490,000.
     e. None of the above.

_____7.   The Chapter 15-2 worksheet shows total variable expenses of:

     a. $205,000.
     b. $90,000.
     c. $505,000.
     d. $711,000.
     e. None of the above.

_____8.   The Chapter 15-2 test worksheet shows a net income of

     a. $16,000.
     b. $90,000.
     c. $0.
     d. $75,000.
     e. None of the above.

_____9. On the Chapter 15-2 analysis a worksheet, the contribution margin is:

   a. $280,000.
   b. $205,000.
   c. $125,000.
   d. $536,905.
   e. None of the above.

_____10. On the Chapter 15-2 analysis b worksheet, the total variable expenses are:

   a. $1,053,333.
   b. $1,333,333.
   c. $771,190.
   d. $976,190.
   e. None of the above.

True/Make True: If the statement is true, write the word "True" in the space provided. If the statement is *not* true, write the correct answer in the space provided.

11. Changes in prices, costs and volume affect profitability.

   _____

   _____

12. The break-even analysis spreadsheets show the calculation of Mike's Surf and Sea's net income.

   _____

   _____

13. On the break-even analysis worksheet, variable costs are determined by multiplying the number of units by unit variable costs.

_____

_____

14. The Chapter 15-1 test worksheet shows 700 units sold.

_____

_____

15. On the Chapter 15-1 analysis worksheet, variable costs and contribution margin are the same amount and percentage.

_____

16. The income statements prepared in Chapter 15 used the break even analysis margin format.

_____

_____

17. On the Chapter 15-2 test worksheet, Mike's Surf and Sea recognized sales of $800,000.

_____

_____

18. Variable cost of goods sold on the Chapter 15-2 test worksheet is 14% of sales

_____

_____

19. On the Chapter 15-2 analysis a worksheet, variable selling expenses are $136,667.

_____

_____

20. On the Chapter 15-2 analysis b worksheet, net income/(net loss) is ($16,000).

_____

_____

Exercise 15-1: Break-Even Analysis

1. The surfboard sales division of Carol's Surf Shop has a contribution margin of 70%. The average selling price of surfboards is $480. The division's fixed cost for the month is $165,000. During the month of September 2004, Carol's Surf Shop sold 825 units.

2. Prepare a spreadsheet to calculate the net income for Carol's Surf and Shop. The spreadsheet should show the number of units sold, unit selling price, total sales, variable cost per unit, total variable cost, variable cost ratio, contribution margin per unit, total contribution margin, contribution margin ratio, total fixed cost and net income.

3. Enter the data from above and calculate the remaining amounts.

4. Set up a header for the sheet that includes your name, the file name, and today's date. Save the file as Exercise 15-1.

5. Print the worksheet.

Exercise 15-2: Test and Analyze Data

1. Change the unit sold to 910 units.

2. Change the contribution margin ratio to 65%.

3. Change the fixed cost to $170,000.

4. Save the file as Exercise 15-2 test.

5. Print the worksheet.

6. Carol's Surf Shop would like to show a net income of $120,000. Carol believes the shop can sell more surfboards by paying commissions to sales associates. Commissions increase the variable cost ratio to 50%. Fixed cost will remain the same.

7. Open the Chapter 15-2 test file.

8. Adjust the contribution margin ratio to reflect the increased variable cost ratio.

9. Using the Goal Seek tool, determine how many surfboards Carol's Surf Shop will have to sell to recognize $120,000 in net income.

10. Rename Sheet2 Column Chart. Insert a column chart.

11. Rename Sheet3 Bar Chart. Insert a bar chart.

12. Save the file as Exercise 15-2 analysis.

13. Print the worksheet.

Exercise 15-3: Contribution Margin Format Income Statement

1. Prepare an income statement using the contribution margin format. The following table shows the allocation of costs between variable and fixed.

	Variable	Fixed
Cost of goods sold	$ 300,000	$105,000
Selling expenses	$ 90,000	$30,000
Administrative expenses	$ 18,000	$50,000

2. During the month of September 2004, Carol's Surf Shop recognized sales of $750,000.

3. Prepare an income statement using the contribution margin format.

4. Show all numbers as whole numbers and use proper number formatting.

5. Use indents to show the difference between detail and category titles.

6. Set up a header for the sheet that includes your name, the file name, and today's date. Save the file as Exercise 15-3.

7. Print the worksheet.

Exercise 15-4: Test and Analyze Data

1. Open the Exercise 15-3 file.

2. Adjust the sales amount to $850,000.

3. Adjust the variable expenses to the following percent of sales (use formulas):

Cost of goods sold	60%
Selling expenses	12%
Administrative expenses	8%

4.   Save the file as Exercise 15-4 test.

5.   Print the worksheet.

6.   Open the Exercise 15-4 test file.

7.   Determine how much sales should be in order to break even.

8.   Save the file as Exercise 15-4 analysis a.

9.   Print the worksheet.

10.   Determine how much sales would be to make $80,000 in net income.

11.   Save the file as Exercise 15-4 analysis b.

12.   Print the worksheet.

CHAPTER 15 INDEX

Chapter 16 Budgeting and Analysis

SOFTWARE OBJECTIVES: In Chapter 16 you will use the software to:

1. Complete part of a master budget.

2. Complete a manufacturing overhead budget report.

3. Compare the results of the budgets to determine the best course of action.

4. Test your models.

5. Solve what-if scenarios.

6. Save your spreadsheets.

7. Complete the exercises and activities in Chapter 16.

WEB OBJECTIVES: In Chapter 16 you will do these Internet activities.

1. Use your Internet browser to go to the book's website.

2. Complete the Internet Activities.

GETTING STARTED

In this chapter, you will use Excel to prepare part of a master budget. You will also prepare a manufacturing overhead budget report and compare the results of your operations with your budget.

MASTER BUDGET

In this section, you will prepare a sales budget, production budget and direct materials budget for Mike's Surf and Sea's wax factory. The budget should be prepared for the year ending 12/31/2004. You should have a column for each quarter as well as a total for the year.

Use the following information to prepare your budget:

Expected unit sales	1,000 units in Quarter 1 increasing 5% each quarter after that
Selling price	$12 per unit
Beginning finished goods inventory	100 units
Desired ending finished goods inventory	10% of next quarter's unit sales
Direct materials per unit	2 pounds per unit
Beginning raw materials inventory	201 pounds
Desired ending raw materials inventory	10% of next quarter's pounds required for production.
Cost per pound of direct materials	$2 per pound

Instructions

1. Using the information above, prepare a sales budget, production budget, and a direct materials budget for the year ending 12/31/04. (*Hint: You may want to create an additional column for the first quarter of 2005 in order to estimate the ending inventory amounts for quarter 4.*)

2. Setup the worksheet so that three budgets print on one page.

3. Set up a header for the sheet that includes your name, the file name, and today's date. Save the file as Chapter 16-1.

4. Print the worksheet.

Mike's Surf and Sea
Master Budget
For the year ending 12/31/04

Sales Budget

	Quarter 1	Quarter 2	Quarter 3	Quarter 4	Total
Expected unit sales	1,000	1,050	1,103	1,158	4,310
Selling price	$ 12	$ 12	$ 12	$ 12	$ 12
Total sales	$ 12,000	$ 12,600	$ 13,230	$ 13,892	$ 51,722

Production Budget

	Quarter 1	Quarter 2	Quarter 3	Quarter 4	Total
Expected unit sales	1,000	1,050	1,103	1,158	4,310
Desired ending finished goods inventory	105	110	116	122	122
Total units required	1,105	1,160	1,218	1,279	4,432
Less: Beginning finished good inventory	100	105	110	116	100
Required unit production	1,005	1,055	1,108	1,163	4,332

Direct Materials Budget

	Quarter 1	Quarter 2	Quarter 3	Quarter 4	Total
Required unit production	1,005	1,055	1,108	1,163	4,332
Direct materials per unit (pounds)	2	2	2	2	2
Total pounds needed for production	2,010	2,111	2,216	2,327	8,663
Desired ending raw materials inventory	211	222	233	244	244
Total pounds required	2,221	2,332	2,449	2,571	8,908
Less: Beginning raw materials inventory	201	211	222	233	201
Direct materials purchases	2,020	2,121	2,227	2,338	8,707
Cost per pound	$ 2	$ 2	$ 2	$ 2	$ 2
Total cost of direct materials	$ 4,040	$ 4,242	$ 4,454	$ 4,677	$ 17,413

Test Data

1. Open the Chapter 16-1 file.

2. Change the expected unit sales in Quarter 1 to 1,200 units.

3. Change the selling price to $10.

4. Save the file as Chapter 16-1 test. Check Figure: The total cost of direct materials is $20,896.

5.   Print the worksheet.

What-If Analysis

Mike's Surf and Sea is considering reducing the unit price to $6 per unit. They believe this will cause unit sales to increase 100%. Because such an increase in sales will also increase their production requirements, Mike's Surf and Sea will be able to purchase its raw materials for $1.50 per pound.

1.   Open the Chapter 16-1 test file.

2.   Make changes to the data to reflect the information above.

3.   Save the file as Chapter 16-1 analysis. Check Figure: The total sales are $62,066.

4.   Print the worksheet.

     Question: Compare the results of the three budgets and determine which would be the best course of action.

MANUFACTURING OVERHEAD BUDGET REPORT

In this section, you will prepare a manufacturing overhead budget report for the Packaging Department of Mike's Surf and Sea and compare the budgeted results to the actual.

Instructions

1.   Using the information in the following table, prepare a manufacturing overhead budget report for Mike's Surf and Sea for the year ending 12/31/03.

Variable Costs	
Indirect labor	$8.00 per hour
Indirect materials	$5.00 per hour
Utilities	$0.75 per hour
Fixed Costs	
Depreciation	$ 2,000
Rent	$ 1,200
Insurance	$ 600
Property taxes	$ 800

2.   The budget should be based on expected direct labor hours of 5,000 and actual hours worked of 4,500.

3.   Use the information that follows for the actual amounts.

Variable Costs	
Indirect labor	$ 27,000
Indirect materials	$ 27,000
Utilities	$ 4,500
Fixed Costs	
Depreciation	$ 2,000
Rent	$ 1,200
Insurance	$ 600
Property taxes	$ 800

4.   Create a column that will automatically enter an "F" if the budgeted amount is greater than the actual amount and a "U" if the budgeted amount is less than the actual amount. (*Hint:* Use the =IF function with F and U in quote marks [=if(...,"F","U")])

5.   Set up a header for the sheet that includes your name, the file name, and today's date. Save the file as Chapter 16-2.

6.   Print the worksheet. Compare it to the one shown on the next page.

Mike's Surf and Sea
Manufacturing Overhead Budget Report
For the year ended 12/31/03

Packaging Department

Direct Labor Hours
Expected	5,000
Actual	4,500

	Budgeted	Actual	Difference	Favorable F Unfavorable U
Variable Costs				
Indirect labor	36,000	27,000	9,000	F
Indirect materials	22,500	27,000	(4,500)	U
Utilities	3,375	4,500	(1,125)	U
Total variable costs	61,875	58,500	3,375	F
Fixed Costs				
Depreciation	2,000	2,000	-	U
Rent	1,200	1,200	-	U
Insurance	600	600	-	U
Property taxes	800	800	-	U
Total fixed costs	4,600	4,600	-	U
Total manufacturing overhead	66,475	63,100	3,375	F

Test Data

1. Open the Chapter 16-2 file.

2. Change the variable costs data to match the table below.

Variable Costs		
Indirect labor	$	54,000
Indirect materials	$	33,000
Utilities	$	3,000

3. Change the budgeted variable cost for indirect materials to $6.00. Change the actual hours to 6,000.

4. Save the file as Chapter 16-2 test. Check Figure: The "Unfavorable" difference between the Actual and Budgeted amounts is (1,500).

5. Print the worksheet.

What-If Analysis

1. Open the Chapter 16-2 test file.

2. Change the actual indirect labor costs to $44,000.

3. Determine the fewest number of actual direct labor hours in order to show no difference between the actual and budgeted total manufacturing overhead cost.

4. Save the file as Chapter 16-2 analysis. Check Figure: The "Favorable" difference in utilities is 1,068.

5. Print the worksheet.

INTERNET ACTIVITIES	
1.	From your Internet browser, go to the book's website at www.mhhe.com/yachtexcel. Link to Internet Activities, then WEB EXERCISES, PART 3-Chapter 16.
2.	Link to this this website http://office.microsoft.com/home/office.aspx?assetid=FX010380471033&CTT=98.
3.	Link to two quizzes of interest to you. For example, in the Office (general) section you could select Are you an Office whiz? Or, select an Access quiz.
4.	Go to the FINANCIALjobs.com presents website at http://www.financialjobs.com/Financial%20Web1130.htm.
5.	Read the article, "As Easy as ASP..." Write a brief summary of the article.
6.	Go to the website http://www.financialjobs.com/Financial%20Web%203301.htm.
7.	Read the article, "Part 2: The Lowdown on Financial ASPs..." Write a brief summary of the article.

SUMMARY AND REVIEW

SOFWARE OBJECTIVES: In Chapter 16, you used to software to:

1. Complete part of a master budget.

2. Complete a manufacturing overhead budget report.

3. Compare the results of the budgets to determine the best course of action.

4. Test your models.

5. Solve what-if scenarios.

6. Save your spreadsheets.

7. Complete the exercises and activities in Chapter 16.

WEB OBJECTIVES: In Chapter 16, you did these Internet activities:

1. Used their Internet browser to go the book's website.

2. Completed the Internet Activities.

Multiple-Choice Questions: In the space provided, write the letter that best answers each question.

_____1. The master budget includes a sales budget, production budget and a/an:

    a. Indirect materials budget.
    b. Direct materials budget.
    c. Cost per unit of production.
    d. Total cost per pound.
    e. None of the above.

_____2. On the Chapter 16-1 worksheet, the formula for determining the expected sales for Quarter 2 is:

    a. Quarter 2 expected unit sales times quarter 3.
    b. Quarter 2 expected unit sales times 5%.
    c. Quarter 1 expected unit sales times 1.05.
    d. All of the above.
    e. None of the above

_____3. On the Chapter 16-1 worksheet, the expected unit sales in Quarter 4 are:

a. 1,158.
b. 1,200.
c. 1,050.
d. $1,389.
e. None of the above

_____4. In order to complete what-if analysis on the Chapter 16-1 test worksheet, you reduce the unit price from:

a. $10 to $6.
b. $10 to $5.
c. $14 to 7.
d. $16 to 8.
e. None of the above.

_____5 On the Chapter 16-1 analysis worksheet, the total cost of direct materials is:

a. $62,066.
b. $16,436.
c. $19,723.
d. $29,585.
e. None of the above.

_____6. The Chapter 16-1 analysis worksheet's direct materials budget shows cost per pound of:

a. $2.00
b. $1.50
c. $1.00.
d. $1.75.
e. None of the above.

_____7. On the manufacturing overhead budget report shown on the Chapter 16-2 worksheet, actual hours worked are:

a. 5,000.
b. 5,424.
c. 6,000.
d. 4,500.
e. None of the above.

_____8. To test the manufacturing overhead budget report, you change the actual indirect materials variable costs to:

a. $54,000.
b. $33,000.
c. $44,000.
d. $22,500.
e. None of the above.

_____9. To complete what-if analysis on the manufacturing overhead budget report, you change actual indirect labor costs to:

a. $44,000.
b. $54,000.
c. $48,000.
d. $33,000.
e. None of the above.

_____10. On the Chapter 16-2 analysis worksheet, the difference between the budgeted and actual total manufacturing overhead is:

a. $84,600.
b. $93,100.
c. $94,609.
d. ($1,500).
e. None of the above.

True/Make True: If the statement is true, write the word "True" in the space provided. If the statement is *not* true, write the correct answer in the space provided.

11.   In Chapter 16, you prepare a manufacturing overhead budget report and compare the results of your operations with your budget.

_____

_____

12.   The master budgets prepared in this chapter are for the year ended December 31, 2004.

_____

_____

13.   The Chapter 16-1 master budget shows the sales budget for three quarters.

_____

_____

14.   What-if analysis on the master budget assumes that Mike's Surf and Sea will be able to increase unit sales by 100%.

_____

_____

15. When you compare the results of the three master budgets, the best course of action is shown in the Chapter 16-1 test worksheet.

_____

_____

16. When the actual amount is greater than the budgeted amount, the manufacturing overhead budget report shows the difference as unfavorable.

_____

_____

17. On the Chapter 16-2 worksheet, the total manufacturing overhead is unfavorable.

_____

_____

18. On the Chapter 16-2 test worksheet, the total budgeted amount for manufacturing overhead is $93,100.

_____

_____

19. On the Chapter 16-2 test and analysis worksheets, the variable costs for indirect labor are unfavorable.

_____

_____

20. On the Chapter 16-2 analysis worksheet, the budgeted and actual amounts are the same for total fixed and variable costs.

_____

_____

Exercise 16-1: Master Budget

Expected unit sales	1,200 units in Quarter 1 increasing 6% each quarter after that
Selling price	$14 per unit
Beginning finished goods inventory	120 units
Desired ending finished goods inventory	10% of next quarter's unit sales
Direct materials per unit	2 pounds per unit
Beginning raw materials inventory	241 pounds
Desired ending raw materials inventory	10% of next quarter's production
Cost per pound of direct materials	$3 per pound

Instructions

1. Using the information shown above, prepare a master budget for Carol's Surf Shop's wax factory for December 31, 2004. Format your worksheet similarly to the ones completed in this chapter.

2. Set up a header for the sheet that includes your name, the file name, and today's date. Save the file as Exercise 16-1.

3. Print the worksheet.

Exercise 16-2: Test and Analyze Data

1. Open the Exercise 16-1 file.

2. Change the expected unit sales in Quarter 1 to 1,300 units.

3. Change the selling price to $10.

4. Save the file as Exercise 16-2 test.

5. Print the worksheet.

Carol's Surf Shop is considering reducing the unit price to $5 per unit. They believe this will cause unit sales to increase 100%. Because such an increase in sales will also increase their production requirements, Carol's Surf Shop will be able to purchase its raw materials for $1 per pound.

1. Open the Chapter 16-2 test file.

2. Make changes to the data to reflect the information above.

3. Save the file as Exercise 16-2 analysis.

4. Print the worksheet.

    Question: Compare the results of the three budgets and determine which would be the best course of action.

Exercise 16-3: Manufacturing Overhead Budget Report

1. Using the information in the following table, prepare a manufacturing overhead budget report for Carol's Surf Shop's Packaging Department, for the year ended 12/31/03. Format your worksheet similarly to the one done in the chapter.

Variable Costs	
Indirect labor	$9.00 per hour
Indirect materials	$4.00 per hour
Utilities	$0.85 per hour
Fixed Costs	
Depreciation	$ 1,750
Rent	$ 1,000
Insurance	$ 500
Property taxes	$ 850

2. The budget should be based on expected direct labor hours of 5,200 and actual hours worked of 4,750.

3. Use the information that follows for the actual amounts.

Variable Costs	
Indirect labor	$ 25,000
Indirect materials	$ 25,000
Utilities	$ 5,000
Fixed Costs	
Depreciation	$ 1,750
Rent	$ 1,000
Insurance	$ 500
Property taxes	$ 850

5. Create a column that will automatically enter an "F" if the budgeted amount is greater than the actual amount and a "U" if the budgeted amount is less than the actual amount.

6. Set up a header for the sheet that includes your name, the file name, and today's date. Save the file as Exercise 16-3.

7. Print the worksheet.

Exercise 16-4: Test and Analyze Data

1. Open the Exercise 16-3 file.

2. Change the actual variable cost data to match the table below.
3.

Variable Costs	
Indirect labor	55,000
Indirect materials	32,000
Utilities	5,500

4. Change the actual hours to 5,850.

5. Save the file as Exercise 16-4 test.

6. Print the worksheet.

6. Open the Exercise 16-4 test file.

7. Change the actual indirect labor costs to $50,000.

8. Determine the fewest number of actual direct labor hours in order to show no difference between the actual and budgeted total manufacturing overhead cost.

9. Save the file as Exercise 16-4 analysis.

10. Print the worksheet.

CHAPTER 16 INDEX

Part 4

Case Problems

In Part 4, you will be asked to prepare projects similar to the ones you worked on in Parts 2 and 3 of *Excel Accounting*. You may refer to those parts for help in preparing the case problems presented in Part 4.

In Part 4, you complete four case problems.

Case Problem 1: Accounting Worksheets. You open a partially completed accounting worksheet from your student CD—Case 1.xls. The trial balance data has already been prepared for you. After completing adjusting entries, you complete financial statement worksheets.

Case Problem 2: Financial Statement Analysis. You complete vertical, horizontal and ratio analyses. The Case 2.xls file included on the Student CD contains all of the financial data you need to complete the analysis.

Case Problem 3: Cost of Goods Manufactured. You prepare a cost of goods manufactured schedule and an income statement. To start, open the Case 3.xls file on the Student CD.

Case Problem 4: Master Budget. You prepare a master budget for one year organized by quarters. To start, open the Case 4.xls file on the Student CD.

Case Problems	File Name	Page Nos.
1	Case 1 answer.xls	416-418
	Case 1 test.xls	419
2	Case 2 answer.xls	419-421
	Case 2 test.xls	422
3	Case 3 answer.xls	423-424
	Case 3 test.xls	425
4	Case 4 answer.xls	426
	Case 4 test.xls	427

Case Problems

In this section, you will be asked to prepare projects similar to the ones you worked on in Parts 2 and 3. You may refer to those sections for help in preparing the projects presented in this section.

CASE PROBLEM 1: PREPARING FINANCIAL STATEMENTS

In this problem, you are presented with a partially completed accounting worksheet for Mike's Surf and Sea for 2003. The trial balance data has already been prepared for you. Complete the steps that follow.

1. Open the Case 1.xls file from the Student CD.

2. Make the sheet labeled Worksheet the active sheet.

3. Enter the following adjustment data into the appropriate cells in the adjustments columns. Be sure the debit column is equal to the credit column.

> You may have to refer to your accounting textbook for procedures on adjusting entries and completing accounting worksheets.

> a. The value of the inventory at the end of the year is $3,550,000.

> b. Depreciation for the year is $1,000,000.

> c. $15,000 of prepaid insurance has expired.

> d. Accrued salaries at the end of the year are $250,000.

> e. Supplies on hand are $150,000.

4.   The adjusted trial balance columns are completed automatically. Be sure the amounts in this column are correct and the total debits are equal to the total credits.

5.   Enter conditional formulas into the income statement and balance sheet columns to reflect the correct amounts from the adjusted trial balance columns.

6.   Enter a formula to calculate the subtotal of the debits and credits in the income statement and balance sheet columns.

7.   Enter a conditional formula to calculate the net income or loss.

8.   Enter a formula to calculate the total debits and credits in the income statement and balance sheet columns. Be sure the total debits equal the total credits.

9.   Set up the file so the entire spreadsheet prints on one page (landscape), is centered horizontally and includes gridlines. The header should include your name, the file and sheet name and today's date.

10. Save the file as Case 1 answer.

11. Print the worksheet. Check Figure: Total debits on the worksheet's Balance Sheet column are $11,185,000.

Financial Statements

In this section, you will create 2003 financial statements from the data you prepared in the worksheet. Use a separate sheet for each financial statement.

Income Statement

1.   Open the file Case 1 answer.

2.   Rename Sheet 1 to Income Statement.

3.   Rename Sheet 2 to Owners' Equity.

4. Rename Sheet 3 to Balance Sheet.

5. Make the Income Statement the active sheet.

6. Enter appropriate header data in cells A1:A3 (who, what and when).

7. Create an income statement by linking the data from the Worksheet sheet. (*Hint: Do* not *separate other expenses into selling and administrative*.)

8. Be sure to use proper formatting for all numbers and labels.

9. Use Indent to show detail.

10. Use underlines and double underlines where necessary.

11. Set up the page so the entire spreadsheet prints on one page, is centered horizontally, and the header includes your name and today's date.

12. Save the file.

13. Print the Income Statement sheet. Check Figure: Cost of Goods Sold should be $5,400,000.

Statement of Owners' Equity

1. Make Owners' Equity the active sheet.

2. Enter appropriate header data in cells A1:A3 (who, what and when).

3. Create a Statement of Owners' Equity by linking the data from the Worksheet sheet and the Income Statement.

4. Be sure to use proper formatting for all numbers and labels.

5. Use Indent to show detail.

6. Use underlines and double underlines where necessary.

7. Set up the page so the entire spreadsheet prints on one page, is centered horizontally, and the header includes your name and today's date.

8. Save the file.

9. Print the Owners' Equity sheet.

Balance Sheet

1. Make Balance Sheet the active sheet.

2. Enter appropriate header data in cells A1:A3 (who, what and when).

3. Create a Balance Sheet by linking the data from the Worksheet sheet and the Statement of Owners' Equity.

4. Be sure to use proper formatting for all numbers and labels.

5. Use Indent to show detail.

6. Use underlines and double underlines where necessary.

7. Set up the page so the entire spreadsheet prints on one page, is centered horizontally, and the header includes your name, and today's date.

8. Save the file.

9. Print the Balance Sheet. Check Figure: Total Assets should be $7,985,000.

Test Data

1. Open the Case 1 answer file.

2. Enter the following data into the adjustment columns.

    a. Ending inventory is $3,750,000.

b. Depreciation expense is $1,500,000.

c. Prepaid insurance expired during the year was $12,000.

d. Accrued salaries were $300,000.

e. Used $75,000 of supplies during the year.

3. Save the file as Case 1 test. Check Figure: The Net Loss is $187,000.

4. Print all of the sheets.

CASE PROBLEM 2: FINANCIAL STATEMENT ANALYSIS

In this case, you will prepare a vertical, horizontal and ratio analysis for Mike's Surf and Sea. The file Case 2 contains all of the financial data you need to prepare the analysis. Refer to you accounting textbook for procedures on calculating vertical, horizontal and ratio analysis.

Input

1. Open the Case 2.xls file from the Student CD. All of the financial data you need is contained in the sheet labeled Input.

2. Save the file as Case 2 answer.

3. Format the sheet so that it prints on one page, is centered horizontally, and the header contains your name, the file name, and today's date.

Vertical Analysis

1. Rename Sheet 2 to Vertical.

2. Enter the header information in row 1 and 2.

3. Prepare a vertical analysis for years 2000–2003 by linking to the data in the Input sheet. *(Hint: use absolute referencing for the denominator.)*

4. Be sure to use two decimals and the percent style.

5. Format the sheet so that it prints on one page, is centered horizontally, and the header contains your name, the file name and today's date.

6. Save the file. Check figure: 2003 Net Income is 1.10%.

7. Print the sheet.

Horizontal Analysis

1. Rename Sheet 3 to Horizontal.

2. Enter the header information in row 1 and 2.

3. Prepare a horizontal analysis for years 2000–2003 by linking to the data in the Input sheet. Use data from the year 2000 as the base year. *(Hint: use absolute referencing when referencing the base year.)*

4. Be sure to use two decimals and the percent style.

5. Format the sheet so that it prints on one page, is centered horizontally, and the header contains your name, the file name and today's date.

6. Save the file. Check figure: 2003 Net Income is 83.51%.

7. Print the sheet.

Ratio Analysis

1. Insert a new sheet into the workbook.

2. Rename the sheet to Ratio.

3. Enter the header information in row 1 and 2.

4. Prepare the following ratios for years 2000–2003 by linking to the data in the Input sheet.

Liquidity Ratios

Current ratio
Acid-test ratio
Current cash debt coverage ratio
Receivables turnover
Inventory turnover

Profitability Ratios

Profit margin
Cash return on sales
Asset turnover
Return on assets
Return on common stockholders' equity
Earnings per share
Price-earnings ratio

Solvency Ratios

Debt to total assets ratio
Times interest earned
Cash debt coverage ratio

---

5. Be sure to use two decimals and the appropriate style (percent, dollar, comma).

6. Format the sheet so that it prints on one page, is centered horizontally, and the header contains your name, the file name and today's date.

7. Save the file.

8. Print the sheet.

Test Data

1. Open the file Case 2 answer.

2. Change the data for the 2003 year to the following:

Income Statement (in thousands)	2003
Net sales	12,000
Cost of goods sold	5,500
Gross profit	6,500
Operating expenses	6,200
Income from operations	300
Interest expense	5
Income before income taxes	295
Income tax expense	89
Net Income	207

Balance Sheet (in thousands)	2003
Cash	600
Accounts receivable	1,450
Inventories	3,000
Prepaid expenses and other assets	1,900
Total current assets	6,350
Property, plant and equipment	2,000
Investments	1,500
Intangibles and other assets	1,000
Total Assets	10,850
Current liabilities	2,450
Long-term liabilities	2,000
Total liabilities	4,450
Stockholders' equity	6,400
Total liabilities and stockholders' equity	10,850

3. Save the file as Case 2 test.

4.   Print all of the sheets.

CASE PROBLEM 3 – COST OF GOODS MANUFACTURED

In this case, you will prepare a cost of goods manufactured schedule and an income statement for Mike's Surf and Sea for 2003.

Input

1.   Open the Case 3.xls file from the Student CD.

2.   Format the sheet so that it prints on one page, is centered horizontally, and the header contains your name, the file name, and today's date.

3.   Save the file as Case 3 answer.

4.   Print the sheet.

Cost of Goods Manufactured

1.   Rename Sheet 2 to COGM.

2.   Enter the appropriate heading in the first three rows.

3.   Use comma and currency style with no decimals.

4.   Prepare a cost of goods manufactured schedule by linking the data from the Input sheet to this sheet as needed. (*Hint: It may be easier to copy and paste link, then delete the rows that are not needed.*)

5.   Format the sheet so that it prints on one page, is centered horizontally, and the header contains your name, the file name and today's date.

6.   Save the file.

7.   Print the sheet. Check figure: Cost of Goods Manufactured is $1,138,000.

Income Statement

1. Rename Sheet 3 to Income Statement.

2. Enter the appropriate heading in the first three rows.

3. Use comma and currency style with no decimals.

4. Prepare a multi-step income statement by linking the data from the Input sheet and the COGM sheet to this sheet as needed.

5. Show selling and administrative expenses separately (Insurance expense is an administrative expense).

6. Sort the expenses by amount in descending order.

7. Format the sheet so that it prints on one page, is centered horizontally, and the header contains your name, the file name and today's date.

8. Save the file.

9. Print the Income Statement sheet.

Test Data

1. Open the file Case 3 answer.

2. Change the input data to the following

Advertising expense	29,000
Depreciation expense - delivery van	20,000
Direct labor	355,000
Direct materials inventory - 1/1/03	35,000
Direct materials inventory - 12/31/03	40,000
Direct materials purchases	655,000
Factory Rent	80,000
Finished goods inventory - 1/1/03	155,000
Finished goods inventory - 12/31/03	158,000
Gain on sale of equipment	50,000
Indirect labor	45,000
Indirect materials	35,000
Insurance expense	41,000
Interest expense	70,000
Net Sales	2,600,000
Office rent expense	30,000
Office salaries expense	130,000
Office supplies expense	15,000
Sales salaries expense	300,000
Store supplies expense	30,000
Work in process - 1/1/03	27,000
Work in process - 12/31/03	25,000

3. Save the file as Case 3 test. Check Figure: The Cost of Goods Manufactured is $1,167,000.

4. Print the workbook.

CASE PROBLEM 4: MASTER BUDGET

In this project, you will prepare a master budget for Mike's Surf and Sea for one year organized by quarters. A partially completed master budget has already been prepared for you.

Instructions:

1. Open the Case 4.xls from the student data files.

2. Review the input information in the Input sheet.

3. Link the appropriate information from the input sheet to the appropriate cells in the operating budgets and financial budgets.

4. Formulas for the balance sheet have already been entered for you. If all of your formulas are correct, the balance sheet should balance.

5. Format the sheets so that the page breaks are in appropriate places (use page break preview), the pages are centered horizontally, and the header contains your name, the file name, and today's date.

6. Save the file as Case 4 answer.

7. Print the budgets.

Test Data

Instructions

1. Change the input information to the following:

Sales Budget		
Expected unit sales in the first quarter		125,000
Sales increase per quarter		5%
Selling price	$	12.00
Production Budget		
Desired ending inventory		20% % of next quarter sales
Beginning Inventory		15,000 units
Cost of beginning inventory	$	7.40
Raw Materials Budget		
Raw materials per unit		1.50 pounds
Cost per pound	$	3.00
Desired ending inventory		15%
Beginning inventory		33,000 pounds

2. Save the file as Case 4 test. Check Figure: The December 31, 2004 balance sheet shows $2,302,160 for the total assets.

3. Print the budgets.

Appendix A

Advanced Excel Applications

Excel is a powerful program that has many features. In this book, some of the features that accountant's use with Excel were shown. It is the purpose of Appendix A to look at some of Excel's advanced features. The features included in Appendix A are Pivot Tables and Vlookup.

PIVOT TABLES

A *Pivot Table* is a table (or list) that quickly combines and compares large amounts of data. You can rotate its rows and columns to see different summaries of the source data, and you can display the details for areas of interest.

Pivot tables in Excel work best for organizing data in a list. The following example shows you how to use lists, then Excel's Pivot Table feature is shown.

Using Lists

Each month, Mike's Surf and Sea keeps track of their monthly sales by using a list. The list displays sales from each store (Ala Monana, Kahala, and Waikiki). The Sales list shows the sales in categories (T-shirts, Shorts, Accessories, Short boards, and Long boards) for each store. The Monthly Sales Summary shown on the next page displays this information as a list.

The McGraw-Hill Companies, Inc., *Excel Accounting*

Mike's Surf and Sea
Monthly Sales Summary

Item	Store	January	February	March	Q1 Sales
T-shirts	Ala Moana	671,532	672,578	680,759	2,024,869
Shorts	Ala Moana	751,678	751,789	789,675	2,293,142
Accessories	Ala Moana	7,685	8,345	8,467	24,497
Short Boards	Ala Moana	854,176	846,765	836,549	2,537,490
Long Boards	Ala Moana	76,589	80,085	80,136	236,810
T-shirts	Kahala	671,532	672,578	680,759	2,024,869
Shorts	Kahala	751,678	751,789	789,675	2,293,142
Accessories	Kahala	7,685	8,345	8,467	24,497
Short Boards	Kahala	854,176	846,765	836,549	2,537,490
Long Boards	Kahala	765,894	80,085	80,136	926,115
T-shirts	Waikiki	671,532	672,578	680,759	2,024,869
Shorts	Waikiki	751,678	751,789	789,675	2,293,142
Accessories	Waikiki	7,685	8,345	8,467	24,497
Short Boards	Waikiki	854,176	846,765	836,549	2,537,490
Long Boards	Waikiki	765,894	80,085	80,136	926,115
		8,463,590	7,078,686	7,186,758	22,729,034

By looking at the list, it is difficult to determine what the total sales from each store are for the quarter or the month. It is also difficult to determine total T-shirt sales.

One way to get the results you need is to sort the data into the categories that you want, then insert rows and total the columns. However, Excel offers a couple of tools that will make this process much easier.

Subtotals

Subtotals will allow you to categorize the data into categories then calculate subtotals for each of the categories. In this case, we will determine the subtotals for each store.

Instructions:

1. Open the file List.xls from the Student CD.

2. Make any cell in the data section (A5:F19) the active cell.

3. From the menu bar, select <u>D</u>ata, then Su<u>b</u>totals.

4. In the <u>A</u>t each change in field, select Store.

5. In the <u>U</u>se function field, select Sum.

6. Check January, February, March, and Q1 Sales in the A<u>d</u>d subtotal to field.

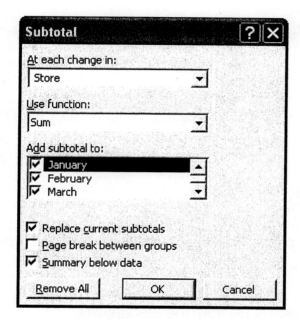

7. Click [OK].

8. Resize columns B, D, C, and E.

9. Delete row 25.

10. Save the file as Subtotal.

11. Set up the page so it prints centered on one page. Include a header that contains your name, the file name, and today's date.

12.   The bar on the left side of the spreadsheet allows you to display, only the grand total, the grand total and the subtotals, or all of the data. To display only the grand total, click on the 1 at the top of the left bar.

13.   To display the grand total and the subtotals, click on the 2.

14.   To display all of the data, click on the number 3.

15.   Save, print, and close the file.

Pivot Table

The subtotal feature is nice but if you wanted to determine how much T-shirt sales were, you would have to sort the data by Item then apply the subtotal feature. An easier way to analyze this data is to use a pivot table.

Before setting up the pivot table, you should know how you want your data displayed. In this case, we want to be able so see how much the sales were for each item by store for the month and the quarter. We also want to be able to see to total sales for the month and quarter.

Instructions

1.   Open the List.xls file from the Student CD.

2.   Make any cell in the data section the active cell.

3.   From the menu bar, select <u>D</u>ata, then <u>P</u>ivot Table and Pivot Chart Report. (If a help screen pops up, click no you don't want to use it.)

4.   From the PivotTable and PivotChart Wizard-Step 1 of 3, click <u>Next ></u> .

5.   Click Next > again.

6.   Click Layout... . Here, you will setup the data the way you want it displayed.

7.   Drag Item to the Row box.

8.   Drag Store to the Column Box.

9.   Drag, January, February, March and Q1 Sales to the Data box. The object should be similar to the following.

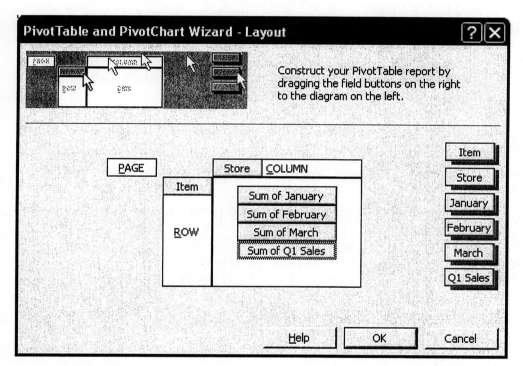

10. Click [OK].

11. Click [Finish].

12. Resize Column A.

13. Format the numbers in columns C-F with the comma style and no decimals.

14. Save the file as Pivot Table.

15.   Insert two additional rows at the top of the page.

16.   Enter appropriate heading information.

17.   Set up the page so the spreadsheet is centered horizontally, prints on one page with a header containing your name, the file name, and today's date.

18.   Save the file.

19.   To display only the data for the Ala Moana store, click the drop down arrow next to the Store header, and uncheck Kahala and Waikiki.

20.   Click [OK].

21.   Do the same to only display the January Data.

22.   Display all of the stores by selecting (Show All) from the Store drop down menu.

23.   To redisplay the other months, click in the data area then drag February, March, and Q1 Sales from the PivotTable Field List back to the data area.

24.   Save and print the file.

VLOOKUP

Vlookup searches for a value in the leftmost column of a table, and then returns a value in the same row from a column you specify. Use Vlookup when your comparison values are located in a column to the left of the data you want to find. (The V in Vlookup stands for Vertical.)

Vlookup allows you to link your work to a list but display only the data you want displayed. Using Vlookup, we will prepare an invoice and link it to the data in a list containing our inventory items, cost and selling price.

Instructions

1.   Open the Items.xls file from the Student CD.

2. Right-click on the sheet tab and select Insert.

3. Select the Spreadsheet Solutions tab then Sales Invoice. When you click [OK], you will insert Excel's Invoice template into the workbook. (*Hint: If necessary install this file from the Excel/Office CD.*)

4. Click on the cell that says *Insert Company Name Here* and type Mike's Surf and Sea, then press <Enter>.

5. From the menu bar, select Tools, then Protection.

6. Select Unprotect sheet.

7. Right-click on the column E header and select Insert.

8. Select the range E19:E35.

9. From the menu bar, select Data, then Validation.

10. Click [Clear All] then [OK].

11. Type **Item** in cell E18.

12. Select the range F19:M35.

13. Format the range with the comma style.

14. Type **shirt** in cell E19.

15. Make cell F19 the active cell.

16. Select Function from the Insert menu.

17. Type Vlookup in the Search for a function: box.

18. Click [Go].

19. Click .

20. Click in the Lookup_value box.

21. Click in cell E19.

22. Click in the Table_array box.

23. Select the range A2:B7 in the Items sheet.

24. Click in the Col_index_num box.

25. Type **2** (The description is in the second column of the range selected in the previous step). The dialog box should look like the following image.

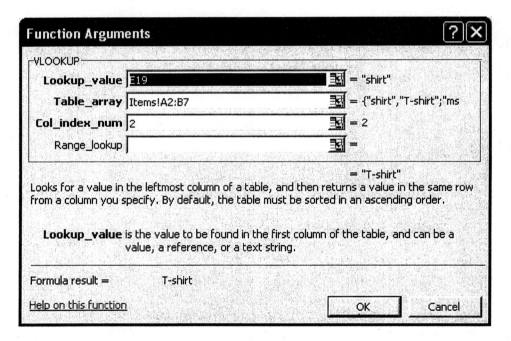

26. Click .

27. The description "T-shirt" should be displayed in cell F19.

28. Save the file as Lookup.

29.   Make cell N19 the active cell.

30.   Insert a Vlookup function.

31.   Click in the Lookup_value box, and enter E19.

32.   Click in the Table_array box.

33.   Highlight the range A2:D7 in the Items sheet.

34.   Type 4 in the Col_index_num box (The item price is in the fourth column of the range selected in the previous step).

35.   Click [OK].

36.   Save the file.

37.   Fill the formula from cell F19 down to cell F35.

38.   Fill the formula from cell N19 down to cell N35.

39.   Save the file.

40.   Test the spreadsheet.

Appendix

B Glossary

Appendix B lists a glossary of terms used in *Excel Accounting*. The number in parentheses refers to the textbook page. Appendix B is also online at www.mhhe.com/yachtexcel. An extensive Microsoft Excel Glossary is available online at http://www.intelinfo.com/microsoft_excel_glossary.html.

absolute reference   An absolute cell reference in a formula, such as $A$1, always refers to a cell in a specific location. When you use an absolute reference, the cell or range references do not change. (p. 61)

active cell   An absolute address in a formula refers to a specific cell location or range. It always points to the location of a specific cell, even if you copy it. Absolute addresses are created by adding a $ sign in front of each character in the cell address. For example, $C$8 always refers to cell C8. (p. 8)

average cost   The average cost inventory method requires that you compute the average cost per unit of inventory at the time of each sale. (p. 241)

bank reconciliation   The process of bringing the balance of the bank statement and the balance of the cash account into agreement. (p. 153)

bond   An issuer's written promise to pay an amount identified as the face value (also know as par value) of the bond along with interest. (p. 315)

bonds payable	The liability account used to identify a company's bonds. (p. 315)
cell reference	When you refer to another cell in a formula. (p. 60)
column header	Column headers are identified by alphabetic characters: A, B, C, D, etc. (p. 8)
conditional formatting	Conditional formatting formats cells based on their contents. You can format up to three conditions per cell. (p. 63)
contribution margin	The difference between sales revenue and variable costs. (p. 375)
cost of good sold	The cost of merchandise sold to customers during the period. (p. 240)
cost-volume-profit analysis	Changes in prices, costs and volume affect profitability. In accounting this is called cost-volume-profit analysis. (p. 377)
depreciation	The process of allocating the cost of a fixed asset (also called plant asset) to expense in the accounting periods benefiting from its use. (p. 159)
drawing toolbar	Allows for the selection of various shapes which can be added to a worksheet or spreadsheet file. (p. 9)
employee earnings record	Shows the pay period dates, hours worked, gross pay, deductions, and net pay of each employee for a pay period. (p. 264)

FICA taxes
This deduction from wages is also called the social security tax and provides qualified workers who retire at age 62 or older with monthly payments from the federal government. (p. 264)

FIFO
An abbreviation for first in, first out. First in, first out method of inventory assumes that the items in the beginning inventory are sold first. (p. 241)

fill handle
The fill handle is a black symbol in the lower right corner of the active cell. Clicking-and-dragging the fill handle can copy cell contents or create a series. (p. 14)

fixed assets
Tangible assets used in a company's operations that have a useful life of more than one accounting period. Fixed assets are also called plant assets; plant and equipment; property, plant, and equipment. (p. 285)

fixed cost
Costs that usually stay the same over time. (p. 48)

formatting
Refers to the ways you can change the appearance of your Excel spreadsheet. (p. 79)

formula bar
Displays the content of the selected cell. The formula bar is located under the toolbars at the top of the working screen. It contains the edit line for working with formulas, and provides information regarding cell addresses. (p. 8)

goal seek
Adjusts the value of a specific cell until a formula that includes that cell reaches the result you want. (p. 113)

general ledger
A record containing all accounts used by a company. (p. 184)

graphical user interface (GUI)	Consists of procedures which enable you to interact with Excel. The key is the Windows environment: the menus, dialog boxes, and list boxes. A mouse simplifies use of the GUI, but it is not required. (p. 1)
gross profit method	Estimates the cost of ending inventory by applying the gross profit ratio to net sales (at retail). This method is often used when inventory is destroyed, lost or stolen. (p.147)
horizontal scroll bar	The horizontal scroll bar allows you to move across the spreadsheet. (p. 8)
Internet	The worldwide electronic communication network that allows for the sharing of information. To read about the differences between the Internet and the Web, go to www.webopedia.com/DidYouKnow/Internet/2002/Web_vs_Internet.asp. (p. 29)
job-order cost system	A cost accounting system designed to accumulate costs by individual products. (p. 345)
LIFO	An abbreviation of last in, first out. Last in, first out method of inventory assumes that the last goods received are sold first. (p. 241)

lower of cost or market (LOCM)　　Market in the term lower cost or market is defined as the current market value (cost) of replacing inventory. (p. 246)

managerial accounting　　The area of accounting aimed at serving the decision-making needs of owners, managers, and others working within a business. The reports used by managers are usually for internal use. (p. 184)

Medicare　　A portion of FICA taxes (also called social security taxes) deducted from wages of qualified workers. Retirees receive medical benefits called Medicare after reaching age 65. (p. 264)

menu bar　　Below the title bar is the menu bar. The horizontal menu bar has 9 selections: File, Edit, View, Insert, Format, Tools, Data, Window, and Help. (p. 7)

mixed reference　　A mixed reference contains both a relative and an absolute component. (p. 61)

mouse　　A pointing device that is used to interact with images on the screen. (p. 1)

name box　　The name box contains information about the selected cell. (p. 8)

nested conditional function　　A conditional function within a conditional function. (p. 64)

notes payable	Issued to obtain assets or cash. Notes are transacted with a single lender such as a bank. (p. 310)
order of precedence	The order in which Excel calculates a formula. (p. 47)
payroll register	Lists the employee with all paycheck information for a specified period of time. The payroll register shows the hours worked, gross pay, deductions, and net pay of each employee. (p. 268)
pivot table	A table (or list) that quickly combines and compares large amounts of data. You can rotate its rows and columns to see different summaries of the source data, and you can display the details for areas of interest. PivotTables are interactive worksheet tables that allow you to summarize data with great flexibility. Their row and column headings can be adjusted to get different looks at original data. (p. 429)
process cost system	Accumulates costs by departments for a specific period of time. (p. 361)
range	A group of cells. (p. 44)
relative reference	A relative cell reference in a formula, such as A1, is based on the relative position of the cell that contains the formula and the cell the reference refers to. When you use a relative reference, the formula will change if you copy the formula to another cell. (p. 60)
row header	Row headers are identified by numbers. (p. 8)

screen tips

To see what each button on the toolbar does, move your mouse pointer over a tool on the toolbar and a description appears. The descriptions are called screen tips. (p. 81)

select-to-do

Highlight data that you want to apply formatting to before the tool shows what it does. (p. 81)

sheet tab

The sheet tab identifies which worksheet you are using. They are located at the bottom of the working screen. Excel includes three sheet tabs for each workbook. Think of the sheet tabs as a subsidiary (or secondary) worksheet related to the first worksheet or spreadsheet created. You can change the name of the sheet tabs. (p. 8).

spreadsheet

A table of values arranged in rows and columns. Spreadsheets allow users to calculate and correct complicated problems quickly. Spreadsheet is the generic term for applications, such as Excel, that you can use to enter, analyze, and calculate data. It performs mathematical calculations and projections based on data entered. Common spreadsheet uses include analysis and budgeting. (p. 4)

status bar

The status bar includes information about applications that are open, the time and date, and other Windows-related information. The status bar is located at the bottom of the screen and provides information about the particular operation in progress. (p. 9)

tabular format	In Excel data tables are arranged in chart or tabular format. Data tables allow you to manipulate columns and rows of facts and figures. (p. 108)
task pane	In Windows XP, the task pane appears automatically when you start Excel. The task pane lists the last spreadsheet(s) saved and other frequently used features. The task pane can be closed by clicking "X" on the "New Workbook" title bar. (p. 8).
taskbar	At the bottom of the Windows screen is a horizontal bar that shows which programs are open. The taskbar identifies an open application with a button or icon. (p. 5)
template	Files that are presaved and can be used with Excel. Excel files end in an .xls extension. The template files included on the CD that accompanies *Excel Accounting* can be used with Microsoft Excel 97 and higher. (p. 2)
title bar	Displays the name of the application and the name of the file being viewed. When you open a new workbook in Excel, the title bar displays "Microsoft Excel – Book1." (p. 7)
toolbar	The toolbar has icons, buttons, menus or combinations of both that allow the user to perform common Excel tasks; for example, clicking on the open folder allows you to open a file or workbook. (p. 8)
trackball	A device that works like a built-in mouse. (p. 2)

units-of-activity	A depreciation method that charges a varying amount to expense for each period of an asset's useful life depending on its usage. (p. 291)
Vlookup	Vlookup searches for a value in the leftmost column of a table, and then returns a value in the same row from a column you specify. The V in Vlookup is for vertical. (p. 434)
vertical scroll bar	The vertical scroll bar allows you to move up and down the spreadsheet. (p. 8)
what-if analysis	The ability to perform calculations that let you see what will happen if you change part of the spreadsheet. (p. 40)
WIMP	The acronym, WIMP, stands for Windows, Icons, Menus, and Pull-downs. This acronym is used to describe the way personal computer software looks and works. (p. 2)
windows	A visual (instead of typographic) format for computer operations. (p. 1)
withholding allowances	Exemptions claimed by the employee. The number of exemptions or withholding allowances often includes one for the employee, one for the employee's spouse, and one for each dependent. (p. 263)
workbook	The Excel file that stores your information. Each workbook may contain numerous worksheets. In Excel 2002, the default workbook consists of three sheets. Each sheet is referred to as a spreadsheet or worksheet. In *Excel Accounting*, the terms spreadsheet and worksheet are used interchangeably. (p. 6)

World Wide Web (Web)   A way of accessing information over the Internet. To read about the differences between the Internet and the web, go to <u>www.webopedia.com/DidYouKnow/Internet/2002/Web_vs_Internet.asp</u>.   (p. 29)

Index
